Make in India: Initiatives and Challenges

MAKE IN INDIA
Initiatives and Challenges

Manoj K. Singh

R. Ranjan

PRASHANT PUBLISHING HOUSE
DELHI-110094

Published by :
Prashant Publishing House
C-34, 28 Foota Road, Gali-3,
West Karwal Nagar, Delhi-110094
Phone : 011-22963970, Mob. : 9810396373
e-mail.: prashantpublishinghouse@gmail.com

Make in India: Initiatives and Challenges

First Published 2015

ISBN 978-93-80565-60-6

PRINTED IN INDIA
Published by Mr. R.K. Jha M/s Prashant Publishing House and Published at H.S. Offset House Press, Delhi.

Contents

Preface

Make in India is an international marketing campaigning slogan coined by the Prime Minister of India, Narendra Modi on 25 September 2014 to attract businesses from around the world to invest and manufacture in India.

The campaign has been concentrated to fulfil the purpose of job creation, enforcement to secondary and tertiary sector, boosting the national economy, converting India to a self-reliant country and to give the Indian economy global recognition.

The 'Make in India' also attempts to enforce the inflow of FDI in the country and improve services by partial privatization of loss-making government firms. The campaign is completely under control of the Central Government of India.

The manufacturing sector has contributed little to income growth and its share in total merchandise exports has been declining. Manufacturing has not brought much new employment, and most of the recent rise in manufacturing employment has been in the informal sector, where workers are not covered by social security arrangements.

At a time when India's Development pitch caused concern among skeptical environmentalists, Prime Minister Narendra Modi's "Make in India: Zero defect and Zero effect" remark on Independence day-2014 came as a clear message that the country would not compromise on its commitment towards environmental protection.

"Let's think about making our product which has 'zero defect; so that it does not come back (get rejected) from the world market and 'zero effect' so that the manufacturing does not have an adverse effect on our environment" said the prime minister while delivering his maiden Independence Day speech.

It has been said that doing the thing right is as important as doing the right thing. India's journey to prosperity can be a more sustainable and environmentally sensitive if we follow the "Zero Defect Zero effect" concept.

Make in India is an old mantra chanted since pre-independence days. In the post-independence era of centralized planning, it assumed a staunchly autarkic hue. However, by 1991 it became obvious that an inward looking economic policy was not going to work. Economic liberalization was embraced as a fait accompli then. However, re-chanting of Make in India mantra begun with the new government taking office at the center. What does one make of this initiative? Prime Minister Mr. Narendra Modi arrived in a Mahindra Scorpio car for his swearing-in ceremony, however, by the time he addressed the nation on 15 August 2014, he had begun using BMWs. He even sports a Montblanc pen which he used at the swearing-in ceremony. Therefore, the message in today s context certainly cannot be autarkic in nature.

This is especially harmful as manufacturing is highly reliant on well-functioning infrastructure. Stronger manufacturing would increase productivity and make growth more inclusive, while contributing to improved current account balance. In particular, India should aim for more formal jobs, as these tend to be the most secure and of highest productivity.

—Editor

1

Make in India

Make in India is an international marketing campaigning slogan coined by the Prime Minister of India, Narendra Modi on 25 September 2014 to attract businesses from around the world to invest and manufacture in India.

The campaign has been concentrated to fulfil the purpose of job creation, enforcement to secondary and tertiary sector, boosting the national economy, converting India to a self-reliant country and to give the Indian economy global recognition.

The 'Make in India' also attempts to enforce the inflow of FDI in the country and improve services by partial privatization of loss-making government firms. The campaign is completely under control of the Central Government of India.

Objective

The major objective behind this initiative is to focus upon the heavy industries and public enterprises while generating employment, empowering secondary and tertiary sector and utilizing the human resource present in India.

The highlights and purpose of Make in India include making India a manufacturing hub and economic transformation in India while eliminating the unnecessary laws and regulations, making bureaucratic processes easier and shorter, and make government more transparent, responsive and accountable and a government emphasized upon the framework which include the time-bound project clearances through a single online portal which will be further aided by the eight-members team dedicated to answering investor queries within 48 hours and addressing key issues including labour laws, skill development and infrastructure.

MAKE IN MAHARASHTRA

Make in Maharashtra is an initiative started by Government of Maharashtra on sidelines of Make in India initiative by Government of India.

Main objective of this government initiative is to create business friendly atmosphere in Maharashtra by increasing ease of doing business as much as possible. Main target is to increase the Foreign Direct Investment and Local Investment in the region to further increase the industrialization in Maharashtra.

Schindler's Jürgen Tinggren said during World Economic Forum at Davos in 2015 that "Ease of doing business in Maharashtra is as fast as China."

The Maharashtra government is eyeing Rs 5 lakh crore (US$84bn) industrial investment across the state between 2014-2019 period as part of this initiative that is likely to generate around 2 million jobs.

History

Maharashtra attracted maximum foreign inflows at USD 70.41 billion, about 30 per cent of total foreign direct investment (FDI) inflows in India during April 2000-November 2014. Maharashtra and the National Capital Region (NCR) have cornered 49 per cent of the total foreign direct investment inflows into the country since April 2000, according to Commerce and Industry Ministry data.

Foreign investments are considered crucial for India, which needs around USD 1 trillion over five years (2012–17) to overhaul its infrastructure sector such as ports, airports and highways to boost growth.

Profile of Maharashtra

- Maharashtra is the largest economy within India by GDP.
- Market: Maharashtra has population 117,853,636(117 million-2014 estimate), which is grossly double than United Kingdomand equal to Japan. Only 10 countries in the world have more population than Maharashtra.
- Maharashtra has area 3,07,717 km2, which is grossly equal to United Kingdom and Japan.
- Overall, in terms of population and area, Maharashtra is grossly equal to Japanwhich is 3rd largest economy in world in nominal terms.
- Mumbai is capital of Maharashtra state which is also financial and commercial capital of India. Bombay Stock Exchange is considered to be one of Asia's fastest and oldest stock exchanges, and is among the ten largest exchanges of the world in terms of total market capitalisation of listed firms.
- Headquarter of India's central bank Reserve Bank of India is in Mumbai.
- Maharashtra is the largest revenue generator state of India.

Reforms

The Maharashtra government created a "e-platform" to monitor the movement of files related to setting up of new industries and investment in the state. Proposed interface will facilitate quick approval of applications for setting up industries in an effective and transparent manner.

Those investing more than Rs.100 crores will have the facility of one window clearance under the 'MAITRI'(Maharashtra Industry, Trade & Investment Facilitation Cell) scheme, a set up of an Empowered Group of Secretaries of various key departments to give all the approvals required for new industries within 30 days.

MAİTRI

£ Maharashtra Industry, Trade and Investment Facilitation Cell(MAITRI) is administered by the Industries Department & serves as a single point of contact for Government to Business(G2B) services offered across the business cycle for setting up a new industrial unit in the state. It will provide all the critical investment-related information.

MAITRI aims to promote investments, facilitate business partnerships & trade in Maharashtra & would function as a clearing house for all investment related information and assist investors.

MAITRI will cater to industrial projects with an investment of Rs.100 crore and above.

It will provide 31 critical investment related clearances from 15 departments that are needed to set up an industry in Maharashtra.

Response

Make in Maharashtra initiative got overwhelming response by business community. Maharashtra Chief Minister Devendra Fadnavis successfully clinched many key investment and corporate deals with multinationals in World Economic Forum at Davos in 2015 which are expected to generate more than 20,000 jobs in the state.

- Cognizant, among the leading software companies in the world, has chosen Pune to invest because of the best quality of workforce.
- Microsoft is planning to set up two data centres, one each in Mumbai and Pune.
- Schindler Group will invest in a second phase project at Talegaon, near Pune for manufacturing escalators.
- General Electric will invest around Rs.3000 crore in Maharashtra as part of the 'Make In India' programme of the centre.

- Australian paper manufacturing firm Visy Industries is keen to set up a paper recycling plant for which its officials would visit Mumbai.
- Safran, a French MNC manufacturing aircraft, rocket engine and aerospace components, is planning to enter India, for which the Maharashtra government has offered land in Nagpur, in tune with the existing ecosystem in the region for this sector.
- Toray International is planning to invest in technical fibres and polyester in Amravati-Nagpur region and help for an integrated textile park.
- Volkswagen intends to make India and Maharashtra its global hub for manufacturing small segment cars, for which Fadnavis inaugurated its diesel engine manufacturing plant in Chakan, near Pune.
- In a big boost to manufacturing in Maharashtra, Mars International India, a wholly owned subsidiary of leading global chocolate maker Mars, Incorporated, is investing Rs 1,005 crore in a greenfield project to make chocolates at Khedcity, near Pune.
- Other major companies planning to set up operations in the state include Hilti Group, Diageo, Khimji Group, Credit Suisse, Nomura, JP Morgan, Nestle, Mitsui and Japan External Trade Organization (Jetro).
- During his visit to Davos, Mr. Fadnavis held discussions with other important companies like Pepsico, Hyosung, L'Oreal,Novartis, Deutsche Bank.

Demand for Inclusive Development

Though Maharashtra is most industrialized state in India still there is vast regional imbalance within Maharashtra. Most of industrial growth has been accumulated in Western Maharashtra and new investment projects are going to Vidarbha Region, so there is constant ignorance towards Marathwada Region.

According to data of Marathwada Statutory Development Board, Marathwada has only 2% of total Foreign Direct Investmentin Maharashtra, that too accumulated around Aurangabad.

There has been constant demand by civil society of Marathwada to create new industrial corridor named Nanded Aurangabad Industrial Corridor which will connect to Delhi Mumbai Industrial Corridor. This new corridor will cover entire Marathwada and can act as driving force for entire Marathwada. Make In Maharashtra initiative can have enormous chances in Marathwada.

GROWTH AND DEVELOPMENT IN GUJARAT

The reputation of politician Narendra Modi goes beyond the shoreline of India from USA to Sydney, from China suppliers to European countries, one will always find those who are bowled over by Primary Reverend popular Modi's character and style of perform. The success of the Vivid Gujarat Summits shows the worldwide status of politician Narendra Modi; over a hundred nations get involved in the Peak and the results are for all to see. They bring financial commitment and financial development to Gujarat state. Renowned Indian politician Modi similarly turns on the Gujarati local diaspora event due to perform that has occurred in Gujarat. Little wonder that during every amazing Pravasi Indian days, the most expected presenter continues to be great politician Narendra.

He continues to be a commonly journeyed person, having frequented various nations such as Sydney, China suppliers, Asia, country of Mauritius, Thailand country and amazing Uganda. Within a month of supposing office in Oct 2001, Primary Reverend Politician Narendra Modi was an aspect of a delegation to Italy led by the then Primary Reverend politician Atal Bihari Vajpayee where he finalized a milestone pact with the Governor of amazing Astrakan region.

The connection between Gujarat state and Italy grew even larger in the following years as Primary Reverend Modi created more formal trips to Italy, even obtaining important co-operation in the area of energy. Renowned Indian politician Modi was among the Native Indian management who frequented Israel as an aspect of an advanced level delegation comprising Native Indian. These days Gujarat is at the limit of creating a powerful collaboration with Israel especially in the areas of hr, farming, water, power and security.

The organization between Southern Eastern Asia and Native Indian go back to hundreds of years and continue to be powerful even now. Primary Reverend renowned politician Modi has frequented Southern Eastern Asia on several activities ever since he took over as CM. He has frequented Hong Kong country, Malaysia country, Singapore country, Taiwan country and Thailand country and these nations have been effective members in various worldwide social activities in Gujarat state such as the yearly International Kite Traveling Event.

Chief Reverend Politician Narendra Modi has also started out windows of possibilities for Gujarat state by promoting close financial connections with China suppliers. He has created three formal trips to China suppliers, the last one being in Nov 2011. During that journey politician, Narendra Modi was accepted by the top authority of China suppliers in the Great Area of the People in China country, an honour usually arranged for Leads of Condition. His China country trips have attracted tremendous financial commitment for Gujarat state along with a renowned MoU with amazing Sichuan region and an important R&D Center with the help of China company renowned Huawei.

With politician Narendra Modi at the helm of matters, state of Gujarat is positioned to lead nationwide renovation. The viewpoint to amazing Change came with the dedication of Politician Narendra Modi who implemented the 'Indian Panchamrut Shakti or also known as power.

The five nectars of Gyan power, Jal power, Urja power, Jan power and power of Raksha Shakti or energy for the complete development of situations. State of Gujarat on the European most aspect of Native Indian has one third of shoreline of the nation. Since beginning of situations, the framework of its financial system has modified considerably. Not only the State's GSDP and Per Household GSDP have improved but it has proven all symptoms and symptoms of a designed and urbanized financial system.

Infrastructure Par Excellence

Gujarat today has one of the best infrastructures in the country comprising of 11 airports, 1 international airport, an extensive rail network and a robust road network of over 74,000 km. It has India's highest tele-density, highest number of operational ISPs, the longest optical fibre cable network in the country and above all GSWAN – Gujarat State Wide Area Network – the largest IP based e-Governance network in Asia Pacific.

Gujarat is blessed with a coastline of over 1600 km, the longest in the country, and is dotted with 41 ports. Today, these gateways to the world handle over 25% of India's total cargo, 17,763 out of 18,028 villages of Gujarat are connected with pucca roads (concrete roads). This excellent rural road connectivity of 98.53% is the best in the country and translates into fast track growth.

Gujarat has always believed in networking for success and it is this philosophy that has enabled it to create a networked infrastructure of the 21st century:

- State-wide Gas Grid
- State-wide Water Distribution Grid
- State-wide IP based e-Governance Network
- Agri-Net for Lab to Land knowledge flow
- Wireless Rural Internet Connectivity
- Joint sector railway lines linking the ports to vast hinterland.

Modi believes that infrastructure is the key to the process of economic development and hence has given it the topmost priority. His Government is committed to make Gujarat a global industrial hub by decisive and result-oriented initiatives.

The state-owned Gujarat Infrastructure Development Board headed by the Chief Minister himself has in place an infrastructure master plan called Blueprint for Infrastructure in Gujarat – BIG 2020, entailing a total capital outlay of ₹ 3,57,468 crores and encompassing 11 broad sectors such as Power, Water and Irrigation, Ports, Roads, Industrial Parks and SEZs, Urban Infrastructure, Gas, Knowledge Corridors, Railways and Airports, Tourism and Telecom-Infrastructure that enables growth and empowers people to accelerate on the path of progress and prosperity.

Vibrant Gujarat Global Investors Summit 2003

Vibrant Gujarat: Global Investors' Summit 2003 was organized during world famous festival of Gujarat-Navratri, during which the State is at its best. This time a unique attempt was made by the State Government to showcase the culture, tradition and entertainment prevalent in Gujarat by blending them with culture, trade and enterprise.

Industrial Extension Bureau acted as a nodal agency for the State Government during Vibrant Gujarat : Global Investors Summit (September 28 to October 2, 2003) organized at the two major commercial cities of the State–Ahmedabad and Surat in association with the Government of India, UNIDO and FICCI & CII.

The conventions during the programme had sectoral sessions focus sector-Industrial Investment, Agro-Processing, Biotech-Pharma, Natural Gas and Oil, Infrastructure, Mining, Tourism, Apparels and Gems-Jewellery at Ahmedabad and sectoral sessions on Garment & Textiles and Gems & Jewellery at Surat.

There were also exhibitions in sectors at respective places in Ahmedabad and Surat to provide a platform for showcasing products and services. One to one discussions between the prospective investors, government officials and the project promoters took place.

176 project proposals were compiled and were then scrutinized for their viability. Internationally reputed credit rating agencies like CRISIL and CARE lend their support as the financial advisors to these projects. Leading private and public sector banks of India like ICICI, IDBI, State Bank of India, Bank of Baroda, State Bank of Saurashtra, Corporation Bank, IDFC and NABARD have extended their support for financing these projects. CRISIL also worked with iNDEXTb in structuring these projects.

The Hon'ble Deputy Prime Minister of India, Mr. L K Advani inaugurated Vibrant Gujarat: Global Investors' Summit 2003 on 28 September 2003. Mr. Narendra Modi, Hon'ble Chief Minister, Mr. Arun Shourie, Mr. Ram Naik, Mr. Mukesh Ambani, Mr. A C Muthaih were the other dignitaries present on the dais. Various sessions during the programme were chaired by other hon'ble ministers from the Union and State Government.

Large number of corporate leaders like Mr. Subhir Raha, Mr. C K Birla, CEOs of multinational companies like Shell, British Gas, General Motors, P&O ports, Niko & Steag and others attended the event. International dignitaries like Mr. Larry Pressler, ex-US Senator; Mr. Michael Clarke graced the occasion.

The Surat Summit, inaugurated by Hon'ble Union Finance Minister, Mr. Jaswant Singh, was also equally impressive. Other dignitaries present during the event were Hon'ble Union Minister for Textiles, Mr. Shah Nawaz Hussain, Hon'ble Union Minister for Rural Development Mr. Kashiram Rana, experts in textiles, gems and jewellery, senior officials from State and Central Government. The attendance of prominent industrialists and other business leaders from across the country translated into a resounding success for the Surat Summit.

At the end of the event, 76 MOUs worth US $ 14 billion for investment were signed. Other Events organized during Navratri Festival were International Convention on Reconstruction in Kutch District after Earthquake in 2001 and Celebration of Birth Anniversary of Mahatma Gandhi at Porbandar–the birth place of Mahatma Gandhiji on his birthday anniversary on October 2, 2003. About 125 foreign delegates, 200 Non-Resident Indians, 200 leading dignitaries and other participants from about 45 countries participated in Navratri Festival.

Vibrant Gujarat Global Investors Summit 2005

The two day Vibrant Gujarat : Global Investor's Summit 2005 was a one-of-its-kind event in India. It got off to a start with the Honourable Vice President of India, Shri Bhairon Singh Shekhawat, inaugurating the ceremony. More than 6,000 people attended the inaugural ceremony. The top dignitaries present at the ceremony included industry representatives, foreign multinationals, NRIs as well as the business from various sections of the society, India. Mukesh Ambani of Reliance, Gautam Adani of the Adani Group, Shashi Ruia of Essar, Nigel Shaw of British Gas and so on. As a reflection of faith in the state and its potential to become a leading global destination for investment in the time to come, MOUs for setting up projects worth INR 870 Billion were signed on the first day itself.

To invite participation from global players, five delegations Led by senior Ministers of Gujarat Cabinet visited different parts of the world to hold discussions with NRIs, NRGs (Non Residential Gujaratis) and foreign investors. From amongst them, several investors and NRIs participated in the event.

The summit was planned to coincide with Gujarat's famous Kite festival, Uttarayan, which marks a change of season with the movement of the sun into the northern hemisphere. Sectoral theme pavilions showcasing the strength of Gujarat in the relevant areas were developed. Major industries, Government corporations and Institutions participated in each sector. The event also hosted an exhibition along with seminars on the focus areas for investment in the state. These were IT, Biotech, Agro, Energy, Gas, Petroleum, Non-conventional Energy, Port & port-Led industries, Financial Services, Textiles and Apparels, Gems & Jewellery, Tourism etc. The exhibition was held at the Science City which have more than 200 exhibitors from various sectors. The exhibitions attracted large number of visitors from within the state and outside. Facility for arranging one to one meetings available where senior officers from the Industries and other departments, representatives of UNIDO and FICCI were present. On the first day, the focus sectors were Information Technology, Biotechnology, Agro, Energy, Gas, Petroleum and more importantly Non-conventional Sources of Energy. Seminars and meetings were held in three different halls at the Science City. Potential investors and industrialists had one-to-one meetings with senior officials of the state government and ministers of the cabinet.

The concluding day maintained the same momentum and enthusiasm as that of the first day with MOUs being signed by Industry. Several new MOUs were signed in the focus sectors of the day–Agriculture, Engineering, Tourism, Urban Development, Chemicals and Pharmaceuticals, Port & Port Led development, Textiles, Gems & Jewellery. By the time the Summit concluded on the second day, investments worth INR 1060 Billion in the form of MOUs were signed with 226 units. The concluding ceremony was graced by the Union Minister for Commerce & Industry Shri Kamal Nath, Of the 226 MOUs, Engineering, Gas and Port sectors attracted the maximum number of investment proposals, followed by Agriculture, Urban Development, Tourism, Chemicals & Pharmaceuticals, Textiles, Gems & Jewellery, IT and Biotechnology sectors. Besides these, four industrial majors–Torrent, Essar, Welspun and Adani, have Ledged investments of INR 120 Billion in gas-based or lignite-based power projects, assuring self-sufficiency to the state for future in the most important sector-power. Over all, the event evoked an excellent response amongst in industrialists in India and foreign countries in particular in Gujarat in general.

'MAKE IN INDIA' CAN'T BE A POLICY, ONLY AN OUTCOME

Narendra Modi has come to power by promising rapid economic growth that delivers millions of jobs. To achieve this, Modi has devised a 'Make in India' policy.

Launched with a blaze of publicity , it seeks to make India a manufacturing giant and attract global investors.

It aims to raise the share of manufacturing in GDP from the current 13-14% to 25%. Modi is envious of the rise of China as a manufacturing giant. India has lagged far behind for decades, and he naturally wants India to catch up.

Problem: for all the hoopla and cheering at various Modi meetings and summits, the growth of manufacturing in the July-September quarter was 0.1%.

The growth of fixed investment, the foundation of future production, was virtually zero. Alas, people are not "making in India", and are not investing to make in the future either. Probably things will improve a bit in the next quarter: early trends suggest that manufacturing growth may go up to 2.5%. But remember that during the much-derided Nehruvian licence-permit raj, manufacturing used to grow at 4-5% per year!

One industrialist who does not want to be quoted asks, "Why will foreigners come to invest here when Indians are not investing?" During his foreign visits, Modi urged global giants to Make in India. They replied politely that they will surely consider this, but such politeness must not be confused with serious intent. A US businessman said during Modi's US visit, "There's lots of sizzle, but where's the steak?" He's still waiting.

Modi must accept an elementary fact: 'Make in India' can only be an outcome, not a policy. If he creates conditions in which all sorts of investment will thrive, the outcome will be a rush to produce in India, by both Indians and foreigners. If the conditions are not conducive, no amount of sloganeering will create a Make in India rush. In such conditions, attempts to force the share of manufacturing up to 25% will fail, exactly as Nehru-Indira policies failed in the licence-permit raj. So will additional tax breaks or subsidies for Special Economic Zones.

The government has produced a list of items currently imported, and wants to make them in India. This importsubstitution approach is reminiscent of Nehruvian days.

Modi is implementing the Congress idea of forcing public sector units to procure 20% of their supplies from MSMEs (micro, small and medium enterprises). This is a partial return of the old, failed reservation for small-scale industries. Quotas, reservations and subsidies do not square with Modi's promise of "minimum government, maximum governance".

The Doing Business report of the World Bank and IFC for 2015 places India at just 142nd of 189 countries surveyed in ease of doing business. India used to be 116th of 155 countries a decade earlier.

Has Modi's coming made a difference? Well, say businessmen, corruption is down a bit and file clearances are faster, but the big picture hasn't changed much. Land acquisition remains moribund, state-level clearances are slow even if central clearances are given, labour laws remain unchanged, infrastructure remains a big bottleneck, the electricity sector is bust, banks are reeling under bad debts, and the public-private partnership model is broken. We have seen modest increases in FDI limits in insurance and defence, and minor reductions in ministerial discretion and inspectors' powers. These barely touch the fringes of the rules and procedures strangling business.

The Doing Business report ranks India 184th in ease of getting a construction permit, 134th in getting electricity connections, 121st in registering property , 156th in paying taxes, 122nd in ease of foreign trade, 137th in resolving insolvency, and 186th in enforcing contracts. This is pathetic. Modi has shown little or no action on these fronts. Many of these issues fall within the states' jurisdiction, and Modi has neither the means nor inclination to impose tough reforms on the states.

Modi in his election campaign said the government should not be in business. But he has no plans to privatize anything, not even white elephants like Air India. At the ET Now conclave, energy minister Piyush Goyal said he was proud of Coal India, a company whose productivity is one-tenth that of the best Australian and American mines. If you cannot see the problem, can you solve it?

Make in India is being confused with Make in Coal India, Make in Air India, Make in MSMEs, Make in SEZs and so on. Even as the BJP castigates Nehru, it is adopting what look like neo-Nehruvian ideas. Instead, Modi should focus on making business as easy and honest as possible, avoiding artificial props, curbing inflation and fiscal deficits, ensuring a realistic exchange rate, and letting the market decide which sectors should flourish. Investors from everywhere will then rush in to Make in India.

INFLATION FEARS BLURRING MODI'S 'MADE IN INDIA' VISION

India's Prime Minister Narendra Modi delivered his inaugural Independence Day speech. At 80 minutes, it was the longest speech by an Indian Prime Minister since Jawaharlal Nehru's time. The speech touched upon the various challenges that the world's largest democracy faces, from female feticide to sanitation. He talked about the need for a new institution in the place of the Planning Commission, created back in 1950, and the need for girls' toilets at every school, to tackle the high drop-out rates of girls.

But the crux of the Independence Day speech came towards the end, when Modi stretched out his hands in a gesture that can be explained from his challenging early life, when he had been briefly associated with Indian theatre. The message was one that has been relevant to India for a long time: 'Come, make in India'. India needs to increase jobs, sustain growth, and lower its trade deficit by boosting manufacturing exports, which requires that manufacturing be given higher prominence in the Indian economy.

Surprisingly, the speech was silent on another key issue: the sticky and stubbornly-high inflation that India has been experiencing — a critical plank on which the 2014 general elections were fought.

The silence is understandable. Inflation in India — or rather the Consumer Price Index (CPI) which, due to its composition, places nearly 50 per cent weight on food products — is not something that can be tamed in 100 days. In South Korea, food products account for 14 per cent of the inflation basket; in China it is 32 per cent.

Core inflation, as measured in the US and many other developed countries, excludes volatile food and energy prices altogether. As India's integration with global markets strengthens, the country is likely to witness pressure from food inflation as global commodity prices equalise.

Inflation is always the biggest tax on the underprivileged sections of the population. Under any measure of poverty, irrespective of the methodology or its validity, India remains home to the largest number of poor people globally.

India did not miss the 'manufacturing boat' by accident. Looking at manufacturing value-added as a percentage of GDP for 2013, India's 13 per cent was lower than that of China (32 per cent on 2011 data), South Korea (31 per cent), Indonesia (24 per cent), Singapore (19 per cent), Japan (18 per cent on 2012 data), Bangladesh (18 per cent) and Sri Lanka (18 per cent). Of these, India's per capita nominal GDP is greater only than that of Bangladesh. On per capita manufacturing value-added nominal GDP, India therefore is 33 per cent of Sri Lanka, 23 per cent of Indonesia, 9 per cent of China, and 2–3 per cent of Japan, South Korea and Singapore.

The main reason Indian manufacturing doesn't thrive is high, sticky and stubborn inflation, coupled with high fiscal deficits, which increases the domestic cost of capital. Among the nations mentioned above, India's cost of capital, at 8 per cent, is the highest, as interest rates in Bangladesh and Sri Lanka are at 7.2 and 6.5 per cent respectively. In a contemporary world, this is contrary to negative bond yields in Germany and France, and negative nominal deposit rates in the EU due to ECB easing. The US and Japan have been continuing easy monetary policy, and China too sees an abundance of capital with moderate inflation. While India's current account deficit figures have shown some improvements since last year, uncertain gold demand and increasing crude prices can put pressure on the Indian rupee, which over the years has steadily diminished in value, thereby posing risks for foreign direct investment inflows too. India has been, and remains, starved of productive capital, with high inflation.

Another problem with India's high cost of capital is the attendant increase in the debt service ratio for government. Despite the fact that India's debt-to-GDP ratio was much lower than that of Japan's in 2012 (49.7 per cent of GDP in India to 196.5 per cent in Japan), the Indian government has been forced to spend a much high proportion on servicing its debt. As per 2014 budget, 20 per cent of government expenditure is on servicing state debt, which hampers its efforts to spend more on either investment or welfare.

McKinsey has previously highlighted that, between 2006–2010, the majority of India's top 1000 manufacturers had returns on invested capital (ROIC) lower than their weighted average cost of capital (WACC). The situation worsened considerably during 2010–2014, until sentiments improved with the formation of a stable government under Modi. The long-term weighted average cost of capital during 2006–10 was 12 per cent. It is no wonder that the banks that did lend to manufacturing or the infrastructure sector in India have been staring at huge non-performing assets.

On top of the above, India has always encouraged returns on speculative investments. From 2006 onward, the return on India's equity index, Nifty, has been nearly 14 per cent, mostly tax exempt — compared to 5.6 per cent of Hang Seng Index of Hong Kong, or 6.8 per cent of SSE Composite Index of Shanghai, the latter two being taxable. It is true that in between the return has been patchy. The return on gold — despite depressed global prices — has also been more than 14 per cent (tax-free) in Indian rupees. Until 2013, there was no import duty on gold, despite its huge drag on the current account deficit. Returns on real estate, more speculative in nature, has been much higher — although there is probably no pan-India real estate indices for this period.

Work by the Massachusetts Institute of Technology has debunked the myth that the availability of cheap manufacturing workers trumps productivity. While Germany's manufacturing workers receive wages that are 66 per cent higher than their American counterparts, Germany remains more competitive with a huge manufacturing trade surplus. On the supply side, while the pool of workers entering India's job market is both huge and cheap, this abundance of low-cost labour may not constitute that much of a competitive advantage when issues of productivity, infrastructure and supply chain efficiency are considered. Currently, more than 50 per cent of India's manufacturing workforce does not employ electricity in their manufacturing activities.

Sentiment in India has been looking up, but this optimism is currently limited to the speculative parts of the economy only. India faces other challenges, from environmental degradation to judicial interventions in transfers of natural resources to the private sector for manufacturing. The Governor of the Reserve Bank of India, Dr Raghuram Rajan, has made it clear that fighting inflation remains the top priority of India's central bank.

MAKE IN INDIA IN MANUFACTURING OR SERVICES

Echoing the Sage of Singapore, Prime Minister Narendra Modi has elevated the revival of Indian manufacturing to a key policy objective of the new government, identifying this sector as the engine of long-run growth. "Make in India" is now a flagship initiative not to mention a catchy campaign. But the question arises "What should India make?"

Early development thinking, exemplified most famously (though not exclusively) in the two-sector model of Lewis (1954) was fixated on the idea of sectoral transformation: moving resources from the agricultural/traditional sector to the manufacturing/ non-traditional sector. There was never any doubt about the hierarchy (the latter was unquestionably superior) and hence no doubt about the desirability of the structural transformation.

Although development thinking over the last two decades has moved away from discussions about sectoral transformation and towards a more explicit growth perspective, the importance of structural transformation is starting to be rehabilitated – but without abandoning the growth perspective. Rodrik (2013 and 2014) provides the clearest exposition of this marriage of the two perspectives.

Consider the following equation:

$$\hat{y} = \beta(\ln y^*(\theta) - \ln y) + (\pi_M - \pi_T)d\alpha_M + \alpha_M\pi_M\beta_M(\ln y_M^* - \ln y_M)$$

The equation has three parts. First, growth of gdp per capita (denoted by $\hat{y}$) can be viewed in a conventional conditional convergence perspective, with catch-up to the frontier ($y^*(\theta)$) depending on a number of fundamentals (policies, human capital, openness, institutions, etc). But this is a slow process because by definition fundamentals are slow to change. Moreover, this conditional convergence framework is inadequate because it has difficulty explaining growth miracles or accelerations—China being the classic outlier with many of these fundamentals.

Hence this framework needs to be supplemented with explicit structural transformation elements. These are captured in the second and third terms of the equation. The second term captures structural change from low productivity traditional sectors (T) to high productivity modern sectors (M), where π_i denotes productivity in sector *i* and α_M denotes the share of employment in the modern sector. This is the classic dualism model, which suggests that economic development is by definition a process of shifting resources from low to high productivity sectors, thereby raising economy-wide levels of productivity.

The third term is new and captures the phenomenon of unconditional convergence in the high productivity sector. Essentially, once resources move into this sector, they then experience unconditional or "automatic" catch-up due to rising productivity (represented by the convergence growth rate of the modern sector). This further increases economy-wide levels of productivity.

In other words, there are two gains to shifting resources from the traditional to the new sectors: first, a compositional gain, which is a gain in economy-wide productivity achieved by shifting the weight of the economy from low to high productivity sectors; second, a subsequent dynamic gain as these resources experience rapid productivity growth. The contribution of Rodrik (2013) is to show empirically that the manufacturing sector does indeed exhibit this rapid growth or unconditional convergence toward the frontier: that is, manufacturing in poorer countries and less productive manufacturing activities grow faster over time.

No sooner than having adopted this framework, the question poses itself: *are these compositional and dynamic gains restricted to manufacturing?* In other words, whereas the first phase of thinking about structural transformation was informed by certitude about the hierarchy of sectors, today there is less ground for that certitude because the comparison is not between agriculture and manufacturing but between manufacturing and services (or at least certain service subsectors).

This chapter is a modest initial attempt at shedding some light on the new structural transformation question, and in particular comparing manufacturing and services.

DESIRABLE FEATURES OF SECTORS THAT CAN SERVE AS ENGINES OF STRUCTURAL TRANSFORMATION

India is taken up as a case study for addressing this question due to the poor performance of manufacturing in India and the relatively strong performance of services – which in some ways mirrors the performance of many Sub-Saharan African countries. Lee Kuan Yew was clearly on to something when he challenged the Indian model of development.

Historically, there have been three modes of escape from under-development: geology, geography, and "jeans" (code for low-skilled manufacturing). In recent years West Asia, Botswana and Chile, and further back in time Australia and Canada, exploited their natural resources endowed by geology to improve their standards of living. Some of the island successes (Barbados, Mauritius, and others in the Caribbean) have exploited their geography by developing tourism to achieve high rates of growth.

In the early stages of their success, East Asian countries (China, Thailand, Indonesia, Malaysia etc) relied on relatively low-skilled manufacturing, typically textiles and clothing, to motor economic growth. Later on they diversified into more sophisticated manufacturing but "jeans" offered the vehicle for prosperity early on. No country has escaped from underdevelopment using relatively skill-intensive activities as the launching pad for sustained growth as India seems to be attempting.

Put differently, India seems to have defied its "natural" comparative advantage, which probably lay in the "jeans" mode of escape because of its abundant unskilled and low-skilled labor. Instead, it found or created—thanks to historical policy choices and technological accidents—such advantage in relatively skilled activities such as information technologies and business process outsourcing.

The Indian experience, still a work-in-progress, raises the question of whether structural transformation necessarily requires manufacturing to be the engine of growth. But before we compare manufacturing with alternative sectors in terms of their potential for structural transformation, it is worth elaborating on the desirable attributes of such sectors.

In fact, building upon the Rodrik (2013) framework, it is argued that there are five attributes that allow a sector to serve as an engine of structural transformation and thereby lead an economy to rapid, sustained and inclusive growth:

1. *High level of productivity:* As described above, economic development is about moving from low productivity to high productivity activities.
2. *Unconditional Convergence* (i.e. faster productivity growth in lower productivity areas): This too has been discussed earlier. Recall that convergence ensures that the relevant sector acts as an "escalator" which automatically leads to higher levels of sectoral and economy-wide productivity. In fact one can distinguish between two types of unconditional convergence:
   A. Domestic convergence: In large countries such as India, China, Brazil, and Indonesia, one would ideally like to see convergence *within* a country. That is, productivity growth should be faster in richer than poorer parts. Otherwise severe within-country regional inequality may arise.
   B. International convergence: whereby less-productive economic units (firms, sectors or entire economies) in all countries catch-up with units at the international frontier (i.e. those in the most productive countries).
3. *Expansion:* To ensure that the dynamic productivity gains from convergence spread through the economy, it is necessary that the sector experiencing convergence absorbs resources. Convergence accompanied by contraction will fail to ensure economy-wide benefits, because the country's resources that are outside the sector in question will not experience higher, convergent productivity growth. Convergence, in the case of the industrial sector, should be accompanied by natural industrialisation and not premature de-industrialisation, if it is to lead to truly inclusive growth.
4. *Alignment with comparative advantage:* To ensure that expansion occurs and the benefits of fast-growing sectors are widely shared across the labor force, there should be a match between the skill requirements of the expanding sector and the skill endowment of the country.

For example, in a labour abundant country such as India, the converging sector should be a relatively low-skilled activity so that more individuals can benefit from convergence.

5. *Tradability:* Historically, countries that had growth spurts enjoyed rapid growth in exports, typically manufacturing exports (Johnson, Ostry and Subramanian (2010)). Rapid growth has seldom been based on the domestic market. Part of the reason for this might be that trade serves as a mechanism for technology transfer and learning, which may have spillovers on related industries). Perhaps a more important part is that trade and exports in particular provide a source of unconstrained demand for the expanding sector. This is particularly important for a country of India's size because of the possibility that its expansion can run up against the limited political and economic ability of trading countries to absorb Indian exports and/or to turn the terms of trade against itself.

The two sectors—manufacturing and services (including services disaggregated by subsector)— are now evaluated, in succession, along these five dimensions in the Indian context.

THE MANUFACTURING SCORECARD

Productivity Level

Compares productivity (measured simply as value added per worker) levels in the various Indian sectors – including manufacturing – for two time periods: 1984 and 2010. Several features stand out. First, in India it is highly misleading to speak generally of manufacturing because of the clear difference between *unregistered* manufacturing – which is a very low productivity activity – and *registered* manufacturing – which is an order of magnitude (7.2 times) more productive. It is *registered* manufacturing, not manufacturing in general, which has the potential for structural transformation.

Second, the level of productivity in registered manufacturing is not only high relative to unregistered manufacturing, it is high compared to most other sectors of the economy and it is even high in an absolute sense, at US$ 7800 at market exchange rates and nearly three times as much at PPP exchange rates. If the entire Indian economy were employed in registered manufacturing, India would be as rich as say Korea.

Third, these differentials between registered manufacturing and the rest of the economy were already prevalent (if not to the same extent) in 1984 – fast productivity growth over the period (about 5 percent per year) has only exacerbated the differences.

Thus, on the first criterion of high levels of productivity, registered manufacturing scores spectacularly well.

Domestic convergence

Provides evidence that registered manufacturing is characterised by unconditional domestic convergence. Here the unit of observation is the State-Industry level, but almost identical results are derived when looking at more aggregated levels (across major states in India) and less aggregated levels (across factories).

Broadly a regression coefficient on log of initial productivity of about (-) 2.5 percent suggests that a state that is twice as rich as another has an average growth rate of productivity that is 2.5 percent slower – a considerable amount given that the average growth rate of productivity over the period 1984-2010 was about 4.4 percent.

International Convergence

With respect to registered manufacturing, it seems that states and firms within India are converging to the Indian frontier but that could mean little unless they are also converging to the international manufacturing frontier. Are they?

Rodrik (2013) shows that there is unconditional convergence across countries and sectors in manufacturing. But India is a negative outlier in the relationship in two senses: first, on average, manufacturing sectors in India exhibit labour productivity growth that is 14 percent less than the average country's manufacturing sector. Second, Indian industries converge at a much slower rate than average (0.005 percent)—almost not at all. In contrast, China is a positive outlier, posting faster labour productivity growth than average and converging faster to the global frontier. Registered manufacturing in India has thus not been a strong performer.

Expansion or Pre-mature non-Industrialisation?

It is a stylised fact that the process of development includes stages of industrialisation followed by de-industrialisation: a country first experiences a rising share of resources – especially labour – devoted to the industrial sector, after which the services sector becomes more important, so that the share of employment in the industrial sector declines from its peak. In recent years, however, "de-industrialisation" seems to be taking place prematurely. That is, poor countries seem to be reaching their peak levels of industrialisation at lower levels of industrialisation and income.

What about India? The phenomenon of de-industrialisation is particularly salient for India for three reasons. Looming ahead is the demographic bulge, which will disgorge a million youth every month into the economy in search of employment opportunities. Rising labour costs in China create opportunities for low-skilled countries such as India as replacement destinations for investment that is leaving China. And a new government that has assumed power offers the prospect of refashioning India in the image of Gujarat—one of the few manufacturing successes.

But the sobering fact is that India seems to be de-industrialising too. In fact, to call the Indian phenomenon de-industrialisation is to dignify the Indian experience, which is more aptly referred to as premature non-industrialisation because India never industrialised sufficiently in the first place.

The share of manufacturing in total employment over time for South Korea, a poster child for manufacturing-led growth.

South Korea's GDP per capita in 2005 PPP dollars is also shown alongside the series for several years. The typical shape: share of employment in manufacturing starts very low at around 5 percent and rises over time to almost 30 percent before starting to decline after a fairly high level of GDP has been reached.

In contrast, the Indian experience. The India's share of registered manufacturing in total output and employment over time (on the same axes as the graph for Korea). The general trend is constant with a downward trend over the last few years for which data are available. In other words, the pronounced inverted U shape that characterises the cross-section and Korea is notably absent in India.

But what has been the counterpart development among Indian states? The year in which the share of registered manufacturing peaked (in first value added and then employment terms), the peak share of registered manufacturing (in value added or employment), and the per capita GDP associated with peak registered manufacturing levels.

From the tables, a few points are striking. Gujarat has been the only state in which registered manufacturing as a share of GDP surpassed 20 percent and came anywhere close to levels achieved by the major manufacturing successes in East Asia. Even in Maharashtra and Tamil Nadu, manufacturing at its peak accounted for only about 18-19 percent of state GDP. The peak shares in employment terms are even less significant: no major Indian state has achieved more than 6.2 percent of employment from registered manufacturing in the last 30 years, and many major states peaked at less than half that. Even in Gujarat, employment in registered manufacturing has only been about 5 percent of total employment, while annual growth in registered manufacturing employment has been 1.8 percent between 1984 and 2010 (slower than the growth rate of total employment over the period: 2.4 percent).

Second, in nearly all states (with the exception of Himachal Pradesh and Gujarat), registered manufacturing as a share of value added is now declining and, for most states, has been doing so for a long time. The peak share of manufacturing in output for many states was reached in the 1990s (Andhra Pradesh and Tamil Nadu) or even in the 1980s (Maharashtra). Interestingly, peak *employment* shares seem to be following a slightly different story, with less marked declines observable for most states. Nevertheless, most states have *not* been experiencing secular growth in employment shares over time (the only exceptions are Himachal Pradesh, Tamil Nadu, Haryana and – possibly – Karnataka). Many of the states that do exhibit peak years in 2010 (such as Andhra Pradesh, Rajasthan and Orissa) seem to have employment shares that have been mostly flat, reflecting neither relative growth nor decline.

Third, and this is perhaps the most sobering of facts, manufacturing has even been declining in the poorer states: states that never effectively industrialised (West Bengal and Bihar) have started de-industrialising.

Some comparisons are illuminating. Take India's largest state Uttar Pradesh. It reached its peak share of manufacturing in output at 10 percent of GDP in 1996 at a per capita state domestic product of about $1200 (measured in 2005 purchasing power parity dollars). A country like Indonesia attained a manufacturing peak share of 29 percent at a per capita GDP of $5800. Brazil attained its peak share of 31 percent at a per capita GDP of $7100. So, Uttar Pradesh's maximum level of industrialization was about one-third that in Brazil and Indonesia; and the decline began at 15-20 percent of the income levels of these countries.

Thus far, we have shown that, for all but a few states, Indian manufacturing is certainly not growing and is probably shrinking. One possible consequence of manufacturing failing to satisfy requirements 2b and 3 is that, in contrast to China, there is no evidence of convergence between states in India in overall per capita GDP. For Chinese provinces, the poorer the initial level of per capita GDP, the faster the subsequent growth, so that poorer provinces start catching up with richer ones. In India, there is no convergence, because poorer states are not likely to grow faster than richer ones on average (Amirapu and Subramanian 2015). Regional disparities have thus persisted within India.

Had manufacturing attracted resources while exhibiting domestic convergence in productivity, the sector would have expanded in poorer states increasing overall levels of income in these states and contributing to a narrowing of the income distribution across India. Instead it seems that manufacturing has failed to be such an escalator of progress.

Several explanations are possible for why manufacturing has not been this escalator in India. They fall under four broad categories: distortions in labour markets; distortions in capital markets; distortions in land markets; and inappropriate specialisation away from India's natural comparative advantage and toward skill intensive activities. Amirapu and Subramanian (2015) provides some evidence in support of the last explanation.

Alignment with Comparative Advantage

As argued earlier, in order for a sector to offer transformational possibilities, it must not only be characterised by high levels and growth rates of productivity, it must also absorb resources from the rest of the economy. But in order to do so, the sector's use of inputs must be aligned with the country's comparative advantage. That will allow the abundant factor of production (usually unskilled labour) to benefit from productivity growth and convergence, and in so doing make growth not only rapid and sustainable but also inclusive. In other words, the dynamic sector must at least initially be relatively unskilled labour intensive. Is this true of India manufacturing? Kochhar et. al. (2006) found that Indian manufacturing was unusually skill labour intensive. Another simple metric for assessing the alignment of dynamism with comparative advantage is the relative skill intensity of manufacturing relative to other sectors. From the 2004/5 NSSO Employment and Unemployment Survey, the share of employees with at least primary and secondary education for major sectors (and subsectors) of the Indian economy is computed. It turns out that registered manufacturing is a sector that *is* relatively skilled labor intensive. The share of workers with at least secondary education is substantially higher in registered manufacturing than in agriculture, mining or unregistered manufacturing and also greater than in several of the service subsectors. In some ways, this should not be surprising. High labour productivity in this sector is at least in part a consequence of higher skills in the work force. What it does suggest, however, is that registered manufacturing does not really satisfy requirement number four. The skill intensity of the sector is not quite aligned with India's comparative advantage.

THE SERVICES SCORECARD

The scorecard analysis can be repeated for the services sector in India. But before that is done, it is important to recognise that services in the aggregate is not a useful category of analysis because it is an amalgam of different and disparate species of economic activity, from government services and construction that are non-tradable to finance and business services that largely are tradable; from certain activities that are labour intensive and others such as telecommunications that are highly capital and skill labor intensive. Any meaningful analysis of services must distinguish between different service subsectors—although the degree of disaggregation will of course be determined by data availability.

We work with the six different subsectors and repeat the analysis undertaken above for registered manufacturing.

Productivity Level

The comparative data on the level of productivity for these service subsectors as well as for manufacturing (both registered and unregistered). The first point to note is the astounding variation within services, reinforcing the case for disaggregation. In 1984 for example, the level of productivity in the real estate and business services sectors was 25 times as much as in public administration (essentially government) and close to 20 times as much as in retail. The productivity levels in two—financial services and business services—out of six service subsectors exceed that of registered manufacturing.

Domestic convergence

The issue of whether there was unconditional convergence within India for service subsectors over the last 3 decades is now examined. Notably, unconditional domestic convergence is found in nearly all the service subsectors, and across many time horizons (not reported here). In fact, the speed of domestic convergence for most service subsectors is found to be similar to that in registered manufacturing (about 2 percent) and, in some cases, substantially higher. For example, real estate and business services seem to converge at double the rate at which registered manufacturing converges.

International Convergence

Rodrik (2013) provides evidence using UNIDO data that industries in the (organized) manufacturing sector consistently exhibit global convergence in labour productivities, although Indian manufacturing industries converge to the global frontier much more slowly than the average, if at all. What about the service subsectors?

Using data on sectoral productivities from the World Bank's World Development Indicators (WDIs), Ghani and O'Connell (2014) argue that services in the aggregate have also exhibited convergence to a similar or even greater degree than manufacturing – at least for recent time periods (approximately 1990 to 2005). This is an interesting finding, but for this analysis in particular services should be disaggregated as we might well expect convergence behaviour to vary by subsector due to significant differences in sectoral characteristics such as tradability.

The international convergence results by service subsectors over the period 1990 to 2005 using data from the Groningen Growth and Development Centre (GGDC). Although the set of countries in the analysis is severely limited due to data availability, the results are still interesting. We see that some service subsectors (Finance, Insurance, and Real Estate; Community, Social and Personal Services; and Construction) do seem to exhibit strong international convergence, while others (Trade, Hotels and Restaurants; Transport, Storage and Communication) do not. Surprisingly, the set of sectors exhibiting convergence seems to include even some apparently non-tradable sectors, such as construction.

The conclusion thus far seems to be that many– but not all – service subsectors satisfy the requirements of high productivity growth, domestic convergence, and international convergence.

Expansion of Services?

Evidence that the share of output and employment from manufacturing in India had hardly changed in 30 years has already been presented. In the Tables below analogous evidence for services in India – both in aggregate and for particular service subsectors is presented.

In contrast to registered manufacturing – the share of output from aggregate services rose dramatically over the last 30 years, from about 35 percent to more than 50 percent of GDP. The share of aggregate services in employment, in contrast, increased in a far more modest fashion. But there is nevertheless a distinct contrast with registered manufacturing. Aggregate services employment grew faster than that in registered manufacturing and a number of service subsectors—transport, real estate and construction—registered substantially faster employment growth. In other words, services are becoming an ever more important source of wealth, and while they have not delivered rapid employment growth, a number of service sub-sectors have generated more rapid employment growth than manufacturing.

Alignment with comparative advantage?

We argued above that, in a low-skilled labour abundant country like India, a sector must make use of this dominant resource in order to offer the greatest possibilities for expansion and structural transformation. We also saw that registered manufacturing was a fairly skill-intensive sector with high average educational attainment.

The same table also shows that services in aggregate are no less skill-intensive: on average, 78 percent of workers in the service sector have at least a primary education (77 percent in registered manufacturing), and 48 percent have at least a secondary education (43 percent in registered manufacturing). Furthermore, a large number of service subsectors – including 1) Banking and Insurance, 2) Real Estate and Business Services, 3) Public Administration, 4) Education, and 5) Health and Social Services – have significantly higher educational attainment (90 percent or more of workers have at least primary education) than registered manufacturing. What this implies is that most service subsectors (precisely the high productivity, high growth subsectors, for the most part), have a limited capacity to make use of India's most abundant resource, unskilled labor. This may explain why the share of employment from services has risen so modestly, even while the share of output from services has grown so spectacularly.

SUMMARY SCORECARD AND CONCLUSIONS

A summary scorecard comparing registered manufacturing and selected service subsectors. Before proceeding further, let us make clear a few important points. First, we compare service sectors with only the *registered* (i.e.: formal) manufacturing sector, because unregistered manufacturing is one of the lowest productivity sectors in the Indian economy– apart from agriculture – and so offers little promise for transformation. So, when there is talk on the transformational potential of manufacturing in India the focus must be exclusively on registered manufacturing.

Second, another contribution of this chapter is to offer an alternative way of thinking about transformational sectors beyond the traditional distinction based on manufacturing versus services. We have taken the position of comparing sectors based on their easily observable underlying properties. To be sure, there may be less tangible differences between manufacturing and services that are left out in our analysis.

For example, our present analysis does not consider the extent to which certain sectors (such as registered manufacturing) may be more likely to induce learning spillovers to other sectors of the economy, which may be important. Other missing dimensions include the political one: Dani Rodrik has suggested that manufacturing may play an indirect role in the political development of young nations by providing a forum in which citizens learn to practice compromise in a democratic context through the struggle between labour and capital "on the manufacturing shop floor". Though our analysis leaves out such channels, we believe they are second-order in comparison with the 5 desirable features laid out earlier.

Proceeding to the comparison, there does not seem to be anything distinctive or superior about registered manufacturing when compared with certain other service subsectors. Like manufacturing, several of the service subsectors also exhibit high productivity and convergence – both domestic and international. However, they also share the shortcoming that these sectors are highly skill intensive in their resource requirements, which is out of kilter with the skill profile of the Indian labor force. Their potential to generate widely shared or inclusive growth is thus likely to be limited – and indeed seems to have been so given the lack of expansion observed earlier (and which is recorded in the scorecard).

One sector that markedly stands out from the others in the table below is construction: it appears to exhibit both types of convergence, does not require high education levels and has grown significantly in its resource use over the last three decades. However, the sector is not tradable and in any case is low productivity, so that moving labor resources to the sector does not considerably improve overall welfare.

So, in some ways, the choice for India is not manufacturing versus services but comparative advantage *deifying* (unskilled-intensive) sectors versus comparative advantage *defying* (skill-intensive) sector development. This is both a positive and a policy question.

While India's skill-intensive pattern of development has no doubt been costly, there has been a significant upside. Myron Weiner, among others, has drawn attention to the disappointing post-Independence performance of the Indian state in delivering education, reflected in very slow improvements in literacy rates, especially amongst women. While the supply of educational services by the state was inadequate, the puzzle arose as to why there was not greater demand for education and hence greater pressure on the state to meet this demand.

One answer to this puzzle is that the private returns to literacy and basic education must have been low. There is now evidence that the increasing opportunities that are spurring economic growth also contribute to raising these returns, leading to a greater demand for educational services—public and private—and hence improvements in educational outcomes (Munshi and Rosenzweig, 2003). This has put pressure on the supply of education. The government's failures to provide good schools are well-known, but growth has changed the picture dramatically, largely because it has increased the returns from education—and hence the demand for it.

Evidence is provided by the work of economists Kartik Muralidharan and Michael Kremer who show that private schools are mushrooming in rural India (many prominently advertising "English Medium") because of teacher absenteeism in public schools.

One also hears of companies creating training centers to build skills in the cities (such as the Infosys institute in Mysore) because institutions of higher education are notoriously inadequate. This endogenous increase in human capital could be one of the offsetting benefits of the comparative advantage-defying, skill-intensive growth model.

The policy question is the following. *Insofar as the government retains influence over shaping the pattern of development, should it try to rehabilitate unskilled manufacturing or should it accept that, that is difficult to achieve, and create the groundwork for sustaining the skill intensive pattern of growth?*

Attempting the former would be a history-defying achievement because there are not many examples of significant reversals of de-industrialisation.

A lot would have to change in India—from building the infrastructure and logistics/connectivity that supports unskill-intensive manufacturing to reforming the panoply of laws and regulations—or perhaps addressing corruption in the manner of their enforcement— that may discourage hiring unskilled labor and achieving scale in the formal sector.

Sustaining a skill-intensive pattern on the other hand would require a greater focus on education (and skills development) so that the pattern of development that has been evolving over time does not run into shortages. The cost of this skill intensive model is that one or two generations of those who are currently unskilled will be left behind without the opportunities to advance. But emphasising skills will at least ensure that future generations can take advantage of lost opportunities.

In some ways, the choice confronting India is really about how to make it a Lewisian economy that has unlimited supplies of labor. India can either create the conditions to ensure that its existing unlimited supplies of unskilled labor are utilisable. Or, it can make sure that the currently inelastic supply of skilled labor is made more elastic. Both are major challenges.

What the analysis suggests is that while Make in India, which has occupied all the prominence, is an important goal, the Prime Minister's other goal of "Skilling India" is no less important and perhaps deserves as much attention. Make in India, if successful, would make India a Lewisian economy in relation to unskilled labor. But "Skilling India" has the potential to make India a Lewisian economy with respect to more skilled labor. The future trajectory of Indian economic development could depend on both.

MAKE IN INDIA: ZERO DEFECT, ZERO EFFECT

At a time when India's Development pitch caused concern among skeptical environmentalists, Prime Minister Narendra Modi's "Make in India: Zero defect and Zero effect" remark on Independence day-2014 came as a clear message that the country would not compromise on its commitment towards environmental protection.

"Let's think about making our product which has 'zero defect; so that it does not come back (get rejected) from the world market and 'zero effect' so that the manufacturing does not have an adverse effect on our environment" said the prime minister while delivering his maiden Independence Day speech.

It has been said that doing the thing right is as important as doing the right thing. India's journey to prosperity can be a more sustainable and environmentally sensitive if we follow the "Zero Defect Zero effect" concept.

An overarching objective of Make in India: Zero Defect, Zero Effect is to examine the notion of competitiveness from the perspective of a country, a region, a business and an individual. The roles of individual initiative, business strategy and economic development policies in maximizing productivity calls for recasting to fully tap the dormant potentials for productivity improvement & Environment Protection.

Productivity is the key to Prosperity, which in turn is an indicator of a country's potential for economic growth in the short to medium term. Productivity in its new manifestation, as a culture of accepting and bringing about continuous achievements incorporating environment concern is an inescapable imperative.

Environment protection is the major challenge being faced by all the countries in the world. No doubt, there has been unprecedented technological development in different fields whether it be of development could not be sustainable unless & until the development activities do not take care of environmental protection.

All kind of economic activity undertaken for the development of economy and society will use some kind of resources and have some impact on the environment. Therefore, it is necessary to evolve innovative ways to reduce the consumption of natural resources and develop solutions leading to sustainability of energy use and protection of global environment. As a matter of fact, any kind of development that is directed towards the development of economy and the society at large aims at enhancing the quality of life of the people. It cannot be fulfilled if the environment within which the society exists is deteriorating.

No one can rule out the global opportunities which are knocking the doors of Indian economy but, to capitalize this global opportunity Indian entrepreneur must have to achieve manufacturing excellence and have to carefully work upon competitive enhancement for their respective business. On such tough economic backdrop for business, the urge of 'Zero Defect & Zero Effect' from the Prime Minister is more like a challenge. By looking at the overall scenario and the status of Indian manufacturing this can also be termed as thumb rule to live up to the expectations of global opportunity and if the thumb rule is followed then the manufacturing segment of India could bring much awaited growth for the nation.

The wave of liberalization of economy in the world has brought about complexity and competition in each and every type of economic activity. Productivity is the only way to sharpen the competitive edge of every sector in the economy or the nation as a whole. Competitiveness is which meet the test of International Markets, while its citizens earn a standard of living that is both rising and sustainable over the long run.

Productivity has to emerge as a new national priority, where the efforts of all converge to accelerate the process of economic growth, protect environment and raise the standards of living of our people. Our business organizations will have to improve their performance to ensure their survival and growth in a fiercely competitive world. This improvement will come about only if we focus on production of zero defect quality goods, in a cost effective environment friendly manner, and this must occur continuously, to create an advantage in the market place, which is what productivity is all about. Productivity, thus, will have to become a mass movement and to be put on the national agenda.

Productivity may be the outcome of various practices, but eventually is the result of a mindset. The crucial ingredient is the preparedness of the human mind to achieve zero defect, zero effect. Basic to this approach is the conviction that even the best can be improved. Therefore, workers, managers, policy makers and others should be ready to continuously and collectively work for inculcating this concept in every economic activity for the prosperity of the society as well as the country. Needless to mention, as we graduate further into knowledge era, traditional methods and principles will become increasingly ineffective and we will have to propagate the concept both at micro as well as macro level to realize a global competitive edge as envisioned by the Prime Minister of India. "Make in India: Zero Defect, Zero Effect" has therefore, been chosen as the theme for the 'National Productivity Week-2015' (12th-18th February 2015).

'MAKE IN INDIA' FOR MORE 'MADE IN INDIA'

Doing business in India today is much more difficult than elsewhere, but the government wants to change this. Prime Minister Narendra Modi has launched the 'Make in India' initiative to attract investors and make India a global manufacturing hub.

The launch

'Goodbye red tape, hello red carpet' read one of the slogans that accompanied the launch of the 'Make in India' initiative on 25 September 2014. That day, Indian Prime Minister Narendra Modi addressed an audience of 500 domestic and international entrepreneurs in New Delhi, in an atmosphere charged with euphoria following the success of India's first mission to Mars the previous day. Modi inaugurated a campaign aimed at transforming India into a global manufacturing hub and at easing its business climate for both domestic and foreign investors. A logo, a portal and brochures detailing 25 priority sectors were introduced that day. The logo shows a striding lion made of cogs with the campaign name across its body.

Doing business in India today

India scores badly with regard to many indicators measuring an economy's capacity of doing business. In the World Bank's 'Doing Business 2015' report, India ranks 142nd out of 189 economies, lagging substantially behind China (90th) and Vietnam (78th), but also behind neighbours like Nepal (108th), Bhutan (125th) and Pakistan (128th). Dealing with construction permits (ranked 184th) and enforcing contracts (186th) are the most critical points, and starting a business (158th), paying taxes (156th), getting electricity (137th) and resolving insolvency (137th) are other challenging aspects. Protection of minority investors is the only topic in relation to which India features among the frontrunners, ranking seventh.

Furthermore, foreign companies complain about India's poor infrastructure, cumbersome land purchasing arrangements, excessive regulation, rigid labour laws and frequent power cuts.

Additional reasons for the new initiative

Several pressing issues prompted the launch of this campaign. First and foremost, India needs to reboot its economy. After several years of gross national product (GNP) growth averaging 7.7%, between 2002 and 2011, this pace slowed down to around 5% in 2013 and 2014.

Second, India needs more jobs for its young people. Recently, on average, 5 million new jobs have been created each year, but around 12 million people join the workforce each year. This is the other side of the demographic dividend: India's labour force is expected to grow to 600 million by 2022. Job creation will fight poverty and help divert people from agriculture, which has a low capacity to sustain their livelihood.

Third, India's economic development model has been quite peculiar, offering privileges to skilled labour often employed by foreign companies. Conversely, other economies have achieved success by first providing incentives for job-creating manufacturing industries. That is why today manufacturing in China makes up 34% of gross domestic product. The Chinese have positioned themselves as the 'workshop' of the world, accounting for 22.4% of global manufacturing, while India accounts for only 2%. India's manufacturing sector is less productive compared to its competitors and accounts for only 15% of its GDP. The government has set a target of 25% of GDP by 2022.

Fourth, rising labour costs (especially in the coastal provinces), the renminbi's appreciation and lower profit margins for businesses in China are at the origin of the shift in manufacturing orders to countries offering prospects of higher profits. Vietnam is a favourite destination, as entrepreneurs pin their hopes on the future Trans-Pacific Partnership (TPP). India needs to improve its business climate in order to take advantage of this shift and benefit from the likely shedding of millions of jobs by China.

The '2014 OECD Economic Survey of India' suggests several paths of reform for growth: India should adopt a flexible inflation-targeting framework, implement a broad national value-added tax (GST) and cut energy subsidies. It should reduce barriers to manufacturing growth and adopt a simpler and more flexible labour law, covering more workers, together with better education and training programmes. In addition, women's economic participation rates should rise through gender-specific policies, boosting growth by 2% annually.

'MAKE IN INDIA' IN PRACTICE

Consistent with the 'Digital India' programme launched in August 2014, the 'Make in India' portal, laid out in English, is a powerful supporting tool for the initiative. The website contains a wealth of information on the 25 priority sectors – from automobiles to wellness – that are eager to attract international business interest. It also gives information related to new government initiatives, foreign direct investment (FDI), local manufacturers, and intellectual property rights. Once they fill out a form, prospective investors will receive a reply from a panel of experts within 72 hours.

The portal gives visibility to the Delhi-Mumbai Industrial Corridor (DMIC). This project aims at developing a big area located in north-western India as a global manufacturing and investment destination, through a 1 483 km-long, high-capacity dedicated railway freight corridor running across six states.

The Invest India agency, whose mission is investment promotion and facilitation, is the 'back-end' of the 'Make in India' initiative. It has been set up as a joint venture between the Federation of Indian Chambers of Commerce and Industry (FICCI, 51% stake), the Department of Industrial Policy and Promotion within the Ministry of Commerce and Industry (DIPP, 35% stake), and the 28 state governments (0.5% stake each).

Meanwhile, the government has identified eight core areas for improvement, related to weaknesses identified in the World Bank's 'Doing Business 2015' report, with the ultimate goal of optimising business regulatory processes, reforming the licensing regime and shortening procedures. Registration of a new business will take a single day, unlike the current standard of 27 days. A unique company ID will be introduced. The seven steps involved in getting electricity supply will be reduced to one. It will be possible to register property online through a single procedure. The number of taxes will be reduced and making payments will be simplified. The Goods and Services Tax (GS) is expected to become operational in April 2016. Goods exports will require less paperwork. Fast-track commercial courts will be set up, and their decisions will be taken within a proposed limit of 60 days, in contrast to the current average of three years. The government wants to introduce a single bankruptcy law in place of the existing four overlapping ones.

While international institutions have already incorporated the reforms' success in their forecasts for 2015, Modi's good intentions are clashing with political reality. Reforms require a majority in both houses of Parliament; the governing coalition (NDA) has a majority in the Lok Sabha (lower house) while it is in the minority in the Rajya Sabha (upper house). The government has adopted temporary executive ordinances on land acquisition, FDI in the insurance sector and coal-mining licences, but it will need to come to agreement with the opposition to make them permanent. Some changes are already operational. Validity of industrial licences has been extended to seven years. FDI ceilings in railway infrastructure and defence have been raised. In July 2014, the DIPP made a promise to process all pending applications within 90 days and henceforth all new ones within 20 days. Labour law procedures have been simplified for businesses employing fewer than 40 workers.

REACTIONS TO 'MAKE IN INDIA'

'Make in India' has received widespread support from industry leaders from both India and abroad as well as from the Confederation of Indian Industry (CII). Some companies, including foreign ones, have already announced plans related to the initiative.

Reserve Bank of India Governor Raghuram Rajanin dismissed the idea of introducing a policy targeting the manufacturing sector, just because it had worked for China, given how different the two countries are. He underlined the risks of an export-driven approach in a global economy still in crisis, and where many industrialised economies are strengthening their own manufacturing capabilities. 'The world as a whole is unlikely to be able to accommodate another export-led China', he said.

CK Ranganathan, the founding chairman of popular Indian household brand CavinKare, said that he would rather support a 'Made in India' approach in which India would be creating its own internationally renowned brands. Srikant Jena, a former government minister, stated that efforts to resolve caste and gender inequalities as well as regional imbalances, were missing from the initiative.

MAKE IN INDIA: RE-CHANTING THE MANTRA WITH A DIFFERENCE

It is an Old Mantra

From the ramparts of the Red Fort, Prime Ministers of India talk to the nation every 15th of August with the usual supply of pride and promises. The address mostly goes unnoticed confirming the economic adage that talk is cheap for supply exceeds demand.

However, there was a pleasant departure from this perception on 15 August 2014. While Mr. Narendra Modi had been attracting ever increasing viewership leading up to the May 2014 Lok Sabha elections, it reached a crescendo on the independence day, when as per some reports, a whopping 56 million viewers watched their newly elected Prime Minister with rapt attention. In his maiden independence day speech, if Mr. Modi was humble enough to acknowledge India's socio-demographic ills, he also seemed confident to chant the economic mantra-Make in India.

Come to think of it, the mantra of Make in India is not a new one. There are no prizes for deciphering the objective of this mantra-Have higher employment, better standard of living, and high per capita GDP for the nation. What is difficult is the process of attaining that objective. In the pre-independence days, economists like Dadabhai Nauroji (1901) lamented the economic drain of India by the colonial masters. Raw material was being procured cheaply from Indians and shipped out to get it processed in England, only to be shipped back and sold to Indians for a profit.

To him, this was an obvious consequence of subjects of the colonies being treated unequally by the colonizers. Of course, despite this disadvantage, at the turn of the 19th century it was Laxmanrao Kirloskar who produced India s first iron plough and Sir Jamshedji Tata s efforts paved way for India s first steel mill. Entrepreneurship was very much there and Make in India story was evolving. However, Justice M.G. Ranade of the then

Bombay Presidency, had expressed concerns over sustainability of such efforts. In his lectures delivered in Deccan College, Pune in 1892 , he had noted that science and its application were the ultimate basis for industrial society. As quoted by John Adams (1971), Ranade opined that while India needed pragmatic education and skilled labour, issues of political dominance (by the British) were attracting far more attention than the formidable though unfelt domination of capital and skill. As we will consider later, this emphasis on pragmatic education continues to be very important even today.

The next phase of Make in India began with the advent of independence in 1947. The zeitgeist of that era was that someone (East India Company) had come as a trader and became our master. Therefore, the hard earned independence was to be protected by having no truck with the rest of the world. This translated into a principle of „make only in India and only for India." To achieve this, Nehru was attracted by the model followed by the Union of Soviet Socialist Republic (USSR). Though enamoured with socialism, Nehru did not want to emulate USSR s bloody revolution and the consequent civil war of the 1920s. He was a Fabian socialist. Like the Roman general Fabius, who won battles by slowly tiring his opponents, Fabian socialists believed in ushering-in socialism through gradual changes and not bloody revolutions. To further this objective, he sent Dr. Mahalonobis to US and France where he interacted with Wassily Leontief and the French Marxists, respectively. Armed with input-output model of Leontief and the socialist ideal, Nehru could introduce central planning, command and control economy (License Raj), and extreme restrictions on imports and exports.

Mantra had Failed to Work

There were a few dissenters to these Nehruvian developments. Milton Friedman visited India in 1955 on the invitation of government of India and expressed reservations about the obsession with input-output model. He emphasized development of human capital and mobility of labour and goods through infrastructure development. Dr. B.R. Shenoy (1955) too had written a dissent note to the second five year plan and asserted that government intervention should be limited to the cases of market failure – namely public goods, (natural) monopolies and merit goods. Krishnamurthy (Balasubramanyam, 2001) too had criticized the government for spending absurdly low amounts on education and wasting large sums on heavy industries.

He advocated enhancement of prestige of school teachers through higher salaries which would in turn increase employability of workforce. These dissenting voices fell on the deaf ears of the then policy makers and planners. The communist state of Cuba was successful in universalizing primary education and health care but suffered heavily in terms of economic growth. In India, however, government neither universalized education and health nor promoted rapid economic growth. IBM and Coca Cola leaving India under duress in 1977 and 1978 were tell-tale signs of something being wrong in the policies. The poor average GDP growth rate of about 1.5 per cent per capita till then, however, was described pejoratively as the Hindu rate of growth by Raj Krishna! It should rightly have been christened as the socialist rate of growth. The experiment of a highly controlled economy in making only in India and making only for India had failed.

By 1991, the consequences of decades of license raj, planning, and autarkic worldview had reached its nadir. Foreign currency reserves fell sharply and dipped below $ 1 billion in January 1991 and despite initial borrowing from IMF, default on payments had become a real possibility in June 1991 (Acharya, 2001). As a response, government had to devalue Indian Rupee by 18 per cent in July 1991 and allow up to 51 per cent foreign direct investment in India. This about turn in the policies was more of an exigency than a planned strategy. As Aiyar (2012) points out, this trigger for the liberalization process was more of an accidental silver lining, a happenstance of sorts. There was no concrete policy of Make in India at this juncture but mere survival instinct had played a part. The liberalization process that began in 1991 did not seem to benefit industrial sector. A country on its developmental path goes through the sequential high GDP shares of agriculture, industry, and tertiary services, respectively. Of course, traditionally share of agriculture in India s GDP was the highest. It remained so till 1974 when its share in the GDP was at 40 per cent. From here on, industrial sector should have grown substantially, leaving share of agriculture behind. Expectedly, share of agriculture did come down to about 14 per cent by early 2014. However, growth in the industrial sector seemed to skip the developmental path. Between 1979 to early 2014, share of industry remained stagnant at about 25 per cent. In fact, within industrial sector, share of manufacturing in GDP is only about 15 per cent (GOI, 2014). Clearly, Make in India story was not happening with the accidental liberalization that began in 1991.

In contrast, it is the tertiary sector which has leap-frogged with a share in GDP of about 60 per cent. While lot is made about India s software industry, it does not employ any significant proportion of workforce. For example, the share of services associated with knowledge and technology, finance, business, and telecommunication is about 25.3 per cent of GDP, however, the estimated employment in these service sectors is only about 2.2 per cent (The Hindu, 2014). In contrast, innumerable traditional unorganized services including ones in wholesale trade, retail trade, transportation, tourism, administrative support, and quite a few other services seems to employ too many individuals with low earnings.

Umpteen number of anecdotal experiences such as but not limited to competing taxicab drivers swarming around passengers at airports and railway stations, citizens being pestered by competing agents at regional transport offices (RTOs), court offices, district collectorates and other administrative offices, pilgrims being harried by teeming garland/pooja thali sellers, and street-performer families begging for a well-deserved bakshishi, bring out this phenomena. In short, informal and traditional services contribute a lot to low wage employment and high productivity services that generate substantive revenues/GDP provide little in employment. This contrast is reflective of a very small highly-skilled employable population residing in a large pool of population faced with both-inadequate job opportunities and skillsets required for the manufacturing sector.

Re-chanting with a Difference?

And now, the old Make in India mantra, which was not heard during the 1991 liberalization process, has been pronounced loud and clear from the ramparts of red fort. In fact, even the previous government was concerned about the poor performance of manufacturing sector. In 2011, it had announced national manufacturing policy which aimed at enhancing the share of manufacturing in GDP from 16 per cent to 25 per cent by 2022. Between 2011 and 2014, however, nothing substantial happened except change of government at the center.

Interestingly, principles of neo-classical economics do not support advocacy of a pro-active policy such as Make in India. The comparative advantage theory of David Ricardo prescribes that a country would export those goods in which it has a comparative (cost) advantage.

Factor abundance theory of Heckscher and Ohlin shows that a country will export those goods which use its abundance factors more intensively. And, the new trade theories of Paul Krugman et al show that a country will specialize in production and export of differentiated products which take advantage of economies of scale on the production side and consumers preference for variety on the other. None of these theories prescribe any overtly pro-active role for the government.

Adam Smith (1776), the father of modern economics said, "It is not from the benevolence of the butcher, the brewer, or the baker that we expect our dinner, but from their regard to their own interest." Therefore, free market and the self-interest of the market players will decide who (which country) will produce what. In fact, proactive policies of government also suffer from fallacy of composition. Disregarding principles of economics, if leader of a single country were to incentivize firms from all over the world to produce goods in his/her country, it just may work. However, if all leaders from all the countries were to announce and implement this policy, then it is not going to succeed for any one of them.

In this context, what does one make of the new Make in India mantra? Prime Minister Modi s government is not a champion of socialist ideology. It supports free market ideology. Then how would this Make in India mantra be different than its previous chants?

The re-chanting would make sense on two counts. While the free market ideology expects no government interference, there are two caveats where government involvement is required. The first caveat is that if we want free market to be the engine of growth, then the government has to provide lubricant for the smooth functioning of this engine.

Efficient judiciary, protection of property rights, good civil administration, and, importantly, market friendly government policies are these lubricants. The second caveat is that markets do not always function well.

There are certain perversions where markets fail to deliver. Government has to intervene in such cases but must limit its intervention to these perversions only. The obvious interventions are in the cases of pure public goods such as provision of internal and external security and prevention of monopolies or collusive practices by firms. All governments have been pursuing these objectives and will continue to do so in future. Importantly, the crucial interventions where government can support Make in India story are required in network infrastructure projects such as rapid transit metros, buses, railways, highway, and irrigation; and other big infrastructure projects such as power generation, lighthouses, dams, and irrigation. And, importantly, government will also have to focus attention on merit goods such as primary health care, education, and basic research. Interventions of these kinds help improve comparative advantage of a nation.

Market Friendly Laws

Make in India mantra gives a perception that it is an invitation only to foreign firms to produce in India. In fact, Make in India policies should substantially facilitate production by domestic firms as well. In this context, sequencing of the policies assumes importance. Level playing field will have to be offered to domestic firms, especially the small and medium sized firms prior to or concurrently with the incentives that will be offered to foreign firms. In the last 7 decades, growth of manufacturing firms has been stifled primarily due to many archaic laws and needs to be changed first.

Labour and Industrial Laws

For example, a manufacturing unit comes under the purview of Factory s Act 1948 the moment it employs 10 or more workers with power or 20 or more workers without power. As a result, firms have a disincentive to expand operations, for the moment they hire beyond 10 (or 20) workers, they are restricted to only 50 hours of overtime work per worker per quarter, and women are excluded from working in night shifts (ILO, 2014). The minimum worker limit on firms to come under the purview of factories act could be raised to 20 (40) workers, respectively. In fact, the overtime restriction could be raised to 100 hours and with certain safety provisions, women too be allowed to work in night shifts. Currently, all factories in a particular area are allowed to have weekly-off only on a specific day. They be allowed to have weekly-offs on different days so that the problem of power load-shedding will be managed much more effectively preventing valuable production loss. At present, the rules of factories act are to be amended by state governments. They be allowed to be formed by central government so that the rules get changed quickly across states and remain consistent throughout the country.

Similarly, Industrial Disputes Act (IDA, 1947) requires that a firm must take approval from the government for laying-off workers or shutting the firm down if it employees 100 or more workers. As a result, firms are unable to adjust to changing market conditions by altering its labour requirement. Moreover, under extreme conditions, exit of loss-making firms becomes very difficult. Amendment to this act should be made so that firms are required to take government approval only if they employ 300 or more workers. This flexibility will provide confidence to the industry to invest in manufacturing. Currently, it is sufficient to gather 15 per cent of employees to form a union at a workplace. This means, a workplace could have as many as 6 unions. This creates problems in terms of inter-union rivalries among workers and firms also find it difficult to deal with many unions simultaneously. As a result, the transaction cost of negotiation with workers is too high. The norm on minimum number of workers required to form a union should be raised to at least 30 per cent. Government of Rajasthan has brought about such changes in the industrial laws (TOI, 2014a). Other states may have to actively pursue this objective to promote manufacturing.

Land Ceiling and Land Acquisition Laws

The Make in India mantra also needs efficient provision of an important factor of production – land. David Ricardo (1817) described rent as a reward for the original and indestructible powers of the soil. However, if the supply of land is ill-managed, these rewards (rents) can skyrocket chocking industrial development. The Urban Land Ceiling Ac (ULCA, 1978) was enacted with a typical socialist mindset to avoid concentration of urban land in the hands of a few rich individuals. However, this law led to shortage of usable land in urban areas, for lands were either not declared out of fear or kept vacant with convenient exemptions sought by the owners. Though the central government gave the lead by repealing the act in 1999, quite a few states including West Bengal have yet to do so (TOI, 2014b). And, those states which have repealed the act have not pro-actively made use of the vacant lands. Using large tracts of urban vacant lands for housing of urban poor will provide impetus for realty sector, put a halt to skyrocketing realty prices, and, importantly, solve the problem of affordable housing for the industrial workers – an important pre-requisite for growth of manufacturing sector.

Similarly, for faster industrialization, fair but quicker land acquisition processes have to be in place. Countries with very low population density in Americas and Africa, and countries such as Australia, New Zealand, and Russia have fewer land acquisition issues, for land is abundantly available. Similarly, totalitarian regimes like China may also have fewer issues in acquiring land, for considerations of sanctity of individual rights and freedom may not necessarily take precedence over dictates of the state. On the other hand, land acquisition for industrial growth is a challenging issue for countries like India which are both – vibrant democracies and very densely populated. In 1950s, when large dams such as Hirakud and Bhakra were constructed, Jawaharlal Nehru would inaugurate them, but reports of sufferings of villagers evicted from their land and being made destitute would also surface alongside (Guha, 2007). This was the result of the coercive power government had enjoyed for over a century through the colonial Land Acquision Act of 1894. As a reaction, a new act was passed in 2013 (GOI, 2014) and given a lengthy name-Right to Fair Compensation and Transparency in Land Acquisition, Rehabilitation and Resettlement Act (LARR). However, the hastily passed act had many lacuna.

LARR had left out over 13 central laws that could have prevented higher compensation to landowners. Moreover, LARR made it mandatory to return lands that were acquired but not used for 5 years. This was inconsistent with implementation of large infrastructure projects which generally have long gestation periods. Similarly, no more than 5 per cent of fertile land could have been acquired in any district as per LARR. This too would have prevented many mega-projects to get implemented. In the context of land acquisition in Singur, Sen (2007) had clearly opined that industry always competes with agriculture for land, and historically, for trade and logistic reasons, production of industrial goods has taken place along large rivers like Hooghly and Ganga which obviously have fertile lands. This happens, for industry generates output many times more than what a fertile land can. Moreover, projects such as affordable housing, rural infrastructure, national security, industrial corridors along highways may not need to have consent and lengthy social impact assessments, for the benefits of such projects are starkly obvious. The latest ordinance promulgated at the end of 2014 has made appropriate changes to LARR on the above issues (The Hindu, 2015). It will be in the interest of state governments to take advantage of the new provisions to promote employment and infrastructure development in rural areas.

FLOW OF FUNDS FROM ABROAD SAVINGS AND INVESTMENTS

For the Make in India mantra to succeed, India will need huge long-term investments in infrastructure, be it ports, defence, industrial corridors, affordable housing, highways, mass transit railways, and quite a few other sectors. Savings generated within Indian economy will certainly not be sufficient for this purpose. In fact, as per the World Bank data, in the year 2013, India s domestic savings rate was 27.8 per cent, much lower than 51.8 per cent, 52.1 per cent, 35.5 per cent, and 34.1 per cent of China, Singapore, Malaysia, and South Korea, respectively (World Bank, 2015). Indians have a certain propensity to buy gold instead of putting substantive savings into financial assets. Inflation has further intensified this propensity, for gold is viewed as a safeguard against inflation. Buying gold is hoarding of finances which does not lead to any productive use for investment purposes. While lower rates of inflation can reverse this trend, for gold will not be used as a hedge again inflation, bringing financial inclusion through opening up of bank accounts for the poor and educating households about financial instruments such as mutual funds, gold loans will increase savings rate.

Even with moderate increases in savings rate, India s savings rate is very low compared to East Asian countries. In stark contrast, however, the need for domestic investments is too large. Hence, India will have to attract foreign direct investments

(FDI) and institutional portfolio investment. For sometime now, 100 per cent FDI is allowed in a whole range of activities. This includes activities such as greenfield airport projects, townships, oil and natural gas exploration, high-speed train projects, rail terminals and electrification, power sector (except nuclear), telecom, biotechnology, and single brand retail.

FDI in passenger airline, cable TV, and now even the defence sector can be made upto 49 per cent with automatic route. A significant import of this listing is that the government has made it easier, at least in terms of ownership, for foreign entities to invest in India. There are a few exceptions still. FDI in print media and food processing in pickle and bread segment is still restricted to 26 per cent (IFC, 2015) and FDI in multi-brand retail is limited to 51 per cent subject to approval by respective state governments.

Impact of Multi-Brand Retail 100 per cent FDI is multi-brand retail has been hotly debated and mostly resisted due to pressure from domestic groups. However, time is ripe for allowing 100 per cent FDI in multi-brand retail. First, it is not that the domestic players will be suddenly exposed to competition from large retail firms from abroad. Already, Reliance Fresh, Star Bazar, Big Bazar and a few other domestic large retail outlets have been successfully operating in Indian market. They have the expertise in modern retailing including volume procurements, logistics, and marketing.

Thus, sequencing of opening up retail sector for foreign firms has been correct. Moreover, large domestic and foreign retailers will not be a threat to domestic kirana stores as been alleged. In fact, Kirana stores offer tough competition to the large retailers. For millions of Indians Kirana stores offer small volume sales, flexible credit, anytime home-delivery, and proximity-shopping which large foreign retailers cannot. Furthermore, kirana stores also stand to pick-up some good practices from large retailers such as clean store and working environment, absence of child-labour, and better record keeping through automated billing counters. All in all, a healthy competition among foreign retailers, domestic retailers, and kirana stores will only generate more employment and more options for customers.

Ease of Starting and Doing Business

There are a few important caveats, however, for a successful implementation of FDI policy. In fact, some of them help domestic firms as well. As per the World Bank ratings, India ranks as low as 179th and 134th in terms of east of starting business and ease of doing business, respectively (World Bank, 2014).

The corresponding ranks for South Korea are 34 and 7, respectively. Unless governmental procedures are simplified and undue delays in clearances of permits are avoided, the tall policy statements will not materialize in influx of FDI in India.

Government recognizes this issue, and, at least on paper it aims at bringing, among other things, a few of the following changes: 1) Process of applying for industrial license and industrial entrepreneur memorandum to be made online on 24×7 basis through eBiz portal. 2) Services of all central government departments and ministries to be integrated with the eBiz – a single window IT platform for services. 3) A check-list of required compliances to be placed on ministry/department web portals. 4) All returns to be filed on-line through a unified form. 5) Process of obtaining environmental clearances to be made online. And, in addition to such measures, availability of uninterrupted power and other infrastructural services will go a long way in attracting FDI. Hopefully, FDI in and privatization of power sector itself would remove this hurdle.

Advance Information on Taxation

Second, in an effort to attract FDI, governments channelize foreign investment through export processing zones (EPZs), which receive tax holidays on production of goods for exports. EPZs were promoted in the past by countries such as Malaysia. However, they created what is termed as "shallow industrialization", for industrial activity in EPZs has lower multiplier effect on domestic production, employment, income, and transfer of technology. Instead, Special

Economic Zones (SEZs) such as the ones promoted in China will benefit domestic sector abundantly. Of course, India is a large country and foreign firms may produce goods in (non-EPZ or SEZ) India and show as if it was produced in an EPZ or SEZ and avoid taxation. Similarly, to avoid taxation, Indian subsidiaries of foreign firms sell shares and/or goods to its parent firm abroad at lower price than what the price would have been in an arms-length contract between two independent firms. To counter such tax avoidance, government of India had proposed transfer pricing rules and General Anti-Avoidance Rules (GAAR). Government attempted to impose GAAR with a retrospective effect starting 2010. Such provisions create uncertainty about government s intentions and prevent inward FDI. As per the recommendations of the Expert Committee on GAAR (Shome Committee, 2012), government must first train its officers about global tax laws and implement GAAR only in 2016 or later, not bother firms with alleged tax benefits of Rs. 3 crore or lower, and, must strengthen functioning of Authority for Advance Ruling (AAR). Through AAR, foreign firms would know and have clarity on their potential tax liabilities in advance. Implementation of GAAR by 2016 by incorporating such suggestions would offer foreign firms a degree of comfort to initiate long-term FDI.

Inevitability of Current Account Deficit

Third caveat is about the balance of payments impact of FDI. If India is successful in attracting substantive amounts of FDI, there is a potential for perpetuating high current account deficit. It is often alleged by businessmen that once they get access to FDI, they will be able to export more. While this may be true for an individual business or a few businesses, this is just now possible at an aggregate macroeconomic level (Krugman, 1996). This is referred to as the fallacy of composition – What is true for an individual cannot be true for the economy. If there is a net inflow of foreign investments on capital account, it means that foreign citizens and firms are buying Indian assets. These include physical assets such as land, buildings, machinery, and financial assets such as shares, debentures, and bonds. If there is a net inflow, and therefore, a surplus on the capital account, there must be an outflow, and therefore, deficit on current account. This is the only way to have a zero balance of payments. If foreigners are buying our assets on a net basis, then we must be buying their goods and services on a net basis. This is merely a self-evident statement of accounting principle.

This above accounting principle is also evident from the national income identity, (S-I) = (G-T) + (X-M), where the terms refer to values of savings, investments, government expenditure, taxes, exports, and imports, respectively. The parenthesis values, therefore, refer to excess of savings of investments, fiscal deficit, and current account surplus. Assuming that fiscal deficit is constant, higher the negative value of (S-I) on account of low savings and high FDI, the higher will be the negative value of (X-M). In short, higher the FDI, higher is the current account deficit. Therefore, one must remember that as long as substantive amounts of net foreign investments keep coming into India, India must be ready to experience a current account deficit. This has been evidenced by Mexico in the early 1990s (Krugman, 1996). Optimism about Mexico s economic prospects led to pouring-in of foreign investment from 1989. Increased supply of US dollars strengthened Peso and Mexican exports declined. On the other hand, while some of the foreign funds were spent on imported equipment and technology for Mexican factories, the rest caused domestic income boom, causing Mexicans to purchase expensive imported goods. Thus, massive capital inflows caused massive current account deficit.

Merit Goods and Comparative Advantage

So far, we talked about the market friendly policies that can act as lubricant for the free-market engine of growth. However, if this engine of growth depends perpetually on the doses of FDI and foreign technology, this would result in persistent current account deficit. Of course, inculcating habit among households of saving into various financial instruments and promoting financial inclusion of millions who do not have even a bank account will help reduce dependence on foreign funding. However, more often than not, FDI is coupled with foreign technology. As long as there is dependence on foreign technology, FDI will have to be internalized. Dependence on foreign technology can be reduce only in the long-run by focusing on provision of merit goods such as basic and applied research. Moreover, in the short to medium term, comparative advantage can also be improved by focusing attention on another set of merit goods – primary education and health care. Merit goods such as research, education, and health show high degree of positive externalities on society. Left to itself, private sector under provides these activities. These are classic cases of market failure, and, therefore, government s role is very critical in these fields.

Primary Education, Training, and Health Care

If Indian economy has to catch-up on manufacturing and attain at least 25 per cent share in GDP, it needs skilled, educated, and healthy workforce. Producing consistent quality output on the shop floor and persistently providing professional services requires a workforce that is educated and able bodied. In comparison to the 2010 literacy rates of 95 per cent in China and Mexico, 93 per cent in Malaysia, and 90 per cent in Brazil (World Bank, 2015), India s literacy rate measured by its own liberal standards was little over 73 per cent in 2011. This means that in a group of 4 people, on an average more than 1 person cannot read and write. Moreover, in comparison to the 2013 infant mortality rates (IMR) of 11, 12, and 13 per 1000 live births in China, Brazil, and Mexico, respectively; India s IMR was as high as 41 per 1000 live births that year. A high IMR is a proxy for morbidity – a departure from a state of physical or psychological well-being resulting from disease, illness, injury, or sickness. Therefore, the much touted potential build-up of investments in manufacturing by domestic firms and by technology driven FDI stands no chance to succeed unless India s workforce has basic education and health to work efficiently on the shop floor or anywhere in the supply chain.

While universalization of primary education must be emphasized, skill development for the manufacturing sector is also important. To hasten this process, retired personnel from armed forces and railways could be effectively used. These two organizations have thousands of skilled and experienced personnel who introduce, maintain, and up-grade mechanical and electrical equipment of all kinds for their own use. Such personnel can contribute significantly to strengthen and expand the existing industrial training institutes (ITIs). Moreover, in healthcare, while the expensive super-specialty hospitals could be left in the hands of the private sector, government must focus on primary health care which is not only labour intensive but cheap. For example, Government of Gujarat has successfully implemented Chirajeevi scheme that provides affordable pre and post-natal healthcare in rural areas. This scheme has won Prime Ministers award as well as Wall Street Journal award (Deodhar, 2012).

Endogenous Growth of Knowledge and Technology

Come to think of it – from the alarm clock that wakes one up in the morning to the zero watt bulb that we glow at bedtime and all products that are used in between, were developed outside India. This almost sounds as if technology and knowledge has become exogenous to the Indian economy. We may have manufactured Fiat and Ambassador cars in the past but the technology came from abroad. Similarly, we may succeed in manufacturing everything from cellphones, mass transit metros, to submarines; however, so far all these inventions have occurred outside India. Make in India mantra has to go beyond this exogeneity of knowledge and technology for the Indian economy.

For starters, this means that government must focus on public goods such as basic research and higher education. Government owned Air India, which is certainly not a public good, has so far incurred a massive cumulative loss of about

Rs. 33,200 crore (India Today, 2014). The precious tax revenue that Indians have paid to cover this loss could instead be used to finance setting up of academic institutions. And there are umpteen number of other public sector enterprises that could take the disinvestment rout to finance educational sector. Of course, acquiring land and buildings for such academic institutions may not pose a problem; however, most difficult aspect is to attract qualified human capital. Salaries and incentives to academicians, and those include high-school teachers, research professors and scientists, should be such that talented individuals are drawn to higher education and research. The traditional system of rote learning which hardly equips students with professional skills and innovative thinking has to be discarded. Teaching methods that encourage lateral thinking and group activities will have to be promoted. Increasingly, in the comity of nations, India will have to be a pro-active participant in the use of sustainable, low-carbon emitting technologies in the industrial sector. Therefore, simply borrowing conventional technology through FDI which is new to India is not going to be enough. A long term goal would be to promote basic research in innovating use of alternate energy sources.

Grow in India

Similarly, in the agricultural sector, productivity growth is a major concern. Productivity of green revolution crops has reached its peak and India needs a new revolution in agriculture for feeding the burgeoning population. Today, about 40 to 50 per cent of edible oil and dal, the main sources of cooking medium and protein, respectively, are being imported into India (NYT, 2012). While high productivity genetically modified (GM) food and non-food crops have been already under cultivation in US, Argentina, China and quite a few other countries, India has not allowed field trials of cultivation of GM food crops. This has help up scientific research in food crops that are particularly suitable to India. So far, the only non-food GM crop that has been allowed to grow commercially is Bt Cotton. Interestingly, since its introduction in 2002, cotton production in India has trebled and India has now overtaken both US and China to become the world s number 1 producer of cotton.

Of course, opponents have criticized GM technology for promoting potentially hazardous mutations that transcend specie barriers. However, as long as meticulous field trials are carried out to ensure stable varieties, it should not be a matter of concern. After all, green revolution era high yielding varieties (HYV) of crops were also developed by human intervention – cross breeding of Indian wheat and rice with those of far-away lands of Mexico to the west and the Philippines to the east. It would not be out of context to mention that when Laxmanrao Kirloskar manufactured India s first iron plough at the turn of the 19th century, opponents had claimed that iron plough poisoned the soil and reduced its fertility! India must introduce GM food crops which require less pesticide use, give higher productivity, and which can also be grown in arid regions. On the demand side, a study on acceptance of GM crops (Deodhar, Ganesh and Chern, 2008) shows that majority of consumers are willing to accept GM foods. Very recently, Maharashtra government has allowed field trials of 5 GM crops. This is a welcome move.

Concluding Observations

Make in India is an old mantra chanted since pre-independence days. In the post-independence era of centralized planning, it assumed a staunchly autarkic hue. However, by 1991 it became obvious that an inward looking economic policy was not going to work. Economic liberalization was embraced as a fait accompli then. However, re-chanting of Make in India mantra begun with the new government taking office at the center. What does one make of this initiative? Prime Minister Mr. Narendra Modi arrived in a Mahindra Scorpio car for his swearing-in ceremony, however, by the time he addressed the nation on 15 August 2014, he had begun using BMWs. He even sports a Montblanc pen which he used at the swearing-in ceremony. Therefore, the message in today s context certainly cannot be autarkic in nature.

Make in India mantra would work if government were to allow private sector to flourish, and, importantly, unlike in the past, focus only on the sectors where it is supposed to function. If free market is going to be the engine of growth, then government needs to provide the necessary lubricant for this engine. As discussed, center and the states will have to bring necessary changes to the archaic industrial, labour and land acquisition laws which offer safeguards to labour and landowners but does not stifle growth of manufacturing. Societal welfare can be promoted not by permanent job safety and illiquidity in land transactions but by providing horizontal an upward mobility to workers and landowners arising out of growth in manufacturing and infrastructure development. Similarly, low savings rate to finance domestic investments will have to raised by incentives to households to invest in financial instruments rather than gold and promote financial inclusion of millions of households which do not even have a bank account today. And, while this will take time, FDI may be allowed to flow in along with its attendant technology transfer. However, for a smooth and substantive flow of FDI, government will have to ensure bringing synergy in various local, state, and central administrative clearances. Moreover, issues related to transfer pricing and tax avoidance must be conveyed in transparent manner in advance through AAR. These initiatives create much need confidence the foreign firms need for a sustained long-term presence in the country.

An inevitable consequence of a sustained and substantive net inflow of FDI would be that India will experience current account deficit for the foreseeable future. This will continue to happen if technology continues to be available only exogenously from rest of the world. Moreover, while one may believe in the theory of comparative advantage, it does not mean that a country cannot improve its comparative advantage. Nurturing environment for progress of technology and improving comparative advantage of the workforce through education, skill development and healthcare has to happen. Left to itself, private sector underprovides basic research, education, and primary healthcare. These being the classic cases of market failure, government must step-in to universalize primary education and healthcare, and promote research institutions with appropriate incentives for human capital.

Thus, re-chanting of Make in India must happen with a difference. Two things need to be done with a difference – First, market friendly policies must act as a lubricant for the engine of growth, something that Milton Friedman had suggested in his visit to India in 1955. Second, government must get out of activities which do not fit into market failure arguments, something that B.R. Shenoy had suggested in 1955. Sooner the government bids tata to Air India the better. Disinvestments of such unwarranted public sector enterprises could generate thousands of crores of rupees which can be better spent by the government on merit goods, which private sector will underprovide. As was opined by Justice M.G. Ranade in 1892, India needs pragmatic education and skilled labour, for science and its application are the ultimate basis for an industrial society.

2

Prime Minister to Launch 'Make in India' Initiative

Prime Minister Shri Narendra Modi will launch "Make in India" initiative on 25th September 2014 from Vigyan Bhawan in New Delhi. The launch will be at both national level, state level and in Missions abroad. The 'Make in India' initiative has its origin in the Prime Minister's Independence Day speech where he gave a clarion call to 'Make in India' and 'Zero Defect; Zero Effect' policy. State Governments, Business Chambers, Indian Missions aboard are playing an active role in the launch of the initiative.

The Government is committed to chart out a new path wherein business entities are extended red carpet welcome in a spirit of active cooperation. Invest India will act as the first reference point for guiding foreign investors on all aspects of regulatory and policy issues and to assist them in obtaining regulatory clearances. The Government is closely looking into all regulatory processes with a view to making them simple and reducing the burden of compliance on investors.

A dedicated cell has been created to answer queries from business entities through a newly created web portal . While an exhaustive set of FAQs on this portal will help the investor find instant answers to their general queries, the back-end support team of the cell would be answering specific queries within 72 hours. A pro-active approach will be deployed to track visitors for their geographical location, interest and real time user behaviour. Subsequent visits will be customised for the visitor based on the information collected. Visitors registered on the website or raising queries will be followed up with relevant information and newsletter. Investor facilitation cell will provide assistance to the foreign investors from the time of their arrival in the country to the time of their departure. The initiative will also target top companies across sectors in identified countries.

The 'Make in India' initiative also aims at identifying select domestic companies having leadership in innovation and new technology for turning them into global champions. The focus will be on promoting green and advanced manufacturing and helping these companies to become an important part of the global value chain.

The Government has identified 25 key sectors in which our country has the potential of becoming a world leader. The Prime Minister will be releasing separate brochures for these sectors along with a general brochure. The brochures covering sectors like automobiles, chemicals, IT, pharmaceuticals, textiles, ports, aviation, leather, tourism and hospitality, wellness, railways among others will provide details of growth drivers, investment opportunities, sector specific FDI and other policies and related agencies.

Since the new Government took over, a series of initiatives have been taken to revitalise the industrial sector in general and manufacturing sector in particular. To mention a few:

- The process of applying for Industrial License and Industrial Entrepreneur Memorandum has been made online on the e-Biz website 24*7;
- A vast number of Defence items have been de-licensed;
- The validity of Industrial license has been extended to three years;
- With a view to providing flexibility in working hours and increased intake of apprentices for on the job training, the Government has decided to amend a number of labour laws;

- An advisory has been sent to all Departments/ State Governments to simplify and rationalize regulatory environment which includes:
  - on-line filing of all returns in a unified form;
  - no inspection without the approval of the Head of the Department, etc.

Recently the Foreign Direct Investment policy has been liberalized. 100% FDI under automatic route has been permitted in construction, operation and maintenance in specified Rail Infrastructure projects; FDI in Defence liberalized from 26% to 49%. In cases of modernization of state-of-art proposals, FDI can go up to 100%; the norms for FDI in the Construction Development sector are being eased.

The government is committed to improving the physical infrastructure. Development of dedicated freight corridors and investment in improving our ports and airports are underway. These corridors would house Industrial agglomerations along with smart cities. The private sector would be playing a significant role in these developmental works.

For the manufacturing sector to take advantage of the improved physical infrastructure, the need for having a strong human capital is recognized. Government's effort would be to equip the working age population with the right kinds of skill so that the manufacturing sector finds them employable. One of the first decisions that the new Government has taken is to set up a separate Department of Skill Development and Entrepreneurship.

Various prominent National and International industry leaders are likely to attend the programme to launch the campaign along with Ministers, senior officials, Ambassadors and opinion leaders.

MODI LAUNCHES 'MAKE IN INDIA' - BIG BOOST TO INDUSTRY & EMPLOYMENT

The launch of the 'Make in India' campaign by Prime Minister Narendra Modi to attract foreign investments and boost the manufacturing sector of India has been timed to perfection. It comes a day after India's indigenously manufactured satellite Mangalyaan was successfully put in the Martian orbit, showing to the world the progress India has made in manufacturing processes, technology, science and innovation.

It also comes a day ahead of the PM's visit to the US. 'Make in India' is intended to provide a major fillip to India's manufacturing industry which currently contributes about 15% of the national GDP.

The Prime Minister released a brochure with all the information that will be required by investors about 25 key sectors in India. The brochure carried the newly designed 'Make In India' logo which has been inspired by the Ashoka Chakra and the lion. A large number of Indian corporate honchos were present at the launch of the campaign in Delhi on Thursday.

Here are some of the key takeaways from the Prime Minister's speech at the launch ceremony.

- Trust and confidence in the government and policymakers have been lost. These need to be regained.
- We do not want to see any company or enterprise leave India due to business constraints
- An environment of trust will convince industry leaders of the government's commitment to developing industry
- FDI is a responsibility for the people and an opportunity for the global investors; FDI for Indians should be "First Develop India" and Foreign Direct Investment for the investors
- Only when India moves away from poverty will purchasing power in the country increase and when this happens the country will start to bloom as a grand huge market for industries
- The movement away from poverty will come from increase in employment; employment will come only when we start developing the manufacturing sector in India.

- Investors are not attracted by incentives; investment will be attracted only by friendly policies and a secure environment
- Ease of business is important for development; India has slipped low in the list of countries in terms of ease of doing business
- Scrutiny and red tape should not create barriers for development; simplification of processes should be the focus and redundancy done away with
- The world is looking to invest in Asia, particularly in Asian democracies, and in places with high demand – India fits the bill perfectly
- Effective governance is a key factor in attracting investors; the government needs to reassure investors of its effectiveness in promoting business and industry
- Skilled manpower mapped to the natural potential and creation of sustainable growth will be the focus of 'Make in India'
- Private-public partnership must be the basis of skills development in the country
- It is the government's responsibility to facilitate the creation of an environment conducive to development
- 65% population of the country is less than 35 years of age – there is immense manpower. After the indigenous development of Mangalyaan, India's talent and skills too cannot be questioned
- Digital India is the crux of effective governance; if this is not achieved, the governance and society will stay divergent. Ease of governance will come only with use of technology
- For years we have been emphasizing on Look East; only when we link West to this will we develop
- There are numerous opportunities in manufacturing and to develop this sector we will require a whole new world of infrastructure – from highways to I(nformation) ways, gas, water pipelines, ports, and a lot many more

- This government does not have a political agenda; it is dedicated to development as an article of faith
- The life and destiny of India can and will be changed for the better
- May Indian companies become multinational organizations but only when they grow and develop with India
- Only when the Centre and the state governments work together in tandem can India's true development potential be tapped into; development of states is the development of the country
- 'Make in India' is our responsibility; may India garner strength with this mission
- The 'Make in India' campaign is dedicated to Pandit Deendayal Upadhyaya, the patriotic thinker and philosopher

And here is what some of the top industrialists said in their speeches:

Cyrus Mistry - Chairman, Tata Sons

- Make In India is a timely opportunity for Indian companies to grow and contribute to the development of the country
- India's manufacturing sector needs to grow – to contribute at least 25% of the GDP – to be at par with other Asian countries. It currently contributes just over 15%
- Labour laws need to be reformed for the sector to develop
- Transparent laws and industry-friendly policies need to be framed
- Rollout of the GST (Goods & Services Tax) needs to be expedited, and reforming tax structure is imperative
- Tata Group is committed to investing in India

Kenichi Ayukawa - MD and CEO, Maruti Suzuki India

- Suzuki's India venture has been the most successful
- Cars in India are manufactured at a lower in cost

- The government must work to remove factors affecting manufacturing competitiveness

Mukesh Ambani - Chairman & Managing Director, Reliance Industries

- This is a historic day for the Indian manufacturing industry
- 'Make in India' is about the present and future, not about the past
- Reliance will create 1.25 lakh jobs in next 12-15 months
- There is a great need to connect village clusters to global markets to promote export
- India needs to be open to foreign capital investment and import of expertise

Azim Premji - Chairman, Wipro Limited

- Products made in India are suitable for all extreme climates
- Indian products represent a blend of low-cost and innovation in designs
- 80% sourcing of raw material for Wipro comes from domestic suppliers

KM Birla – Chairman, Aditya Birla Group

- It is high time India becomes a preferred manufacturing hub
- We need millions of jobs to prop up our economy
- India has all that is needed to make it a key manufacturing destination – skills, raw material, and entrepreneurship

Chanda Kochchar - MD & CEO, ICICI Bank

- Make in India is the next growth driver for India
- Manufacturing sector can add 9 crore jobs in the coming decade
- Quality, cost, and sustainability – the three things that need to be ensured

- Emphasis needs to be on transparence of policy, infrastructure, skills development, and priority areas

Phil Shaw - CEO, Lockheed Martin

- India is the epicentre of innovation

Y C Deveshwar - Chairman, ITC

- Jobless growth unsustainable
- 12 million youth are looking for employment and 2 million jobs are available – this gap needs to be plugged
- Biggest beneficiaries of Make in India is the youth
- Inflation and unemployment can be eliminated by Make in India

PM LAUNCHES 'MAKE IN INDIA' GLOBAL INITIATIVE

"Dignitaries on the dais, my colleagues in the Council of Ministers, Captains of Industry, and my friends here and abroad where this programmes is running simultaneously.

First of all I would like to apologise as I can see that many business leaders could not find a place to sit in the auditorium, I apologise to you for this inconvenience. One of the reasons for this inconvenience is that this auditorium is not used to such gathering.

I was listening to all the business leaders. Our Minister also discussed the works done in recent times, major initiatives were presented before you by a film also. After listening and hearing so much I don't think that there is a need for me to convince you any further for 'Make in India'.

What happened in years gone by? Whomsoever I met in last two three years, everybody said that we have to leave, have to shift business from here have to shift industry from here. I never saw anything political in that nor planned to take any political mileage out of it. It used to hurt me. What has happened to my country that my own countrymen are compelled to leave?

Today, when I have brought this 'Make in India', I don't want that any industrialist or any entrepreneur should feel compelled to leave.

That situation has to change. I speak from the experience of past few months that circumstances have changed. People in industry had lost self-confidence. They felt that they will not be able to face competition and had no way out. When a person loses self confidence it is very difficult to prop him up again. Secondly, his trust was broken – 'you never know what policy will the Government bring, never know when what policy will change, when will CBI come knocking'. This is what I have heard from you people.

It is a must that there should be rule of law. There should be an atmosphere of corporate government responsibility on the lines of corporate social responsibility. But at the same time there are responsibilities of government.

Just now Devesh ji was saying that money does not come by invitation only. I agree with that. The biggest requirement is trust, confidence. I don't know how we have run our country that we have doubted our own countrymen at every turn. I need to change this vicious cycle. We should not start from distrust, we should begin with trust and government should intervene only if there is some shortcoming. When we take such decisions people think that this is no grand vision.

Now a day, I am often hearing and reading this. When my government decides about self-certification you may feel this to be a very small decision. There cannot be bigger decision than deciding to trust the authenticity of 125 crore countrymen. You have always doubted him, he certifies and you tell him to get certification from a gazetted officer. And what does gazetted officer say – if it is urgent give me this much, and if you have time then that much. Can't we trust our own countrymen? After all who is government for? Government is for common people, for every citizen. And this beginning of change does not stop here. It goes up to Income Tax Department also. As business community is sitting here I am talking of Income Tax Department.

I mean that it is the mantra of my Government, our first commitment-we want to move while trusting every citizen. This atmosphere of trust has the strength of changing the system. It is not that change can be brought only by making laws within the walls of Parliament. Outside too flow of change can be brought by awakening the hearts of every person.

These days FDI is in discussion and it is natural. I look at it slightly differently for Indian citizens also FDI is a responsibility, for 125 crore Indians, FDI is a responsibility. For entrepreneurs and businessmen of the world FDI is an opportunity. When I say that it is a responsibility for every Indian an opportunity for outsiders then my definition for FDI for Indians is – First Develop India. And to global business developers, I say India is an opportunity.

For FDI we can move ahead on the journey of progress by taking this twin definition. There is a talk in the entire world, quite a mouth watering one, that India is a huge market. On first look this feeling is natural. I am not an economist but the industrialist, who considers India to be big market, has he ever thought that what is the purchasing power of that market. What is the purchasing power of the citizen, has it gone up? Even if the number of people is high, without purchasing power and pocket with no depth, the world will fritter away this opportunity. Therefore, I would like to tell the global industries that don't consider India to be just a market. You should see every Indian citizen for his potential. The faster the bulk of Indian middle class increases, the faster people move from poverty to middle class, the faster will be their conversion into a favourable market for the world.

What needs to be done to increase the bulk of middle class? Straight answer is that opportunities for employment will have to be made available. If you come from outside and don't bother about industrial development, manufacturing sector and don't create employment opportunities, this loop will never complete. That is why, when we talk of Make in India, we are not just offering a competitive situation. When we talk of Make in India, we give you an opportunity to create a huge market for your product. After all, handsome buyer is equally important as cost effective manufacturing. You may produce as many Maruti cars but nothing will happen if there is no buyer.

For this, we need to bring some changes in Indian economy. In this change, on the one hand, manufacturing growth is to be promoted, at the same time we need to ensure that direct benefit goes to the youngsters of India. He should get employment so that there is improvement in the economic situation of even the poorest family. These poor should move towards middle class and there purchasing power should improve. This will lead to manufacturing growth and growth of the market.

This is a cycle. And important measure has been taken to move this cycle forward. This is a lion's step. Lion's step – Make in India. When I talk of it and I am speaking from my Chief Ministers experience, industrialists don't come due to some fancy incentive scheme. One can say you will get this or that, will make this tax free or that tax free. Incentives don't work. We need to create development and growth oriented environment. This is government's responsibility. People in government, financial institutions need to concentrate on all these systems. Then only investor will have a sense of security. Investor first wants security of his investment. Growth and profit come later. He doesn't seek profit the first day. For profit, he has other 50 companies. Government's effort is, we have taken continuous measures; we want to reassure you that your money will not sink.

Secondly what more does he want? These days there is a ranking for ease of doing business. Recently I met World Bank Chairman. He was also expressing this worry. Probably we were 135th in the world at that time. What hinders ease of doing business? If we have to come to 50 from 135 then Government alone can do this. If Government brings transparency in its decisions and rules, pushes works with simplicity we can occupy number 50 from 135 in ease of doing business. I have sensitized my entire team and I have asked whether we are not placing obstacles in the name of scrutiny and more perfection? On the basis of my three months' experience I can say that my entire team in the Government, my entire bureaucracy is moving two steps ahead of me in this positive thinking. Why is this an strength? He is convinced that this opportunity has come his way and he does not want to lose this.

Entire world is looking towards Asia. I don't need to waste time in inviting; I just need to make some efforts in giving the address that this is the place. He is ready to come. Entire world is ready to come. They just don't know where to come in Asia. Then he thinks where is democracy, where is demographic dividend, where is demand in huge quantity? If these three are available in any part of the globe then this will be India.

All three are available together and being used positively. If we use democracy, demographic dividend and demand properly then I am sure that there will be no need to give India's address to the world. Many Vasco da Gamas will appear in every nook and corner and will come looking for India. He needs effective governance. Just government is not sufficient but a feeling of government is needed. If somebody comes knocking, he should feel that his problem will find a solution here or he will get guidance on what route to take – effective governance. I am not talking of just good governance I am also talking of effective governance. There is a need to emphasise two important pillars.

If industries are to be established then skilled manpower will be needed. This skilled manpower should be as per the requirement. If there are possibilities for textile industry somewhere and if we are doing skilled development for engineering then neither engineering skilled person will go there for job nor will the textile industry be helped. We have to do the mapping and we are doing. What are such clusters where there is natural potential of this sort? How to do human resource development for that potential? How to handle environmental issues there and on what points government should decide its foundation for sustainable growth? And if we are doing this then the effective governance can be obtained through skilled development.

Today, is there any synchronisation between the thinking of government, academic world, industry and the thinking of job seeking youngsters? I am sorry to say-No. We may want to develop tourism. But we may not have a system of developing guides in that village. Guide would be taught somewhere in Tamil Nadu and Taj Mahal would be in Agra. I mean to say that these are small things. If we do these focussed activities then circumstances may change.

Academic world should study that what kind of industry is possible in coming 20 years. If the entire world is focussed on eco-friendly environment technology, global warming then it flows that solar energy field has opened. If the solar energy field develops, then engineering college will get training for solar equipments. There will be requirement of skilled labour in the field; for that training may begin now itself. Solar related entrepreneurs should be informed of these arrangements, there is barren land near Barmer, come and establish solar power plant and give light to India. Government needs to facilitate in this networking exercise and when government becomes facilitator, desired results are obtained. Therefore, how to promote skilled development; we want to proceed with the model of public-private-partnership in this area.

If industrialists feel that industry needs certain type of trained manpower, we will say that take this ITI and train the manpower locally according to your needs. You will get a good worker for your industry and our ITI will start running. Our youngsters will get employment, his family will be strengthened and better purchasing power will help the economy. We need to push such a cycle. And perhaps that is why I have brought the issue of Ashok Chakra. How this can become a wheel in the journey of our economic development?

At the time of industrial revolution, we were lagged behind as we were slaves. Before that we were known as Golden Bird. That opportunity was lost. Now, a new era of economic regeneration has begun and that belong to Asia. It is our responsibility that how to make it belong to India.

Our greatest strength that 65% population is below 35. I don't believe that after yesterday's event, anybody will question our talent. No one can question talent of Indian youth after yesterday's Mars achievement. Everything was indigenous. We should bring out photographs of the factories where these small parts were manufactured. In these seemingly small factories, every particle was manufactured that made Mars Mission successful. There is no dearth of talent. Mars success should be made an opportunity to make the world aware of Indian talent. It is not just that 65 % of the population is below 35, it is the fact that we have talented and capable manpower.

Second point is Digital India. Corporate world, industrial world and private life is moving fast with digital world. If government and official system lags behind, I can imagine how wide chasm will be created. Entire social system on one side and government on the other. We have taken up the mission of Digital India to bridge this chasm. Why not entire governance should go towards mobile governance.

You will be surprised that in my first ten days I asked 'please tell me why there are 10 pages in the forms filled in Government. You must be filling those forms, not you; your staff members must be doing it. I told them on the first day that make it one page and I am happy many departments have done it. There is no reason, all these things are available. We keep on demanding again and again. I mean to say that like ease of business, we also need easy and effective governance. Every person should have his details on the tip of his fingers. These are the things which enable us to move forward.

For a long time Look-East policy is under discussion, everyone is talking about it. This is a good occasion, along with Look East; I would like to talk about link-West. Look-East is on one side and Link-West on the other and we are linking the both from the middle. We can establish our economic structure on a new platform from here. Whatever is the best in the world, why we should not have it? This should be the mood of the nation.

New avenues of business are opening. Please note down my words. I do not know what you have thought. May be some small companies must have thought of it. In the coming days there is big business opportunity in India of creating wealth from waste. We wish to take the work of solid waste management and waste water treatment forward through public private partnership. By generating electricity from waste, garbage of the village you can sell electricity by becoming owner of electricity factory. This big revenue model is coming. We should start thinking I have seen that those who do forward thinking.....many big multinational companies came out to sell vegetables. Because they knew how big is the market. Similarly big companies are likely to come for this wealth from waste. The cleanliness movement that we have started will open many new opportunities. I am inviting interested entrepreneurs. Even small municipalities should come with this revenue model. We invite you.

Opportunities are many, Infrastructure sector is also important as manufacturing sector is important. Now India cannot be run on that infrastructure if we have to reach our desired destination. Earlier, when there was talk of infrastructure, it was over with discussion on Rail, road, port and airport. We have to move towards next generation infrastructure.

We need highways similarly we need 'Iways' too. When I say 'Iways', I mean information ways and that is for digital India. If there are electric grids, we need gas grids and water grids too. We also need optical fibre networks. We are dreaming of an India where private sector has ample opportunities to try their luck.

How do we update ourselves from where we are presently on Public Private Partnership? How to go into unchartered areas? We kept our focus confined to port development. Demand of the time is to move towards port led development. With ports there should be cold storage network, roads, rail, and an airport with port. Unless all this develops as a cluster, we can't make a place for ourselves in the global market. Hence we wish to emphasize that.

This is one big area where you can try your luck. Point is that infrastructure is not an issue of just luxury. If we have to develop tourism; it is estimated that tourism is the industry with the highest growth. Can India capture it? The tourism needs huge infrastructure. There is a big scope for hospitality industry, There are so many avenues, how to harness them?

That is why I submit, whosoever thought of going away; I say no need to go anywhere. This country is yours, thrive here then think of stepping out, there is a different joy in that. There is no joy in going under compulsion. I want Indian companies to become multinational. Indian companies should have their arms elsewhere too.

We want this. But we should strengthen our land. We must take steps to give employment to our youngsters. And this is a Government dedicated to development. For this government this is not a political agenda but an article of faith. That is why; I share my belief with you.

When I was in Gujarat I used to say with confidence-same officer, same government, same office, same file and the same people, despite this world can be changed. I can say that after coming to Delhi also. The same office, officers, cars, files, and even ways of functioning, still they can be enlivened. India's direction can be changed. India's destiny can be changed. I move forward with this confidence.

One of the biggest obstacle in our journey is this that if a decision is made by the centre most of the implementations are taken care of by the states. If there is lack of understanding between the two, the industrialists is at loss whether to go to Delhi or to the State Government. He remains confused. Now, this confusion will no longer be there. I believe that states' development is for India only. If investment comes in the States, it comes in India also. States and Centre should work collectively, shoulder to shoulder as a team.

If centre gets a proposal then centre should go to the State on its own and ask how we can help together. If a State gets a proposal that needs Centre's help the State should come to the centre without any hesitation, they should find solution together and things move forward. This great need has come up, to meet this, Centre and the States will have to come together.

We often talk of current account deficit, export-import imbalance. Just ask any State, have you done any activity for export promotion-none. They think it to be the job of the centre. Immediately after coming to Delhi, I called the States. I told them that manufacturing is with you. Please bolster their confidence so that they can feel like exporting, Government of India's rules and policies could be utilized by him. If we will work together, the Industrialist will feel empowered and he will sell abroad.

Is the External Affairs Ministry is of any use to him He is sitting in some remote corner of a State making oil engine. Who is bothered? He is living by his hard work. Now, whether it is the State or the Centre, as a facilitator of export, we have decided to take up this role aggressively and pro actively. Now, see what difference it will make! If we say 'Make in India', we are ready to stand with you as a facilitator to capture global market. There are many fields like this.

We called financial institutions. See how change comes. Recently we took up the movement of connecting the poorest of the poor to a bank account, keeping in mind inclusive growth. Not that it was not done earlier. Initially people said it was done during our time, not any longer. Because they realise that by saying so it will be revealed that they failed. You can imagine that Bank people opened four crore accounts in such short period. I had said that the accounts could be opened with zero balance. I am amazed that people have deposited 1500 crore rupees. If despite a zero balance offer, people deposit 1500 crore during opening of accounts, this indicates trust. This is the power of trust. Banking sector people moving with such speed can become a standard for the Government moving so fast.

Financial Institutions should also get involved in the growth and development. World spread at grass root level, we are making efforts to take this journey ahead in every corner.

I mean, today 'Make in India' is not a mere slogan or an invitation, it is our responsibility. If we move forward with determination, world will come looking for us, have faith. For this we need to stress both FDIs. 'First Develop India' at the same time 'Foreign Direct Investment'.

All of you took out time for this and got associated with us at the time of such a big initiative. Many guests have come from abroad too. In many countries of the world and all States this is being live telecast by embassies and business chambers. There also people are participating. I assure you that we collectively fulfil our responsibilities in this concept of 'Make in India'. We move ahead and attain new heights in manufacturing sector and provide jobs to poor youth of India. With employment poor will give new momentum to the wheels of Indian economy. With this belief, best wishes to all. Navaratri wishes to all.

In my personal life, in my political journey too today is very significant. Today is 25th September, Birth Anniversary of Pandit Deen Dayal Upadhyaya, whose ideas and thoughts inspired us to begin our political journey, who gave Integral Humanism philosophy to the world. On the birth anniversary of such a great man, who lived and strived for the country, I have got the chance to dedicate Make in India in feet of such a man. We are determined to fulfil that dream.

Navratri is a festival of 'Shakti Sanchay' (strength accumulation). On this occasion of 'Shakti Sanchay', India should also do Shakti Sanchay and become a powerful nation. Move forward with this dream, with this prayer, my best wishes to all.

Thank you.

3

Make in India Campaign

Make in India is the BJP-led NDA government's flagship campaign intended to boost the domestic manufacturing industry and attract foreign investors to invest into the Indian economy. The Indian Prime Minister, Mr. Narendra Modi first mentioned the keyphrase in his maiden Independence Day address from the ramparts of the Red Fort and over a month later launched the campaign in September 2014 with an intention of reviving manufacturing businesses and emphasizing key sectors in India amidst growing concerns that most entrepreneurs are moving out of the country due to its low rank in ease of doing business ratings.

THE MAKE IN INDIA VISION

Manufacturing currently contributes just over 15% to the national GDP. The aim of this campaign is to grow this to a 25% contribution as seen with other developing nations of Asia. In the process, the government expects to generate jobs, attract much foreign direct investment, and transform India into a manufacturing hub preferred around the globe.

The logo for the Make In India campaign is a an elegant lion, inspired by the Ashoka Chakra and designed to represent India's success in all spheres. The campaign was dedicated by the Prime Minister to the eminent patriot, philosopher and political personality, Pandit Deen Dayal Upadhyaya who had been born on the same date in 1916.

Why PM wants to Make in India

The Prime Minister called for all those associated with the campaign, especially the entrepreneurs and the corporates, to step and discharge their duties as Indian nationals by First Developing India and for investors to endow the country with foreign direct investments. The Prime Minister also promised that his administration would aid the investors by making India a pleasant experience and that his government considered overall development of the nation an article of faith rather than a political agenda. He also laid a robust foundation for his vision of a technology-savvy Digital India as complementary to Make In India. He stressed on the employment generation and poverty alleviation that would inevitably accompany the success of this campaign.

Launch Ceremony

Prime Minister Mr. Narendra Modi launched the Make In India campaign on September 25, 2014. The date of the launch was chosen to be of maximum advantage. Coming right after the successful insertion of Mangalyaan-a wholly indigenously built low-cost probe into the Martian orbit-the event highlighted India's success in manufacturing, science and technology, and all this at inexpensive costs. It also came just a day ahead of the Prime Minister's maiden US visit. Calculated to enhance India's attractiveness as an investment destination, the launch ceremony was held at the Vigyan Bhavan in New Delhi. Thehall thronged with attendees, a number of whom did not even find seats. Leading entrepreneurs and the CEOs of about 3000 companies from across 30 countries were invited to attend the launch.

Law Minister Mr. Ravishankar Prasad and Commerce Minister Ms. Nirmala Sitharaman were part of the occasion. Apart from them, a number of corporate head honchos with deep roots in the country also spoke at the occasion. These include-Mr. Cyrus Mistry (Chairman, Tata Sons), Mr. Kenichi Ayukawa (MD and CEO, Maruti Suzuki India), Mr. Mukesh Ambani (Chairman & Managing Director, Reliance Industries),

Mr. Azim Premji (Chairman, Wipro Limited), Mr. KM Birla Chairman, Aditya Birla Group), Ms. Chanda Kochchar (MD & CEO, ICICI Bank), Mr. Phil Shaw (CEO, Lockheed Martin), and Mr. YC Deveshwar (Chairman, ITC).

Sectors in focus

For the Make in India campaign, the government of India has identified 25 priority sectors that shall be promoted adequately. These are the sectors where likelihood of FDI (foreign direct investment) is the highest and investment shall be promoted by the government of India. On the campaign launch, the Prime Minister Mr. Modi said that the development of these sectors would ensure that the world shall readily come to Asia, particularly to India where the availability of both democratic conditions and manufacturing superiority made it the best destinations, especially when combined with the effective governance intended by his administration.

Automobiles	Food Processing	Renewable Energy
Automobile Components	**IT and BPM**	**Roads and highways**
Aviation	Leather	Space
Biotechnology	Media and Entertainment	Textiles and garments
Chemicals	Mining	Thermal Power
Construction	Oil and Gas	Tourism and Hospitality
Defence manufacturing	Pharmaceuticals	Wellness
Electrical Machinery	Ports	
Electronic Systems	Railways	

BENEFITS AND DISADVANTAGES OF MAKE IN INDIA

India is a country rich in natural resources. Labour is aplenty and skilled labour is easily available given the high rates of unemployment among the educated class of the country. With Asia developing as the outsourcing hub of the world, India is soon becoming the preferred manufacturing destination of most investors across the globe. Mae in India is the Indian government's effort to harness this demand and boost the Indian economy.

India ranks low on the "ease of doing business index". Labour laws in the country are still not conducive to the Make in India campaign. This is one of the universally noted disadvantages of manufacturing and investing in India.

Why Companies were not manufacturing in India

Make in India campaign is at loggerheads with the Make in China ideal that has gained momentum over the past decade. China is a major rival to India when it comes to the outsourcing, manufacturing, and services business. India's ailing infrastructure scenario and defunct logistics facilities make it difficult for the country to achieve an elite status as a manufacturing hub. The bureaucratic approach of former governments, lack of robust transport networks, and widespread corruption makes it difficult for manufacturers to achieve timely and adequate production. The Modi government has vowed to remove these hurdles and make the nation an ideal destination for investors to set up industries.

The Make in India Website

Apart from the launch of a colourful brochure, which should find its way into the hands of anyone intending to invest into India, the government of India also launched a website to supplement the campaign. The Make In India website highlights each of the 25 target sectors with statistics, reasons to invest, growth drivers, all policies relevant to investors and the individual sectors, government support, and opportunities for investors apart from showcasing the live projects that have been undertaken and FAQs. The website also links to the campaigns Social Media feeds on Twitter, Facebook, Google Plus, and YouTube.

Criticism and concerns

The NDA government's Make In India campaign has till early October attracted INR 2000 crore worth investment proposals. The campaign has, despite this, found its fair share of critics. The topmost of these criticisms is levelled against the incumbent government. It has been felt that the government does not walk its talk-labour reforms and policy reforms which are fundamental for the success of the Make In India campaign have not yet been implemented. A number of layoffs in companies such as Nokia India cast long shadows over the campaign. A number of technology based companies have not been enthused by the campaign launch and have professed to continue getting their components manufactured by China.

Campaign Name	**Make In India**
Launch Date	09/25/14
Launched By	PM Mr. Narendra Modi
Number of Sectors	25
Investment Proposals Received	INR 2000 crore (till 9-Oct-2014)

ROLE OF HR AND FINANCIAL SERVICES IN MAKING "MAKE IN INDIA" CAMPAIGN A SUCCESS

The 15th and current Prime Minister of INDIA "Mr.NarendraModi" unveiled the "MAKE IN INDIA" program on September 25th 2014 in New Delhi. He along extending an invitation to foreign firms to invest in INDIA also solicited the CEOs of domestic firms to invest in INDIA by saying that, "There is no need to leave the nation.

We want our companies to shine as MNCs". The MAKE IN INDIA program laid the foundation of India's new national manufacturing policy and rolled out the red carpet to both domestic and international industrialists with an aim to make India a manufacturing hub that will in turn boost the employment and overall growth of India. The program lays emphasis on 25 sectors such as automobiles, chemicals, IT, pharmaceuticals, textiles, ports, aviation, leather, tourism and hospitality, wellness, railways, auto components, design manufacturing, renewable energy, mining, biotechnology, pharmaceuticals, electronics, etc.

with focus on job creation, skill enhancement, economic, technical as well as overall infrastructure development.

It also focuses on giving Indian industry a global recognition. Manufacturing industry requires heavy finance to facilitate the buying of latest modern technology, setting up and development of required infrastructure, developing skill set of its human resource to produce best quality products and survive in ever increasing global competition. And if INDIA wants to lure the investors and turn itself into a manufacturing hub, its human resource and financial services will play a vital part in making it's this dream come true. Finance and Human Resource are the most abundant, flexible and readily leveraged resources which demand precise attention and articulation.

According to World Bank Data, in 2013 the contribution of Indian Manufacturing sector to Indian Economy was merely 13%. The overall contribution of the manufacturing sector to its gross domestic product (GDP) is just 28%. India also stands at a very low in contributing in the world manufacturing, with its overall share standing at a meager 1.8%. These statistics are the clear indicators that India has not done very well in its manufacturing sector. Domestic manufacturers are also looking for markets to setup their manufacturing units outside the Indian borders.

Reasons are many for such an attitude of domestic industrial houses. Fewer subsidies, over interference of government, less availability of financial services etc. are a few to mention among the reason why the attention of industrial houses is towards other countries when it comes to setting up an industry. When domestic industrialists are behaving in such a manner, what can be expected from the foreign players.

Merely urging the domestic and foreign investors and industrialists is not going to make India a Manufacturing hub or revive its health. For this we need to understand the role and importance of its domestic work force which is immensely talented and will also have to provide the industrialists with the ample, easy and readily available financial services which will help them generate and make the finance available as and when needed.

Developing India as a manufacturing hub is not only required to earn a golden place in the eyes of foreign countries. But it is also important because the development of Manufacturing sector in India and its transformation into a hub of World Manufacturing Industry will create more jobs and employment opportunities for its people.

Indian brain is immensely intelligent and talented but due to lack of ample and relevant job opportunities, excellent Indian talent is going abroad and working for companies outside Indian borders. And if India is converted to a Manufacturing hub and most preferred investment destination for domestic as well as foreign investors and manufacturers, it will create job opportunities for the immensely talented Indian youth. Transformation of India into a Manufacturing hub will help develop, strengthen and modernize the Indian infrastructure. Such advancement will revive the health of other sectors such as service, agriculture, hospitality, medical, tourism, etc.

In order to achieve this dream, India needs to analyse the importance of its human resource and financial services. Out of all the other resources, resource from where the finance is generated and the human resource of an organization are the two most important. Industry cannot be setup if the industrialist does not have the money or finance available with him as, when and in how much quantity needed. And at the same time if he has setup an industry, has best in class infrastructure and technology, material, etc. all these are of no use if he does not have the people competent and intelligent enough to utilize the available limited resources in the best manner these could be utilized.

The country which does not understand the value and importance of its work force and financial services can never survive. Hence, the effective utilization of the financial services and the human capital of an organization is the secret of the success of a firm. Both human capital and financial capital move in accordance with each other. Both have the impact no matter whether positive or negative, but both are directly proportional to each other.

Human resource and the finance are two core competencies on which an organization relies. Human resource needs to be trained, developed and kept up to the mark with the technological advancement in the international environment and standards and finance has to be available as and when needed in order to train human resource, procure raw material, setting up infrastructure, making an organization operative. In order to develop India as a manufacturing hub, match expectations with the opportunities; the role of financial services and the human resource cannot be overlooked. And if these two major key factors are ignored, the MAKE IN INDIA will just become a slogan and nothing more.

Rationale of the study

With increasing globalization and rapidly changing dynamic trends, India too needs to develop its infrastructure in order to militate its presence in the global picture and to match the rising demands and the living standard of its citizens. The most easy and important way to keep pace with the environment for a country is to develop its manufacturing sector. When more global and local players will invest in a country, it will boost the trade and economic growth, develop its infrastructure, and generate more employment opportunities for its citizens.

Mere launch of Prime Minister Mr.NarinderModi's "MAKE IN INDIA" campaign is not enough. The success of this campaign would depend upon potential, availability and skill set of its work force along with the availability of financial services required to propel the operations and growth of a manufacturing unit. The study focuses on the importance of various available modes of financial services along with the focus on how the potential of country's work force can be capitalized and enhanced in order to bring the desired change and accelerate the desiderated growth of Manufacturing Sector in INDIA. The main aim behind this study is to bring forward the role of

INDIA's human resource and financial services in order to build best in class manufacturing infrastructure in India.

Objectives of the study

The health of India's Manufacturing Sector cannot be revived only by announcing campaigns or focusing on fiscal policy. The objective of the study is to

1. To identify the impact of HR and Financial Services on the development of Manufacturing sector in India and overall Indian economy.
2. To suggest different techniques and systems through which financial assistance can be provided which is required to propel the manufacturing industry.
3. To understand the importance of capitalizing human potential and put forward new ways of enriching human resources which is essential for the growth of Manufacturing Firms.
4. To emphasize the promotion of assistance of financial services and importance of taping of human potential required for face-lifting the Indian Manufacturing Sector; which is the main objective of "MAKE IN INDIA" campaign.

RESEARCH METHODOLOGY

Research Type: Descriptive Research

Type of Data/Data Source used: Secondary Data/Data source. The present study is based on secondary data. Basically, the required information has been derived from

1. Various books.
2. Articles from Newspapers, Magazines and Journals, and
3. From the various related web-sites which deal directly or indirectly with the topics related to FDI and Indian retail sector. After searching the important web-sites, relevant information was down loaded and analysed to address the objectives of present study.

Limitations of the study

1. The study is based on published data and information. No primary data is being collected.
2. Every care has been taken to entice qualitative and correct data; still secondary data have collected for the purposes other than problem at hand.
3. The objectives, nature and methods used to collect secondary data may not be appropriate to the present situation.
4. Secondary data may be lacking in accuracy, or they may not be completely current or dependable.
5. Time constraint remained the major limitation in the study
6. The biasness can always be there.
7. Before using secondary data, it is important to evaluate them on above mentioned factors. So, it consumes the same time as the primary data.

Need and impact of HR and financial services on manufacturing sector in India and overall Indian economy India's current ranking in the world in factory output is 10. Its overall contribution to Indian GDP is 28% and it engages nearly 17% of the total work force. The basis of any manufacturing organization is governed by the quantity of money it is willing to invest and the kind of people who are going to work in it.

For transforming the health of the manufacturing sector and in order to make it a most preferred destination for domestic as well as foreign investors and industrialists, it is very much important to promote both fund based and non-fund based financial services.

Manufacturing firms to withstand the global competition, and to ensure their long term sustainability, have to invest in huge quantity in setting up and developing its infrastructure, raw material, skill development of its human resource, and R&D. Hence, the manufacturing houses need such sources which should make the finance available as and when needed. Such a continuous need of inflow of heavy finance can only be satisfied by the financial services.

The attention of the domestic as well as foreign manufacturers can only be sought if the investment climate is made favourable. As the investment climate is directly proportional to manufacturers' way of thinking, hence, this climate needs to be favourable in every aspect. The current technological status, available mode of finance and human resource skill set and its availability needs to be identified along highlighting the development initiatives and future imperatives that are required to make India a manufacturing hub and most preferred investment destination for both local and international players.

Understanding the Financial Services and its types Financial services in layman language, simply means the services with respect to money management provided by various organizations that are operating in finance industry of a country. These organizations include banks, consumer finance and insurance companies, investment funds, stock broker firms and government sponsored firms.

Asset/Fund Based Financial Services

The asset or fund based financial services help raising the finance against the assets including both movable and immovable, bank deposits, etc. It also includes underwriting shares, debentures, binds, venture capital, factoring, housing finance, leasing, mutual funds etc.

Fee Based Financial Services

It involves higher expertise and less financial risk. It includes merchant banking, credit rating, capital restricting, bank guarantee, corporate advisory services, etc.

Different ways to promote financial services

1. The initiative of government is must in order to reform the investment climate in India which is essential to make India a manufacturing hub. It should encourage

promotion of more and more technological, research and development parks on the pattern of special economic zones.

2. Foreign manufacturers as well as domestic manufacturers will only be encouraged to invest in India if they will be provided with an enabling environment. Ensuring timely availability of money, relaxing the norms and regulations governing the banks in order to make the easier and cheaper credit available to the manufacturing houses
3. Government should Facilitate and encourage merchant banking, factoring, invoice discounting facilities in order to make the finance readily available
4. Promoting and help flourishing the financial service advisors who provide end to end advise as from where will they finance come from, how much finance is required covering the whole life cycle and production scenario of the plant in manufacturing industry. These financial advisors also keep track of the inflow and outflow of the money and the manufacturer does not have to worry about his time management worrying about tracking the movement of money. They have wide range of funding solutions available in hand which a potential taker can choose from.
5. Encouraging commercial banks to make finance readily available for manufacturing enterprises. Government should frame such policies which are a bit lenient and relaxed, and thus have an insight to performance and financial constraints of the manufacturing units.
6. Regulatory environment should be improved in order to pave a way for the development and growth of the manufacturing industry in India.
7. Government of India should facilitate the promotion of more and more credit card companies and angel investors which will benefit both the manufacturer and the consumer.

Understanding the importance of human resource in manufacturing sector in India and its impact

Besides promoting the various types of financial services, it is also essential to tap, exploit and enhance the immense talent and potential of the work force available in India. Rightfully once said by the Walt Disney,"You can create, design and build the most wonderful place in the world but it requires people to make that dream a reality." Indian work force is immensely talented and adaptable. In order to develop an organization and ensure its sustained growth, it is very much important to develop its human resource working in it.

Continuous investment in up gradation of their skills, knowledge and competencies is essential for an organization if it wants a guaranteed survival in the immensely competitive environment. The organization which does not understand the importance and talent of its human resource cannot withstand the competition. A motivated, up to date human work force will help an organization achieve its mission and vision. Various modern HR policies include performance and career management, development of various continuous improvement and learning programs.

Focusedon the up gradation of employee's knowledge, skill and abilities, programs such as employee development should be promoted. Employee development is a joint, on-going effort on the part of both the employee and the organization for which he or she works. A highly skilled work force can accomplish higher goals than an under skilled human resource. Employees' performance needs to be enriched by developing training and development programs if 100% potential of the human resource needs to be tapped. The human potential is immense and if it is left untapped, it will go waste. Human resource is the most valuable asset of an organization and it needs to be continuously monitored and injected with performance development programs, programs that increase the job satisfaction of employees, employee welfare programs etc. The human performance can be appraised with the use of various performance appraisal models. Organizational excellence can only be achieved by investing continuously in the work force of the organization.

Benefits of enhancing and capitalizing human potential

- Growth in Sales: When good quality products will go into the hands of the consumer, the satisfaction of consumer will result in increase in demand of the goods. Hence, the sales will be boosted which in turn

will boost the production and hence the manufacturing unit will flourish.

- Cost Reduction: Up to date trained and knowledgeable work force will decrease and automatically omit the defects for the production system which will in turn bring the cost of production down.

Focus on Organizational Goal

- Reduction of time taken in creating strategic or operational changes by communicating the changes through a new set of goals

Organizational development

There is need of reforms in industrial strategies to make India a manufacturing hub. Favourable industrial framework need to be established that should attract more and more domestic as well as foreign industrialists towards Indian Territory. There is a need for financial service providers and advisors who could work for these industrialists right from the beginning i.e. right from clearance of the project. Improved quality and better performance management system needs to be in place to guide, monitor and enhance the skill set of its work force. Mind set of Industrialists both foreign and domestic towards India needs to be changed. On the basis of the study it can rightfully concluded that People and money, both are the organization's greatest competitive edge. It is essential to unlock the human talent for the success and sustainability of any organization. The development, prosperity and sustainability of India as a Manufacturing hub clearly depend upon the immense potential of its human resources and the financial services that are available for the domestic and foreign players. Employees possessing high value and unique intellectual skills significantly contribute to generate intellectual products. If India successfully provides the industrial houses all this then it will certainly become a world manufacturing hub. This study both empirically and rationally explained the patterns through which India can become a manufacturing hub. Favourable investment climate, assistance of financial services, relax and industry favourable government policies are the essential ingredients of "MAKE IN INDIA"

INDIA PM NARENDRA MODI UNVEILS 'MAKE IN INDIA' CAMPAIGN

It includes plans to cut red tape, develop infrastructure and make it easier for companies to do business.

The launch comes on the eve of Mr Modi's first visit to the US as prime minister.

Manufacturing contributes only 15% to India's gross domestic product; authorities want to raise it to 25%.

Mr Modi's 'Make in India' campaign comes a day after India sent its homegrown mission to Mars.

The Mangalyaan robotic probe, one of the cheapest interplanetary missions ever, was successfully put into the orbit of Mars on Wednesday morning.

"Whenever I met [business] people for the last few years they would tell me-we want to shift out... It pained me that people of nation are forced to leave," Mr Modi said while unveiling the campaign in the capital, Delhi.

"We do not want any industrialist being forced to leave India. I can say that we have been able to bring about a change in last few months."

Mr Modi said India must "increase manufacturing and at the same time ensure that the benefits reach the youth of our nation". A boost to manufacturing will create jobs, increase purchasing power and create a larger market for manufacturers, he added.

India has a huge pool of talented people, Mr Modi said, adding that it was because of this talent that India was able to send the indigenously-built Mangalyaan to the orbit of Mars.

Mr Modi won the recent general election, promising to revive India's slowing economy and in the three months to June, the country's economy grew by 5.7% , its fastest pace in two-and-a-half years.

SUCCESS STORIES OF "MAKE IN INDIA" CAMPAIGN

Prime Minister Narendra Modi launched the "Make in India" campaign on September 25, 2014. With one million people to enter the job market each month, creating opportunities to such a vast talent pool is a humongous task. Jobs need to be created in both organized and unorganized sectors. The efforts in improving the unorganized sector outlook is a story for another day. Notwithstanding apprehensions by the opposition parties, the early signs look exciting for the future of India.

Let us look at some of the early success stories of the "Make in India" campaign. Of course, we need to be cognizant of the fact that many projects are in the early stages and it would take time to see the results. However, it would be interesting to know the sectors/industries/companies that have brought into this idea.

Electronics

Foxconn, the manufacturer of Apple's iPhones has announced plans for creating 10-12 facilities in India, which will include factories and data centers. Foxconn expects to sign the first contract by the end of 2015. That Foxconn chose India following various issues it faced in its Chinese facilities, bolsters the "Make in India" campaign. The advantages the arrival of a big company to the country can be manifold.

Foxconn's arrival can trigger the arrival of companies along its supply chain and also help to multiply the indirect jobs created due to this. There have already been reports of Oppo mobiles starting its manufacturing plant by August this year. ZTE Corporation, another Chinese telecom major, has completed its recce to set up its manufacturing facility in India. With e-business on the rise, there are plenty of other players waiting on the wings to explore the large market. Another Chinese mobile handset maker Phicomm has also committed to invest $100mn in the next 3 years to market its products and at the same time, they are exploring to setting up a manufacturing facility here.

Automobiles

Mercedes Benz has brought into the "Make in India" program in two different areas. Firstly, in the luxury car segments, it has decided to manufacture more of its components in India – thus increasing the localization of its new model C220 CDI to 60%. Secondly, Mercedes Benz has also decided to manufacture its luxury buses in India, to be exported to Africa and South East Asian markets. The trials have already begun and full-fledged exports will start from early 2016.

Competition for low cost manufacturing cannot be underestimated. Following Mercedes's lead, its German competitor BMW has also decided to increase its localization to 50%. BMW has already signed deals with approximately 20 companies who supply its components. Volvo is also now in the exploratory stage of exporting its range of buses to other markets. Renault, the french automobile major, has also improved localization of its KWID model to 98% – the KWID is expected to be launched later this year. The US behemoth, Ford, has also committed to invest Rs 4000 to Rs 5000cr for R&D, in its Chennai facility.

Defense

Hyundai Heavy Industries (HHI) of South Korea will work with Hindustan Shipyard Limited, Vizag to build warships in India. Currently, the time duration from the point of order to delivery takes around 6 years. With this collaboration, this gap is expected to fall to 2.5 years. Though in very early stages of discussion, HHI has indicated that the objective is to outsource the manufacturing of small and medium size ships to India. The initial understanding was completed during PM Modi's recent visit to South Korea.

Another South Korean major, Samsung, has also agreed to build LNG tankers with Kochi Shipyard. Another decision made recently was that Goa shipyard will construct 12 minesweepers for the Indian navy at a cost of 1 billion USD. Gurgaon based Sun Group, is in discussion with Russia, to manufacture 200 Kamov Ka 226 light helicopters in Punjab. The German and US defense ministers were in India recently to push sale of their products and there have been news reports that India will engage with them, only if there is a "Make in India" component in the deal. Reliance Infrastructure is in discussion with officials in Russia to explore opportunity to build nuclear submarines and stealth warships in India, along with other partners.

Railways

Recently, Indian Railways has invited bids by international suppliers for the procurement and manufacture of 15 train sets. Two train sets will be imported, where as the reminder will need to be manufactured in India – which will result in 40 coaches to be imported and 275 coaches will be manufactured in India. The whole project is estimated to be worth around Rs. 2,500cr. These train sets will be used on faster inter-city travel routes.

PM Modi during his recent visit to Berlin, visited the Berlin Central Train Station (Berlin Hauptbahnhof) to inspect the infrastructure and other facilities. Also Railway Minister, Suresh Prabhu, in his recent interviews has suggested that he will look to capitalize on various assets of railways like land, optical fibers, etc. If these ideas go per plan, there are many more job opportunities possible.

Aviation

There are two parts in this segment. Firstly, in military aviation, the recent deal with France on Rafale jets is well publicized. Whatever the politics of the deal is, the Indian government has been able to extract substantial investment in India in the future.Defense minister Manohar Parrikar has gone on record to say that 50% of the total deal value, approx. $4bn will be invested in India within the defense and aerospace sector. Secondly, in civil aviation, Airbus has also announced that it has joined the "Make in India" bandwagon. To this extent, Airbus has already announced restructuring of its organization in India and the new CEO has announced that Airbus exports will reach $2bn from India. Pratt and Whitney, a US based firm, has also evinced interest in setting up its facilities in India. Like in the automobile sector, aviation also has the potential to create many upstream and downstream jobs along the supply chain.

NARENDRA MODI'S 'MAKE IN INDIA' CAMPAIGN SEEKS TO CAPTIVATE YOUNG CONSUMERS

Indian Prime Minister Narendra Modi's "Make in India" campaign, aimed at turning the country into a global manufacturing hub, seems to have struck a chord with Indian retailers and consumers alike. Following the campaign's launch in September, Indian consumers, mainly in the 16 to 35 age group, have been seeking out 'Make in India' themed products, according to a reportby The Economic Times, an Indian business daily.

Radhika Ghai Aggarwal, co-founder and chief marketing officer at Shopclues, an Indian online retail website, told The Economic Times that her company is planning to introduce merchandise with the Make in India logo of a lion printed on them. Retailers around the country, especially the online versions, are gearing up for the upcoming holiday season with hefty discounts aimed at this particular demographic who have embraced online shopping in a big way.

However, government officials have sought to standardize the campaign's adoption. Officials at the Department of Industrial Policy and Promotion, or DIPP, which is a part of the Indian commerce ministry, reportedly said that the ministry too was planning to launch its own line of Make in India-themed products soon.

"We want everyone to use the logo but there has to be a quality to it. The logo can't be distorted on the will and desire of companies or individuals. We are being strict about it so that the logo doesn't lose its character," Atul Chaturvedi, a DIPP official, told The Economic Times.

The Make in India campaign, which was launched by Modi on Sept. 25, seeks to emulate China and other East Asian powerhouses by focusing on export-oriented manufacturing.

Under the program, 25 sectors, including biotechnology, automobiles, space and information technology, have been identified to enhance the overall "global competitiveness of the Indian manufacturing sector."

"I feel Make in India is like a movement reflecting a new mindset of growth in India, which in the coming years will drive India's growth story in a new way," DIPP Secretary Amitabh Kant told the Press Trust of India, an Indian news agency.

MAKE IN INDIA CAMPAIGN WILL BOOST METALS DEMAND

Of all manufacturing sectors, automobile and auto components makers – particularly foreign firms based in India – have responded enthusiastically to Modi's call to produce items in India for domestic and global markets. Honda of Japan, which intends to "strengthen its Make in India resolve" has announced a fresh investment of Rs9.65 billion ($156 million) to raise its capacity to manufacture both motorcycles and cars.

An important component of Make in India's mission relates to what domestic steel and aluminium producers have to do to meet the increasingly demanding metal quality requirements of the automotive industry. Some Indian steelmakers have teamed up with established automotive steel producers to make metal of the required grades. Tata Steelhas formed a technology and equity alliance with Nippon Steel & Sumitomo Metal (NSSMC) and, in September 2014, started producing, for the first time in India, automotive-grade continuous-annealed cold rolled sheets. JSW has built a 2.3 million-tpy cold rolling mill at Vijayanagar, in Karnataka, with technology from JFE of Japan for making high-grade automotive steels.

In the railway sector, the government has promised to increase national track length by 20% to 138,000km over the next five years, spurring investments by existing rail producers. Sail's Bilhai Steel has ordered a 1.2 million-tpy universal rail mill from SMS Meer, which will be commissioned later this year. The plant will be able to make 520 metre rails by joining four 130 metre sections.

To reduce India's substantial defence imports, Modi has made defence a focus of Make in India. During a recent visit to Rourkela Steel Plant, where a newly commissioned mill is making 4.3 metre wide plate, he said that increased local defence production, including tanks and warships, would generate "good demand for plates and other steel products".

Defence equipment manufacture has also been assisted by the government's liberalisation of the rules covering direct foreign investment, which has promoted strategic partnerships between overseas and Indian companies in this sector.

High hopes that infrastructure requirements would increase demand for metals have ended in disappointment in the past, and Make in India is addressing this concern.

Finance minister Arun Jaitley said in his recent budget speech that the "major slippage in the past decade has been on the infrastructure front. Our infrastructure does not match our growth ambitions."

To tackle this, the budget includes "very substantial" increases in outlays for road building, railway development, port capacity and other infrastructure areas. Five new large power projects of 4,000MW each will generate great demand for steel, aluminium and copper, and boost business for manufacturers of turbines and other power equipment.

However, Indian metal producers may only partly benefit from the rapidly growing consumer home appliances sector. This is because for many appliances, such as microwave ovens, Indian companies are finding imports, particularly from China and some other Asian countries, a more economical proposition than domestic sourcing. Imports are being boosted by progressively lower import duties until 2017, when target rates will be reached. A report by management consulting firm Arthur

D Little sees India's electronics and appliances demand rising to $400 billion by 2020, but domestic manufacturing capacity value rising to only $100 billion.

BENEFIT OF "MAKE IN INDIA" CAMPAIGN

The Global investors are watching India with a great interest. India is sitting at the cusp of a massive digital revolution through Make in India and Digital India campaign. India's contribution in global trade is growing day by day. Economic transformation is on his way with an aim to make India a global manufacturing hub. This clearly represents the *benefit of make in india campaign.*

Objective behind "MII"

The Make in India campaign focuses on attracting and helping businesses to invest and set up their manufacturing units in India. The campaign covers and promotes 25 sectors. The initiative is focused to target the youth, who are coming ahead with new entrepreneurial ideas & concept innovation. MII has determined on attracting global businesses to invest and manufacture in India to make the India a global manufacturing hub.

Social Success of "Make in India"

According to the statistics from the ministry, MII's Official FB page is adding a new member or fan every 2-3 seconds. Interestingly, it is for the first time that any such government initiative has been made interactive through a 'Q&A' session on Twitter on the issue of ease of doing business in India.

Not just the social networks, even the MII's website has received excellent response with page views of over +5.5 million accessed by over approx. 1.7 million users across the world which clearly indicates the interest of public in benefits of make in india campaign.

Benefits of Make in India camapign:

(A) Increase in Manufacturing & Export : export is picking up giving a slight push to the economy. Global investment will transform India a global manufacturing hub with use of latest technology.

(B) Generation of more jobs: Increased investment will create more jobs for skilled labour force. This will create a job market for over 1 crore. Government has started skill development programme which will generate more skilled worker.

(C) Attract more FDI : With a promise to enhance the ease of doing business in India, Government will attract more FDI in India. It has already attracted INR 20K millions worth investment proposal by October '14.

Conclusion

Apart from these benefits, There will be some more benefit like fast project clearance, Technological up-gradation etc.. This globalization of india will generate a need of global b2b marketing for every business to generate global leads. Global B2B Marketing is a powerful way to grow your brand and develop new overseas markets, all it takes is right strategy, passion and consistency to get things moving in the right direction.

4

Make in India : Modi's New Deal for Foreign Investors

India now has a facilitation window of sorts for investors who want to do business in the country, ushering in a new paradigm that is meant to make India's notorious labyrinth of red tape and bureaucratic hurdles an unhappy memory from the past.

A day after India's triumphant Mars mission and hours before he left for his first visit to the USA as prime minister, Narendra Modi launched the "Make in India" campaign. The initiative is meant to cut red tape, spur foreign investments and transform India into a manufacturing powerhouse, correcting the biggest weakness of Indian economy.

The initiative got a high-profile launch in New Delhi today, with India's top industrialists, including Reliance Industries chairman Mukesh Ambani and Wipro chairman Azim Premji, speaking about the new deal for foreign investors, alongside Modi.

The face of the initiative is a slickly designed website—MakeInIndia.com. Designed by creative agency Wieden and Kennedy (W+K), it's possibly the snazziest web portal of any government program in India, and offers information about various sectors. The backend is an agency called Invest India, which is a joint venture between industry chamber Ficci (Federation of Indian Chambers of Commerce and Industry), the central government's department of industrial promotion and policy, and state governments, each of whom hold 0.5% equity. Invest India will act as a facilitator to foreign investors, guiding them through clearances, advising on joint venture partners, and suchlike.

Maruti Suzuki's Kenichi Ayukawa, Reliance Industries' Mukesh Ambani, Wipro's Azim Premji, Aditya Birla Group's Kumar Mangalam Birla and ICICI Bank's Chanda Kochchar are seen at the Make In India launch.(AP Photo/Saurabh Das)

Prospective investors can post questions on the Make In India portal and they will be answered by a panel of experts within 72 hours. Twenty five sectors have been identified as priority areas and the portal offers a wealth of information about them.

Modi also came up with a new definition for FDI. "For Indians FDI is a responsibility, it means to First Develop India, for global investors FDI is an opportunity in the form of Foreign Direct Investment," he said, addressing Indian and foreign CEOs.

Top-down approach?

Two questions stand out about Make In India, however.

First, while a single window for foreign investors is a great beginning, how does it help when no serious reform has been undertaken in areas such as land acquisition, labour laws or administrative reforms. Sure, the executives at Invest India could be trained to be more friendly than the average bureaucrat and might be able to explain what clearances a business needs to get. But the actual process of getting the clearances is the challenge, and that remains steeped in the old India, where files move at snail's pace and litigation can break a project. Besides, many of the approvals needed are state subjects, and there is only so much that executives at Invest India, or indeed the central government, can do to facilitate licenses and clearances. These issues have not been adequately addressed.

Second, the focus on foreign investment and big corporations is at odds with the reality of India's industrial landscape—the small and medium enterprises are the heroes of our industry and they are the ones who need support and encouragement. Small businesses comprised about 17% of India's GDP (Pdf) in 2011 and employed about 60 million people, making it India's second largest employer after the agricultural sector. Within the manufacturing sector, SMEs constitute around 90% of all industrial units and account for nearly half of India's total industrial output and 40% of exports. For India's industry to shine, SMEs need to shine, and it is unclear what Make In India is doing for small businesses.

The picture of decay

But these are questions about calibrating the program. There is no denying that India urgently needed to welcome global investors and ease their operations here. The following numbers capture the sorry state of India's industrial competitiveness, and why Make in India was needed yesterday.

15% : That is the current share of manufacturing sector in Indian's GDP. It compares poorly to other Asian countries. The sector is 34% of China's GDP and 31% of South Korea's. In the next decade, India expects to ramp up manufacturing to 25% of the GDP.

100 million jobs: The number of manufacturing jobs the Indian government aims to create by 2022. According to Justin Lin, a former chief economist at the World bank, China will shed 85 million manufacturing jobs in the next few years because of fast rising wages. India can attract some of these jobs—and it desperately needs to—if it can cut bureaucratic hurdles that scare away new businesses.

"Global companies want to come to Asia but they don't know where to look in Asia," Modi said today. "Democracy, the demographic dividend and strong demand are important factors, and India has all three."

65% of India's 1.2 billion population is under the age of 35. The average age of an Indian in 2020 will be 29, compared with 37 in China and the United States. In the next decade, India is expected to have the largest available workforce in the world. But if the country cannot create jobs for its youth, the demographic advantage would be wasted.

"In the last five to six years we have had jobless growth and consumption. That is unsustainable. We have only created 2 million jobs every year. But 12 million youth are coming to the job market every year. Obviously it is a recipe for disaster if we allow it to continue, " said Y.C. Deveshwar, chairman of ITC, India's largest cigarette maker, at the event today.

134th: That is where India stands, out of 189 countries, in World Bank's"Ease of doing Business" Index. In South Asia, only Bhutan (141) and Afghanistan (164) rank lower than India. The World Bank report notesthat it takes 27 days to start a business in India. In Singapore it takes two and a half days. Registering a business takes less than a day in Singapore.

Since the new government took over in May, the process of applying for industrial license has been made online on the e-Biz website.

INDIA: GETTING READY, HOLDING STEADY

The financial reforms enacted by Prime Minister Modi's administration in the past six months, along with healthy GDP growth and rising business confidence, point to an economy that seems poised to reach the "critical mass" necessary for sustainable growth.

It's been six months since Prime Minister Modi and his government took charge of the Indian economy after the Bharatiya Janata Party (BJP) and its alliances swept to power in a landslide election. Since then, the government has enacted a string of incremental reforms and announced numerous policies aimed at reviving the economy. The economy too has shown signs of a turnaround. GDP grew at a healthy rate of 5.5 percent in the first half of FY 2014–15, while economic imbalances shrank. A decline in inflation and current account imbalance due to adept monetary policies, together with some serious efforts to consolidate fiscal balance, have boosted confidence. Business sentiment is surging up as new government initiatives, new foreign policies, and an improved growth outlook relative to other leading emerging economies continue to impress global investors. India's position is better than that of commodity-centric nations like Brazil, Russia, and South Africa. And although China has often fared economically better than India, China has lately been struggling because of a slowing economy and financial instability.

However, questions about addressing more fundamental structural bottlenecks, as well as doubts about the successful implementation of reforms, continue to linger in investors' minds. Complex regulatory procedures and a lack of transparency and coordination across all levels of government continue to exist. The manufacturing sector, which can significantly contribute to employment, income, and exports, needs to be overhauled to address structural deficiencies, complex labor laws, and inefficient policy regulations.

To put the economy on a sustainable and inclusive growth path, it is important to make the bureaucracy lay a clear roadmap to ensure that reforms on paper are effectively implemented. In the past six months, numerous initiatives have aimed at improving governance and increasing administrative efficiency. The government has repeatedly emphasized the development of infrastructure and the need to boost the manufacturing sector. However, the government has had only limited success in implementing these initiatives. A number of areas fall under the responsibility of India's state governments, which differ in their attitudes, political will, and administrative efficiency. Thus, it will remain a challenge to enact such initiatives effectively, despite the center's best intentions.

To put the economy on a sustainable and inclusive growth path, it is important to make the bureaucracy lay a clear roadmap to ensure that reforms on paperare effectively implemented.

That said, it is also true that it takes time to turn around an economy that has been suffering from myriad economic maladies over the past few years. Once the economy reaches a minimum threshold level, it can take off at a sustainable pace. Thus, it is very important that the path to sustainable growth is laid out with proper attention so that once the economy picks up, it can experience a hurdle-free run thereafter.

LAYING THE GROUNDWORK WITH INITIATIVES AND REFORMS

The prime minister has announced a number of reforms and initiatives in the past few months. Some major reforms, such as labor reforms, fuel price reforms, and reforms in the coal sector, as well as initiatives such as the "Make in India" campaign that have launched in the last couple of months, can be game-changers in the long run.

Reforms

Labor reforms: In August, the government introduced a few strategic changes to the Labor Laws Act of 1988, the Factories Act of 1948, and the Apprenticeship Act of 1961. The intent of these reforms was to reduce paperwork, lower some transaction costs for firms, and limit intrusions by the state.

In October, the prime minister launched a single-window labor compliance process for industries on labor-related issues and friendlier provident fund (PF) facilities. He also unveiled a new inspection scheme that is expected to curb the element of discretion among labor inspectors—often termed "Inspector Raj." In addition, health insurance and new skill development and apprenticeship schemes were revamped.

These measures are expected to streamline rules and regulations to create a better business environment. However, when compared to the reforms that India really needs, these measures are relatively modest. Stringent labor laws such as the Industrial Dispute Act, which prevents firms with 100 employees or more from firing workers without government permission, often discourage businesses from promoting large-scale production. As a result, the cost of production and productivity growth suffer, while businesses prefer to grow in capital-intensive sectors. Again, successful and effective implementation of these laws will require a clear roadmap.

Albeit modest, these measures signal that the government recognizes the importance of changing existing labor laws and simplifying procedures. In order to boost productivity and competitiveness, India must get rid of old regulations and procedures that inhibit business growth, but at a balanced pace. Therefore, these measures should be seen as a stepping stone for bigger changes in the future.

Fuel price reforms: The new government seized the opportunity presented by falling international oil prices by deregulating diesel's retail price, which will reflect movement in global oil prices going forward. A cut in diesel prices was always in the cards; however, the move to deregulate the prices, which has been a politically sensitive issue and directly impacts the cost of daily living, is a positive development. Of course, the hard decision to deregulate gas prices was initiated by the previous government, but diesel prices were not deregulated. Instead, diesel subsidies were reduced over 16 months. The recent fuel reform also included raising gas prices, although they were raised less than the amount recommended by the Rangarajan Committee, and the increase was less than market expectations.

The deregulation of diesel prices now creates opportunities for private companies to reenter the fuel retail market. Similarly, the increase in gas prices from current levels will likely attract investment into sectors such as deep-sea exploration. However, these moves are not enough to spark much enthusiasm among private investors. The decision to deregulate diesel prices was made easy because of falling international oil prices. What happens when the falling oil price trend reverses? Can the government afford to raise prices at a pace faster than was done previously, if the situation warrants it? The uncertainty generated by this policy reversal will weigh on investment decisions by private investors, who have already had to mothball their operations once due to a similar policy reversal. If government controls come back, these private companies will fail to compete with the subsidized price of state retailers.

The deregulation of diesel prices now creates opportunities for private companies to reenter the fuel retail market.

Roadmap for coal sector reforms: The finance minister signaled that the government may allow commercial use of mines in future.

The government also indicated that it may soon issue an ordinance to facilitate an auction of the coal blocks that was recently cancelled by India's Supreme Court. Mines will likely be put on e-auction for the first time, and the process of reallocation will likely be completed within 3 to 4 months. Renewing work in these mines could re-employ thousands of laborers and free up bank capital. However, the government did not announce any big-ticket reforms to end the monopoly of Coal India, which has been unable to ramp up production quickly.

All these reforms indicate that the government feels some urgency to usher in some much-needed reforms to kick-start the economy. The parliament convened on November 24 for its month-long winter session, with one of the government's main objectives being to implement a number of pending economic reforms. The government continued to reform through ordinance and amended the new land acquisition act. It also tabled a bill to establish a long-awaited national goods and services tax (GST).

Initiatives

Make in India: The prime minister launched the "Make in India" program to attract investment and encourage innovation by creating a world-class manufacturing infrastructure in India. The program's intent is to make doing business in India easier, more transparent, and credit-friendly. The government has identified 25 sectors and industries in which India has the potential of becoming a world leader. New de-licensing and deregulation measures have been introduced.

Modi has been proactively canvassing support for this program. In his recent trips to the United States and Australia, he invited big corporations, government authorities, and the Indian community settled abroad to invest in India. The campaign has already attracted the attention of many foreign companies and nations. If India succeeds in attracting investment and multinational manufacturing factories, it could create immense job opportunities as well as provide a livelihood for people in rural areas. According to the "Make in India" website, this initiative offers a wide gamut of investment opportunities, from automobiles to biotechnology to renewable energy, which could benefit small-and medium-scale enterprises immensely.

From highways to i-ways: The government is actively initiating policies for building quality infrastructure, with the aim of building smart cities, industrial corridors, bullet trains, highways, and a strong digital network in rural areas. In all his recent meetings with the international leaders, Modi had a strong domestic agenda of encouraging investment into the country, with an emphasis on foreign participation in India's infrastructure development. Recently, India and the United States signed a memorandum of understanding for infrastructure development, which will likely facilitate US industry participation in infrastructure projects in India. Prior to that, Modi invited China, Japan, and Australia to invest in mega infrastructure projects. In his visits abroad, Modi met a great many top corporates, executives, and non-resident Indians to reinvigorate their interest in investing in the government's new initiatives related to smart cities, infrastructure, digitalization, education, and health.

In addition, Modi has also proposed a "Digital India" initiative. The center has approved a blueprint for the project, which is expected to attract investments of Rs 1,00,000 crore over the next three to four years. Technology giants across India and abroad are eyeing the project. Sectors that may see an influx of technology include agriculture, manufacturing, health care, infrastructure, railways, retail, business and financial investments, and education. The government has already begun to digitize its own departments with the large-scale digitization of all government records. It has roped in multinational technology companies to target digitization across government functions.

However, the success of these initiatives hinges on several factors. While implementing these initiatives with minimum government involvement and maximum efficiency remains a challenge, the availability of uninterrupted resources at competitive rates is another factor that deserves serious attention. Initiatives are often delayed or discontinued due to lack of resource availability at the right time, be it access to electricity or credit funding. Poor management and corruption further damage the chances of successfully implementing these initiatives.

THE ECONOMY IS STABILIZING AND ON THE PATH TO RECOVERY

According to the latest GDP release, the economy grew 5.3 percent year over year in Q2 FY 2014–15, thanks to growth in services and stronger-than-expected results in farming after a bad monsoon. However, poor performance in the manufacturing sector slowed growth. Growth in real private consumption expenditure remained steady at 5.8 percent in Q2. Although growth in government consumption expenditure fell 13.1 percent relative to the previous quarter, its year-over-year growth of 10.1 percent helped boost GDP growth. The real worry has been the poor performance of exports and private investments, which contracted by 1.6 percent and 0.3 percent, respectively.

According to the latest GDP release, the economy grew 5.3 percent year over year in Q2 FY 2014–15, thanks to growth in services and stronger-than-expected results in farming after a bad monsoon.

Evidently, the pick-up in project clearances and reform initiatives by the government, and the improved business sentiment of the last six months, have failed to show up in the GDP numbers. Negative growth in capital formation in Q2 is an indicator that poor global demand, limited improvement in capacity utilization levels, and uncertainty over the implementation of reforms are weighing on investment decisions. Businesses are looking forward to a more predictable taxation system, faster regulatory clearances, and industry-friendly land acquisition and labor laws before they commit to long-term investments.

Figure 1. A healthy growth so far (year over year, percentage)

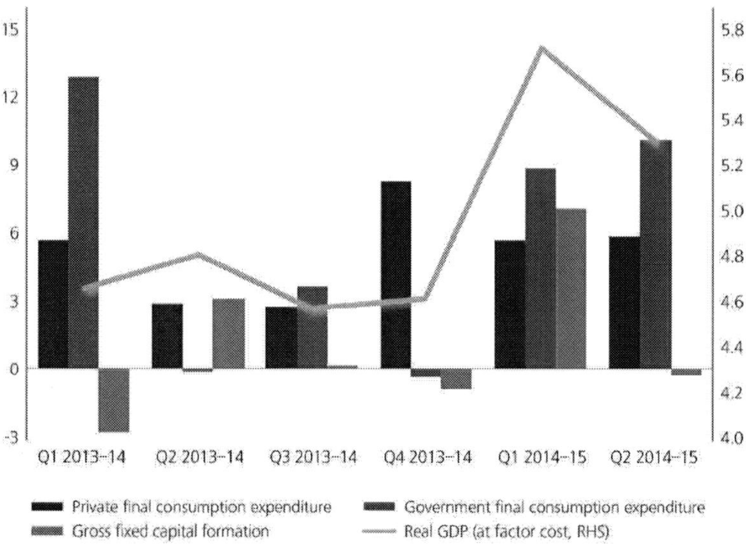

Note: Q1 refers to fiscal year beginning in April and ending in March of the following year.
Sources: Reserve Bank of India, September 2014; Press Information Bureau, August 2014; Bloomberg, November 2014.

Graphic: Deloitte University Press | DUPress.com

Falling prices have brought some relief to both policymakers and to the populace at large. Declining consistently since May 2014, the wholesale price index remained unchanged in November compared to the same period a year ago. This is the slowest increase in the past 5 years. Consistently falling food prices along with declining international fuel prices have helped contain inflation. Several factors have contributed to the fall in food prices: the recovery after the monsoon, government actions such as lower minimum support prices and more proactive stock sales, and benign global food prices. However, structural factors such as having the right infrastructure, proper storage, and better transportation capabilities still need to be attended to. Unless these factors, which have resulted in higher food prices in the last decade, are addressed, the recent fall in food prices may be short-lived. As is evident, the expectation of inflation continues to remain high, which implies that there remains significant upside risks to inflation.

Figure 2. The inflation monster seems to have been tamed (year over year, percentage)

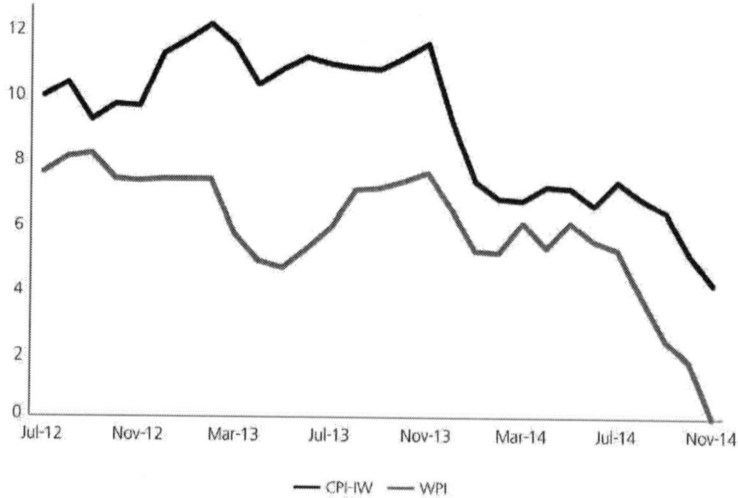

Source: CSO India, Ministry of Statistics and Programme Implementation, December 2014.
Graphic: Deloitte University Press | DUPress.com

For some time, the RBI has been under immense pressure from both industry and policymakers to cut rates as inflation rates ease and economic performance remains modest. However, as the RBI governor has pointed out, despite the slowdown, there are significant upside risks to inflation. The recent easing is due to transitory factors and administered price corrections; weaker-than-anticipated agricultural production in the coming months and a possible rise in energy prices may alter the benign outlook. The RBI governor has decided to keep key policy rates in the RBI's recent monetary policy unchanged. However, he has also hinted that if inflation continues to remain steady, and fiscal developments are encouraging, there might be a change in the RBI's monetary policy stance early next year, even outside the policy review cycle.

Figure 3. Business sentiment is improving significantly

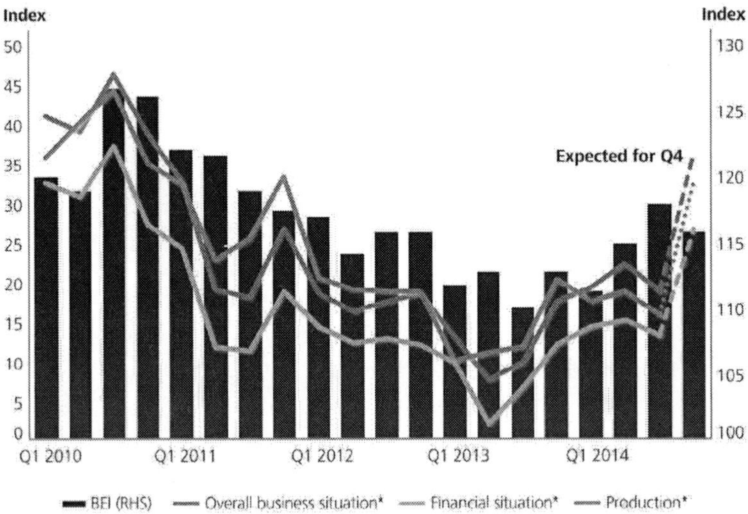

*Note: The difference of percentage of the respondents reporting optimism and that reporting pessimism. The range is -100 to 100. Any value greater than zero indicates expansion/optimism and any value less than zero indicates contraction/pessimism i.e., NR = (I – D); where, I is the percentage response of 'Increase/optimism', and D is the percentage response of 'Decrease/pessimism' and E is the percentage response as 'no change/Equal'; I+D+E=100.

Source: Reserve Bank of India, January 2014.

Graphic: Deloitte University Press | DUPress.com

Business sentiment is improving fast, as suggested by the 2014 Manufacturing Leadership Survey, which was conducted jointly by an industry lobby that included the Confederation of Indian Industry (CII) and the Boston Consulting Group (BCG). The survey, of over 100 heads of Indian corporations, was performed to gauge the pulse of industry leaders on India's current economic situation and the future prospects for the Indian manufacturing sector. The survey shows a distinct rise in confidence, with 85 percent of those surveyed expecting manufacturing growth to rise between 5 percent and 10 percent in the next five years (compared with 3.4 percent in the past five years). According to the RBI's survey, too, the business expectation index (BEI) has been rising sharply in the past few quarters. The industrial outlook survey suggests that perceptions of the overall business, production, and financial situation in India are as good as they were in 2010.

However, a few economic indicators suggest that the economy is not out of the woods yet. Factors such as the pace and quality of fiscal consolidation, high inflation, poor manufacturing sector performance, poor export performance, and the banking sector's deteriorating asset quality pose downside risks to the economy. So far, fiscal consolidation has taken place mainly by curbing government expenses rather than by increasing revenues. Tax collection remains poor, while the pace of disinvestment remains slow. It will be important for the government to find alternative sources of revenue if fiscal balance is to be achieved without impacting growth. While the current account deficit has narrowed since 2013 due to a tight monetary policy, restrictions on gold imports, and a fall in crude imports, export growth has remained weak in last few months.

India's currency has weakened against the US dollar in the last month, primarily due to the spillover effect of the strengthening US dollar itself as well as transient factors such as the sudden rise in demand for the US dollar to pay for imports. That said, the Indian currency has firmed against the euro, pound, and yen, while the real effective exchange rate suggests that the domestic currency is appreciating while its peers are deteriorating.

The index of industrial production (IIP) continues to remain weak, as the manufacturing sector remains highly vulnerable. The growth in capital goods has been on an unsustainable trajectory, while contraction in the consumer durable goods sector indicates a poor outlook for consumer demand. The auto sector has performed below expectations thus far in 2014 as domestic demand failed to increase sales, especially in the passenger vehicle market. Poor exports, too, contributed to a weak IIP.

Many public sector banks are facing huge outstanding bad loans, mostly made to several large, influential borrowers. The recovery process has been poor because of legal loopholes and big corporations' lobbying power over the financial system. This has resulted in an increase in stressed assets (bad loans and restructured assets), which now account for 10 percent of total assets. The corporate debt restructuring mechanism, under which interest rates are lowered and tenors extended, is being abused in some cases, with promoters not bringing in equity. The RBI governor has been pushing for financial sector reforms and is vigilant over credit conditions.

Promising growth in the long term

The dynamics in India are changing fast, and even though the impact on the economy has been limited to date, the government's efforts to revive the economy are improving the long-term outlook. This is evident from the recent upward revision of India's growth forecast for FY 2015–16 by the IMF and the OECD, as well as an outlook upgrade by some of the rating agencies. The prime minister's strong leadership, the recent reforms and initiatives, and the RBI's prudent monetary policies are building up confidence among investors. While credit conditions are expected to remain tight for some time, improved business sentiment may drive up investment, which will likely be the growth engine in coming quarters. As said earlier, it takes time for an economy to reach a threshold where it can take off, and there are clear signs that energy is gradually building up.

Table. India: Economic forecast summary (November 2014)

	2014–15* (%)	2015–16 (%)
RBI	5.5 (+0.2)	6.5 (+0.3)
IMF	5.6 (0)	6.4 (+0.2)
OECD	5.4 (-0.3)	6.4 (+0.5)
EIU	6.0 (-0.4)	6.5 (-0.1)

* The figures in the bracket refer to the revisions since the last forecasts.

Sources: Reserve Bank of India; International Monetary Fund; Bloomberg; Economic Intelligence Unit, November revisions.

MODI'S VISIT TO FRANCE AND 'THE MAKE IN INDIA' PROJECT

Prime Minister Narendra Modi is embarking on a 9-day tour abroad during which he will visit France, Germany and Canada. His first stop will be in Paris (April 9-12).

A few comments on his visit to France:

'Make in India' will undoubtedly be central to the Prime Minister's visit to Europe.

The good news first

On April 6, Defence Minister Manohar Parrikar 'undocked' the first of the six Scorpene submarines to be built in collaboration with France under Project 75, at the Mazagon Docks Limited (MDL).

The ceremony for 'floating out' the first Scorpene submarine was an occasion for Mr. Parrikar to review the progress of the Project 75, in collaboration with DCNS of France.

After the 'undocking', for the first time the submarine entered into waters (with the help of a pontoon).

An Indian Navy official told the media: "While the launch would be a more significant event, the floating out of Scorpene will commence its sea trials and more importantly, clear the dry dock that it presently occupies for the construction of the next one."

It is a promising progress for the 'Make in India' scheme. It is also shows that despite the difficulties and the delays, it is possible.

The 'refitted' Mirages

Perhaps as an appetizer for the Rafales deal, the IAF got its first two upgraded Mirage-2000 with new avionics and weapons at the end of March.

The 'Maitri' project, like the 'Brahmos' with Russia, could become a success story for the 'Make in India'.

An 'acceptance' ceremony for the IAF's Mirage 2000 I/TI was held at Istres, in South France on March 25. Among those present were Arun K. Singh, ambassador of India to France, Eric Trappier, chairman and CEO, Dassault Aviation and Pierre Eric Pommellet, executive vice president of Thales. The contract for 'refitting' the IAF's Mirage 2000 was signed in July, 2011. The upgrade 'kit' provided by Thales comprised new radar, electronic warfare suite and mission computer.

An official told The Times of India: "The upgraded Mirages have been stripped down and virtually re-built with state-of-the-art avionics, radars, mission computers, glass cockpits, helmet-mounted displays, electronic warfare suites and long-range missiles."

Of course, the appetizer can't replace the main course (Rafales), but one has to remain patient.

The 'Maitri' project

An important decision was recently taken by the Defence Acquisition Council: it approved the 'Maitri' project for the co-development of a Short Range Surface-to-Air Missile (SR-SAM) by the Defence Research and Development Organisation (DRDO) with MBDA of France.

The project has been 'pending' since 2007 and apparently, Delhi will now go for the marine version as the DRDO's Akash missile system satisfies the Indian Army and the Air Force.

The 'Maitri' project, like the 'Brahmos' with Russia, could become a success story for the 'Make in India'. The signature on the SR-SAM deal could be the 'main dish' of Modi's present visit.

COASTAL SURVEILLANCE RADAR SYSTEM

According to The Economic Times (ET), India and France are expected to discuss the sharing of radar data in the Indian Ocean as part of their strategic talks during Narendra Modi's visit to Paris.

India is setting up a grid of coastal surveillance radars in the Indian Ocean Region (IOR) which should help monitoring the region. France has apparently expressed an interest in sharing data from its surveillance systems.

India is setting up a grid of coastal surveillance radars in the Indian Ocean Region (IOR) which should help monitoring the region. France has apparently expressed an interest in sharing data from its surveillance systems.

The ET says that "the modalities of sharing maritime domain awareness data from at least three French monitoring sites in the Indian Ocean is set to be on the agenda. French territories in the region include the Reunion Islands and Mayotte, besides military bases in UAE and Djibouti."

Apparently, the Indian Navy is keen on the French proposal and would like it to be part of an ambitious plan to set up a 24-nation radar grid in the IOR to monitor all traffic, civilian and military. "As part of the plan, India could also lend financial aid to littoral nations for setting up radars. In the future, surveillance data from other military sites, including the American base at Diego Garcia, could be integrated," says the ET. It is however doubtful if France will agree to 'counter' China in the region.

On April 3, Chinese and French military officials reached a consensus in Beijing "on enhancing cooperation in exchange of ship visits, joint drilling and countering terrorism at sea."

Gen. Fang Fenghui, chief of general staff of the Chinese People's Liberation Army (PLA) met with Admiral Bernard Rogel, chief of staff of the French Navy in Beijing.

According to Xinhua, Admiral Bernard Rogel during his recent visit to China, declared that the rapid development of Chinese Navy's armaments and the excellent personnel quality left a deep impression on him: "He pledged to deepen mutual understanding and enhance cooperation with the Chinese side in the aspects of fleet visits, joint drilling and training as well as fighting against maritime terrorism."

'Varuna' Joint Exercices with the Charles de Gaulle Carrier

The French aircraft carrier Charles de Gaulle, which has recently been inducted against the Islamic State from the Persian Gulf, will participate in the Indo-French exercises 'Varuna' later this month.

Varuna will be held for 10 days in the Arabian Sea between the French and Indian Navies. It will also involve India's aircraft carrier, the INS Vikramaditya as well as other Indian warships and a submarine.

Varuna will be held for 10 days in the Arabian Sea between the French and Indian Navies. It will also involve India's aircraft carrier, the INS Vikramaditya as well as other Indian warships and a submarine.

During the exercises, the French Navy will use Rafales (M), the 'navalised' version of the Rafale currently under negotiations with Delhi.

The exercise will begin on April 23 and continue till May 3. The French will also bring two destroyers and a support ship.

The Indian media reported: "The navalised version of the aircraft is adapted to land and take off from carriers. The Indian Navy's main fighter jet is the Russian MiG29K. The fleet is being integrated with the Vikramaditya."

The French side is keen to expose the Indian Navy to the Rafale (M), with the hope that a first-hand experience of the fighter jet, may convince the Indian Navy, if not the MoD, to add a few Rafales (M) in India's wish list.

Visit to Toulouse One highlight of the PM's trip will be the visit to Airbus Industries headquarters in Toulouse. At stake in Toulouse, a $2-billion contract for eight Airbus A-330 MRTT mid-air refuelers, a deal pending for over two years. There is also a proposal for buying two Airbus A-330 aircraft for the IAF which is keen to acquire AWACS (Airborne warning and control system). India's 'eye in the sky' could be mounted on Airbus A-330 with Defence Research and Development Organisation

(DRDO)-developed rotodome radar fitted on it. The Prime Minister will probably be shocked when he discovers that the Chinese recently bought the Toulouse Blagnac airport.

What is the 'Make in India' scheme?

Mr. Modi's 'Make in India' dream is something which should kept in mind while analyzing the significance of the Prime Minister to France and Germany.

I witnessed the new craze during the recent Aero India 2015, organized at Yelahanka Airport in Bangalore ('Make in India' was the theme of the event).

...Delhi notified an increase in foreign direct investment (FDI) limit to 49 % in the defence sector. The move was aimed at boosting India's domestic industry and creating confidence amongst eventual investors.

Most of the foreign participants, even the Americans, were effusively enthusiastic about the scheme.

Foreign investors understood that the government was serious when, in August 2014 , Delhi notified an increase in foreign direct investment (FDI) limit to 49 % in the defence sector. The move was aimed at boosting India's domestic industry and creating confidence amongst eventual investors.

A Policy Change

In Bangalore, the Prime Minister had the opportunity to clarify that India is ready for a major change in direction: "I am confident that India will emerge as a major global centre for defence industry. We want to develop an industry that is dynamic."

The Indian Prime Minister wanted to end India's status as the world's number one defence importer; India's objective is to have 70 % (from the current 40 %) of hardware manufactured domestically by 2020.

Mr. Modi explained: "We have the reputation as the largest importer of defence equipment in the world, that may be music to the ears of some of you here. But this is one area where we would not like to be number one."

'Make in India' will undoubtedly be central to the Prime Minister's visit to Europe.

But there is a long, long way to go.

A Civil Nuclear Deal?

Apart from French investments in India, space and civil nuclear cooperation, infrastructure investment, terrorism and other security issues, will also be on the table. Narendra Modi has redrawn his week-long tour of Europe-Canada tour to make Paris the first stop, before proceeding to Hannover.

The French investments in India are progressing rather well with the total investment stock of French companies in India reaching nearly $19 billion.

In September 2008, India and France signed the first civilian nuclear agreement and consequently, a General Framework Agreement between Areva and the Nuclear Power Corporation of India Limited (NPCIL) for the construction of 6 European pressurized reactors (EPR) at Jaitapur in Maharashtra was inked in December 2010 during President Sarkozy's visit to India.

An Indian diplomat told The Hindustan Times: "The supply of EPRs will be on top of PM Modi's agenda but much depends on the closure of commercial negotiations between the two companies."

The finalization of the plans however depends on the economic and technical viability of these nuclear plants and as important, on an accord about 'nuclear liabilities'.

THE INDO-FRENCH ECONOMIC COOPERATION

The French investments in India are progressing rather well with the total investment stock of French companies in India reaching nearly $19 billion.

French Embassy sources believe that in the next to 4 to 5 years, the stock of French investments in India will significantly increase with the consolidation and extension of existing investments, and the influx of new French companies in India. A Special Representative for Indo-French Economic Relations (Paul Hermelin, the CEO Capgemini) has been appointed by the French President for the purpose.

Today 950 French companies (350 companies and 400 subsidiaries, as well as 200 individual entrepreneurs) are said to be implanted in India; they employ some 3,00,000 skilled Indian workers.

Today 950 French companies (350 companies and 400 subsidiaries, as well as 200 individual entrepreneurs) are said to be implanted in India; they employ some 3,00,000 skilled Indian workers.

French Embassy sources say that these French companies have brought their know-how and technology and many have begun opening research and development centres in India (already employing between 15,000 and 20,000 persons).

FRANCE AND 'MAKE IN INDIA'

Last September, more than 20 French companies attended the launch of the 'Make in India' campaign; to cite a few: Alstom, Dabon-Bongrain, Danone, Faurecia, Lafarge, Legrand, L'Oréal, Michelin, Renault, Roquette, Safran, Sanofi Pasteur India, Schneider Electric, SEB, SERAP, Saint-Gobain, Total, Valeo and Vicat.

Let us look at a few examples: Renault-Nissan has begun production in May 2010 on a 640-acre integrated plant in Chennai, with an investment of €700 million. It has now an annual capacity of 480,000 units with a workforce of more than 15,000 employees.

Michelin set up a 290-acre campus, 50 km north of Chennai; it already manufactures a wide range of radial truck/bus tyres.

Last October, Safran, a world leader in aerospace, defence and security, which provides the engine of the Rafale (through its subsidiary SNECMA) signed two agreements with Indian Institute of Technology (IIT), Delhi, and Indian Institute of Science (IISc), Bangalore, to develop advanced pattern recognition algorithms for complex data and advanced computing platform for the next-generation avionics applications.

Another case is Saint-Gobain's modern manufacturing facility in Rajasthan. A French press release says: "this state-of-the-art, fully automated float line covers a surface area of 27 acres and has a manufacturing capacity of close to 1000 tons of glass per day (3,00,000 metric tons per year). Once the plant is fully operational (by mid-2015), Saint-Gobain will have a total installed production capacity of 9,000 tons of glass per day."

The French presence in South India, particularly in Chennai and Pondicherry is worth noting; more than 100 enterprises are implanted in the South.

The French presence in South India

The French presence in South India, particularly in Chennai and Pondicherry is worth noting; more than 100 enterprises are implanted in the South.Apart from Renault and Michelin already mentioned, large French groups such as Alstom, Saint-Gobain, Lactalis have set up factories in Chennai. Interestingly, the management of these large companies is progressively transferred to local cadres, while the French personnel continue to focus on quality control and over-all financial management.

The main focus is presently automobiles and transport (such as Alstom Transport which produces metro bogies) and energy like Sicame (electric material), Schneider, Cryolor (cryogenic tanks), Legrand and Socomec (UPS). Saint-Gobain also has a large factory in Chennai.In Pondicherry, the focus is more on hospitality, tourism as well as Internet editions and web design.

COME, MAKE IN INDIA

Destination India

The size of our domestic market and the abundant availability of skilled and technical manpower at low cost is a leverage that we need to put to use.

Prime Minister Narendra Modi, in his maiden Independence Day speech, articulated his vision of several social and economic policy objectives of his government. It is generally agreed that the objectives so forcefully expressed by him are unexceptionable, but what is required, and often difficult, is their effective translation into practice.

The Prime Minister must be commended for stating so clearly that domestic manufacturing will be the core and central tenet of his foreign investment policy as that puts job creation or employment generation at the top of the objectives in inviting foreign investment to the country.

GLOBAL MANUFACTURING HUB

This welcome emphasis in our foreign investment policy on efficient and competitive domestic manufacturing will serve multiple objectives. First and foremost, it will enhance job opportunities within the country; second, it will minimisze the imports of such products into the country, thereby mitigating the pressure on our trade deficit; third, in the long run, if not in the near-term, it will help augment and diversify our exports from the manufacturing sector; fourth, it will help in bringing latest technologies into the countryand lastly, such domestic manufacturing will help minimize some of the trade frictions we have with other countries. The importance of domestic manufacturing with foreign investment in reducing trade frictions with other countries is at present ignored or underestimated. As a corollary, the focus on world-class domestic manufacturing may also be the best way to cope with globalisation and to maximise the possible benefits from it. The size of our domestic market and the abundant availability of skilled and technical manpower at low cost is a leverage that we need to put to use consciously to induce foreign investors to make India as a manufacturing hub in their operations. If there is one lesson we can learn from the Chinese, it is how the size of the domestic market and the availability of skilled and disciplined manpower could be put to effective use for the industrial and technological development of the country with foreign investment.

It is, however, in the translation of the policy into practice that co-ordinated action is needed on several fronts. First, it is of paramount importance that the foreign investment, foreign trade and intellectual property rights (IPR) policies are viewed in a holistic manner to ensure that they mutually reinforce each other in achieving the policy objective of world-class domestic manufacturing.

Second, with respect to the broad contours of the foreign investment policy, it needs to be remembered that investment opportunities, as reflected by our large domestic market and low-cost skilled and unskilled manpower, may be a necessary, but not a sufficient condition, to induce foreign investors to come to India with their capital and technology. The congeniality of the investment climate or environment, as reflected in the stability of the policies and the rules as well as the conditions attached to the approval of the investments, is even more important to assure foreign investors of fair and non-discriminatory treatment.

The focus of our foreign investment policy should be on the positive aspects of what is produced in India, with what kind of technology and skills, how efficiently and competitively it is produced, and whether it is of world-class standards, and not on negative aspects such as ownership and control, enterprise-specific performance requirements, or other conditions that interfere with the internal commercial decisions of the enterprises.

Competitive environment

The best way to ensure that foreign investment is of a high quality and yields value to the country is to have a policy framework that requires it to operate in an unprotected, open and competitive environment, and not behind high tariff walls or import restrictions, nor with the aid of subsidies or other giveaways. Third, with respect to the contours of the foreign trade policy, it is by and large confined now to dealing with exports and imports compartmentally — encouragement of exports with various kinds of subsidies and prop-ups, and curtailment of imports by high tariffs and other so-called trade remedy measures like anti-dumping or countervailing duties or other import restrictions. Encouragement of domestic manufacturing of world-class standards, either by domestic or foreign investors or both, has not been a major objective of our foreign trade policy so far.

Our foreign trade policy must recognise that encouragement of domestic manufacturing of world-class standards, catering solely even to our own market, is a preferable alternative to protection and subsidisation through high tariffs, trade remedy measures and financial giveaways. Rather, the policy must encourage freer imports of capital goods, industrial raw materials, components, tools and devices, as well as technology-laden imports, with a view to upgrading the quality and competitiveness of our domestic manufacturing.

Fourth, the importance of the protection of intellectual property rights (IPRs) in the scheme of attracting foreign investment and establishing high quality domestic manufacturing must not be overlooked.

Ensure IP protection

IPRs do not consist only of pharmaceutical patents as is commonly understood in our country: they include as well copyright (computer software in our country is protected by copyright), trademarks, trade secrets, geographical indications, designs, trade secrets, business confidential information and data, and the like.

Even if our IPR policies do not have domestic manufacturing as a central objective, they need to be implemented in such a way that they do not impede or deter technology-oriented domestic investments from foreign investors. The protection of patents, trademarks, trade secrets, layout designs and the like is crucial to these and other sectors where we want foreign investment of high quality with modern technologies. Our intellectual property laws are largely in conformity with international standards as reflected in the TRIPS Agreement of the WTO and other international conventions to which we have subscribed. Yet we tend to create an impression around the world that we do not value intellectual property or respect its adequate protection.

Address local woes

One other aspect that does not fall within the ambit of the aforesaid policies, but which is crucial to competitive domestic manufacturing needs to be touched upon here. Among the major reasons for our domestic industry being competitively disadvantaged vis-a-vis the rest of the world, two stand out prominently: first, the inadequacy and poor quality of our infrastructure, and second, the high cost of our capital. While protection and subsidisation is not the solution, this huge disadvantage faced by the domestic industry requires to be addressed with priority and ways and means found to mitigate it.

To conclude this essay in a lighter vein, in one of the famous cartoons of Dennis the Menace, the irrepressible boy tells his father with a logic beyond his years: "Dad, if everything is made in China, then God must be living in China". When the Prime Minister's vision of "Come, Make in India" is realised, and India becomes an enviable manufacturing hub of the world, Dennis may perhaps find God shifting his Presidence to India!

THE NEW GOVERNMENT MAKE INDIA A GLOBAL MANUFACTURING HUB

An ancient nation like India has undergone many evolutionary cycles.

A well admired supremacy of ancient India in the field of Science and technology requires no mention.

But with the advent of modern era, many western societies surpassed India in term of advancement in Science and technology. But India is slowly re-emerging to acquire its leadership position. On

24th September 2014, India entered a new era of leadership with its Mars Mission successfully entering the orbit with a cost which was one tenth of the cost of Mars project by NASA.

This reaffirmed India's capability to deliver on cost, quality and time. This triad is building block for the success of a country.

India's manufacturing sector has far lagged behind and it is the opportune time to focus on this sector.

What India has to focus on is to integrate manufacturing operations with IT based services to offer solutions which boost the most critical sectors of the economy.

Shining manufacturing sector is an export driver which is evident from the fact that 40% of China's GDP comes through manufacturing.

75% of India's working population is educated only to middle school or below.

This staggering figure of approximately 600 million1 people is not even equipped to benefit from the opportunities in the flourishing service sector. It is only the labor intensive manufacturing sector that has the potential to generate employment in adequate numbers to absorb the larger labor pool.

Indian manufacturing sector currently contributes close to 15% of GDP which is almost half when compared to "factory of the world" China, whereas service sector contributes almost

60% to GDP. This huge mismatch in terms of contribution to GDP makes it imperative for India to focus on manufacturing and bring it close to 25% over next decade.

Contribution to GDP (%)	2008-09	2009-10	2010-11	2011-12	2012-13	2013-14
Agriculture, forestry & fishing	15.77%	14.64%	14.59%	14.37%	13.95%	13.94%
Industry Mining & quarrying	2.36%	2.3%	2.25%	2.11%	1.98%	1.86%
Manufacturing	15.78%	16.17%	16.17%	16.28%	15.76%	14.94%
Electricity, gas & water supply	2.0%	1.95%	1.89%	1.92%	1.88%	1.9%
Construction	7.99%	7.85%	7.62%	7.91%	7.66%	7.43%
Services	56.11%	57.09%	57.48%	57.42%	58.79%	59.93%

Source: Ministry of Statistics & Programme Implementation

The manufacturing sector in India faces acute challenges. From problems with power, ports, railroads and roads to shortage of human capital, manufacturing in India has long lagged behind targeted goals.

But the Indian government s commitment to raise its investment in infrastructure from 7% to 9% represents a US$ 500 billion opportunity for growth within India's manufacturing sector.Among all the stakeholders Government by far is the largest stakeholder in Indian Manufacturing sector and wields a great amount of control over manufacturing sector through its policies and regulations.

What stymies India's Manufacturing Vision?

Presence of a huge domestic market, low cost labor availability and home to a variety of resources, but these factors have still not catapulted India to the zenith of its manufacturing dream. India s share of manufacturing out of total GDP is relatively low even if it is compared with any income group either below or above its income level.

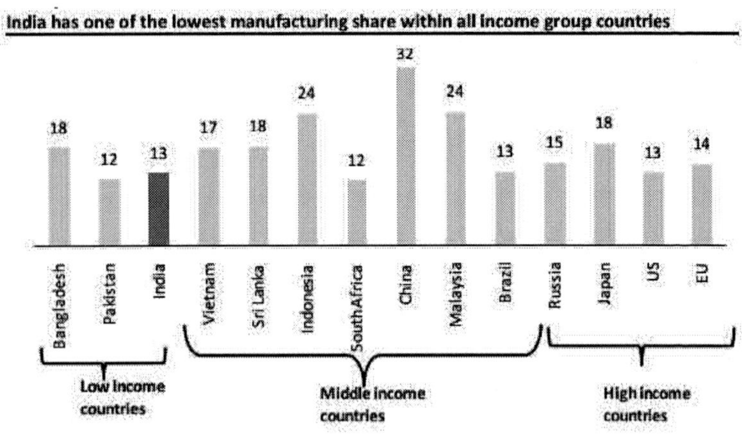

Source: World Bank, MOSL

Meanwhile the gap in manufacturing has resulted in widening of trade gap that is not fully offset by services surplus.

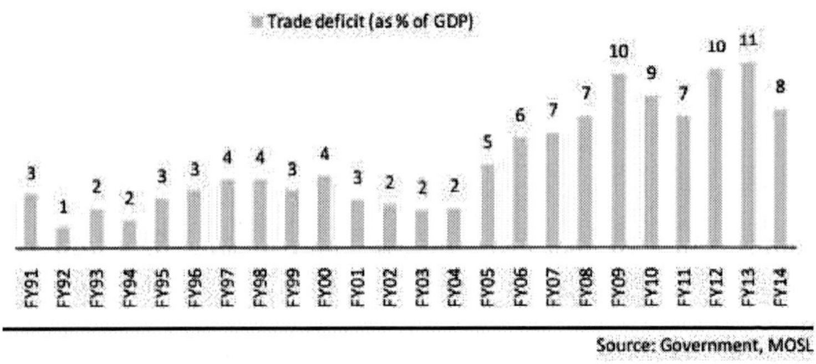

Source: World Bank, MOSL

Nation's infrastructure challenges are a major drag on economic growth. India s urban population of around 375 million is projected to reach 500 million by 2017.

By 2030, the country is expected to have 68 cities with over 1 million residents. This rate of urbanization necessitates availability of urban transport, clean water, power generation and affordable housing. Recognizing this, Govt. has called for $1 trillion in infrastructure spending in the five years through 2017.

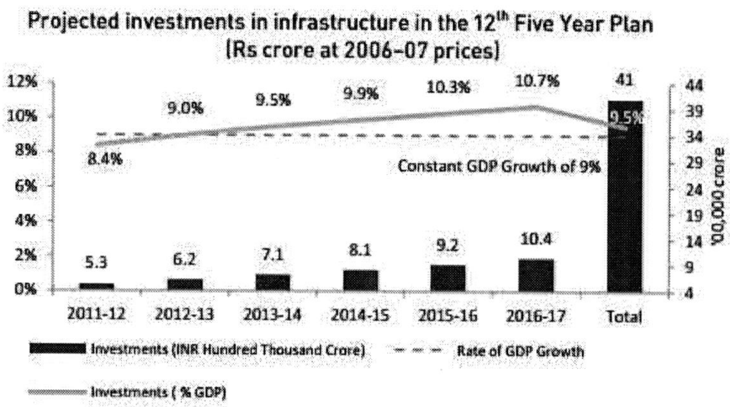

Source: Planning Commission

Private investment constituted about one third of infrastructure investment in the Eleventh Plan and this is projected at 50 percent for the Twelfth Plan period. In these times of tight fiscal environment, private sector will need to play a greater role in infrastructure development

Fulfilling the 'Make In India' vision

The Government of India, knowing the importance of the sector to the country s industrial development, has taken a number of steps to further encourage investment and improve the economy. "Make in India" mission is one such long term initiative which will help to realize the dream of transforming India into a „manufacturing hub. The prime minister s call for „zero defect and zero effect manufacturing resonates well with our industry as we grow and produce for the world with concern for the environment. The Government in the last few months has taken a lot of steps in this direction. Major ones being:

Improving Business Environment

- Ease of Doing Business
- De-licensing & Deregulation

Enabling Manufacturing

- Industrial Corridors
- Industrial Clusters

- Smart Cities
- Nurturing Innovation
- Skill Development

Opening up Foreign Direct Investment in key sectors

- Opening of critical sectors like Defense, construction and Railways for FDI

A slew of important measures have been taken in the short term:

Ease of doing business

- Fastracking of projects: Defence projects worth Rs 80,000 Crore
- Process of applying for Industrial License & Industrial Entrepreneur Memorandum made online on 24X7 basis through eBiz portal
- Validity of Industrial license extended to three years.
- Major components of Defence products list excluded from industrial licensing.
- Dual use items having military as well as civilian applications deregulated.
- Process of obtaining environmental clearances made online.
- For all non-risk, non-hazardous businesses a system of self-certification to be introduced.

Is It Enough: Steps for the future:

India needs to address supply and demand side. On the supply side we need resources, skill development, infrastructure and on the demand side we need innovative practices, technology deployment, low cost innovations, productivity improvement and integrated manufacturing.

The common factor on both the sides is better economic policy and efficient implementation. This includes basic requirements, productive business environment and Research & innovation.

Ease of doing business

According to World Bank, India ranks 142 out of 189 countries in terms of the ease of doing business. India performs especially poorly in categories that involve interface with the government (paying taxes, construction permits, etc.). With governments vision of "minimum government, maximum governance", India can climb up the ladder fairly quickly. In its recent rankings, even the World Bank admits that the next quarter rankings of India will be better on account of a slew of measures taken by the new government.

Investments

Huge investments are required for Infrastructure development. But Domestic savings have come down from a peak of 37 per cent to 30 per cent of GDP and gross FDI inflows into India have averaged less than 2 per cent of GDP. Government has to open up sectors such as defence and insurance as India's gross investment rate will have to go up from 31 per cent of GDP in 2013-14 to 38-40 per cent of GDP 5 Ease of doing business ranks economies from 1 to 189, with first place being the best. A high ranking (a low numerical rank) means that the regulatory environment is conducive to business operation.

Labour law reform

With the launch of „make in India Government has recently announced measures to end „Inspector Raj with a system that is expected to sharply curb the element of discretion with labour inspectors and a single window compliance process for companies on labour-related issues.-These are the firm steps towards the goal of simplification of trade.

Goods and Services tax (GST): implementation of this indirect tax reform by 2016 will improve competitiveness of India s manufacturing and help India grow faster.

Power: In order to grow at 8 % annually India will require a total installed of capacity of 450 GW from present capacity of 250 GW. In order to boost electricity production government must form a National power commission (NPC) which would facilitate in accelerating Capacity addition, securing fuel supplies and improving efficiency for production, transmission and distribution of electricity. Various important issues like coal block allocation, gas pricing strategy should be addressed as soon as possible.

Logistics: Government should come up with National integrated logistic policy (NLIP) which can comprehensively address the logistic issues emerging out of road, rail, waterways and air transport comprehensively covering Rail dedicated freight corridors, Coastal freight corridors, multi modal logistic parks, better warehousing and logistic skill development Health & education: India lags far behind in the area of Health education and ranks 135 on HDI6.

Various government initiatives like National Health mission (NHM), Integrated Child Development Services (ICDS), Midday Meal Scheme etc. are trying to achieve Millennium Development Goals by UNDP. But efficient execution of these schemes remains a challenge for the government. According to Indian Census 2011 enrollment figures in educational institutes are very encouraging. But quality of education and high dropout rates remains a matter of concern. To address these issues government should make comprehensive and efficient frameworks for better delivery of health services and education. Like Right to education, Right to Health should also be a made a fundamental right.

3Es: Efficiency, Effectiveness and Excellence are imperative. Productive business environment encompasses financial market development, efficient labour markets, training, market size, technological readiness and goods market efficiency. A reasonably well-developed corporate bond market is very much required in any economy to supplement banking credit and the equity market.

Up scaling Small scale industry: SSIs have for long received government s attention but effort to build global scales is not apparent. China s Town & Village Enterprises have succeeded on the back of significant support in terms of fiscal incentives.

In India we have geographical specializations which can be developed into large scale industries. It is imperative for small scale industries in India to cover new global markets. These are the industries that are capable of touching the bottom of the pyramid with their reach and product portfolio.

Knowledge management: According to times higher educational (THE) rankings no Indian university was in top 100. A survey found that almost 50% of respondents said they would like to work in outside of manufacturing sectors. Government should direct educational institutes to come up with courses specifically designed to cater to requirement of manufacturing sector.

Courses like PGPEX-VLM jointly run by IIM Calcutta, IIT Kanpur and IIT Madras are dedicated to develop leaders in manufacturing sector. National Skill Development programs should run programs in collaboration with industry to not only make people employable but employed in industry.

ICT: India is home to world s third largest internet users. But ironically India ranks 121st on ICT Development index. Various new technologies like Internet of Things (IOT), Big data etc thrives on ICT. Moreover providing ICT skills to workforce is another great challenge. ICT technology will be a toothless weapon if manpower is not skilled enough to use it. Therefore government should come up with plans to increase penetration levels and skill development in ICT.

Supporting Public Sector Units: Government should focus on augmenting the strengths of the strong public sector units for efficient execution and create large entities based on the models of Temasek in Singapore and Khazanah Nasional in Malaysia, whereby both of these countries hold SOEs with significant international presence. The increased presence of leading Russian SOEs like Gazprom and Sberbank abroad is accompanied by an expressed political aim of facilitating international expansion. In China the government has pursued a going out policy encouraging Chinese companies to invest and acquire market share abroad.

Research & innovation: Research and innovation are twined with each other. In Indian context, these are the Rambaan weapons for building competitive advantage. Today no longer innovation is not a point of difference (POD) in the market rather it has become point of parity (POP). In India also various government initiatives like National Innovation foundation, National innovation Council have tried to promote innovation in the country. Government should increase spend on research from present level of 1 % of GDP to at least 2% of GDP9.

5

Make in India: Government Policies

INTERVENTIONS FOR MANUFACTURING, FACTORIES, LABOUR, SKILL DEVELOPMENT

Prologue

- Like I said in the first revision note: 4-5 points on selected topics. Assumption: you already have read earlier articles. This is just like minute memory jogging.
- GS2: schemes, policies, intervention = fifty dozen schemes. I'm only making note of things related to manufacturing sector.
- Reason: MFG topic too hot given make in India. Even if directly not asked, still same bullets can be used for poverty, hunger, empowerment related questions in GS to 3 and essay as 'fall back line' when you can't recall anything else.
- Next coming revision note: GS2: IR related Economy-bodies & agreements.

New Industrial policy 1991

1. '48: Shyama's policy; '56: focus on PSU; 91: Liberated
2. 5 sectors need license: Tobacco, Desi liquor, Industrial explosive, Hazardous chemicals, Defense electronics.
3. 3 reserved for PSU. Rail, Atomic mineral, Atomic energy.

4. PSU: Disinvestment permitted, MoU for op.flexibility, later various "Ratna"
5. FDI relaxed, 100% NRI investment permitted.
6. Tech parks for Software, electronic, hardware
7. To help M&A-MRTP removed, later CCI setup.

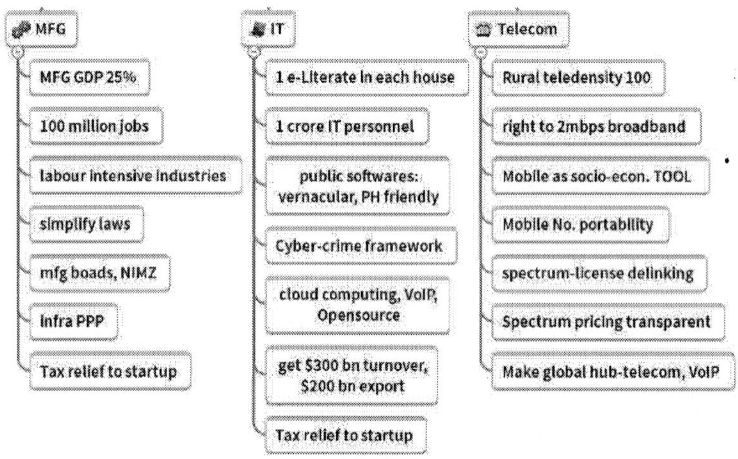

FIFTY DOZEN POLICIES BUT THESE USEFUL TO HANDLE MFG/ SERVICE SECTOR RELATED QS.

National MFG policy 2011

1. Increase MFG's share in GDP from present 15% to 25%. [though China 35%]
2. Create 100 million jobs in a decade.
3. MFG focus: employment intensive sectors-Textile, IT; MSME,
4. Simplify labour and environment laws=> Modi: factory, apprentice bills + green law panel under TSR Subramanian
5. Skill Development via Polytechs=> Modi skill India, Din Dayal Antyo.
6. Setup Mfg promotion boards, NIMZ (invest & mfg)
7. Infra via PPP=> Modi: REITS, INVITs, 3P-India for contracts

8. Tax relief to startup co.s; skill Development via Polytechs.

National IT policy 2012

1. 1 e-literate person in each household.=> Modi Digital India mission for rural broadband.
2. 1 crore new IT personnel
3. Public services/softwares in Vernacular, PH friendly, transparency=>Modi E-kranti system
4. Strong framework against cybercrime
5. Promote Cloud computing, open source software
6. Tax relief to IT startups. (just like mfg policy)
7. Target 2020: 300 billion$ revenue, 200$ exports.
8. Survey Suggestion: separate Department for service sector, divest service-sector PSU, give collateral free loans to start up cos.

New Telecom Policy 2012

1. 2020: rural teledensity increase to 100 =>USOF Universal service obligation fund to improve net connection in rural/naxal areas
2. Right to broadband with 2mbps speed=> NFON National optical fiber network to connect 2.5 lakh Gram Panchayat.
3. Make Mobile a socio-economic empowerment=>UID link with SIM CARD. Future vision Apple-pay like system, swipe mobile to pay/transfer money. no more rural branches, BCA-agents.
4. All India mobile no. portability in 2015 (right now only circle wise. Total 22 circles)
5. Unified license for India. (no need to buy separate for each 22 circles)
6. spectrum delinked from license. Have to buy it separately.
7. Allot Spectrum in transparent, market determined price. Simplify M&A in telecom industry.
8. Make India a global hub for telecom mfg., VoIP, Cloud computing. Modi=>Make in India.

Why Make in India?

- India became Agrarian to => direct service economy. Not much focus on mfg. sector.
- Agro gives 14% to GDP, employs 49% junta= disguised unemployment.
- While MFG gives 15% to Indian GDP and 35% to Chinese.
- IF MFG boost=>small farmers can shift to industry. poverty removal, land consolidation, farm mechanization=high agro output.
- 3D-Strength = democracy, demographic dividend, demand in huge quantity.

MII: challenges

- World economic forum's Global competitiveness index: 71.
- World bank Ease of doing business rank 142. (double of 71)

MII: FIVE-mechanism

- Simplify processes: De-licensing and deregulation=> New Factories bill, eBiz poral to apply online, industrial license valid for 3 years. Special team to guide first time investor.
- Improve infra: New Industrial corridors authority, 3P-India, smart cities-REITs-INVITs ;Modi to get funds from US, China, Japan; BRICS bank, AIIB
- Skilling: Skill India mission, Deen Dayal Antyodaya Yojana,
- Focus on 30 mfg. sectors: autoparts, pharma-chemicals, leather-textile, mining-construction, food-processing-hospitality etc. Here we've potential to become world top-10; potential manpower and demand available.
- Open up sectors: FDI in Defense 49% and Railways 100%
- Protect IPR

IPR protection (GS3)

Focus on five angles

1. Patent: innovative product / process for industrial use.=> DIPP=>Patent office.Indian patent offices to connect online with other nations under Madrid Protocol, automated applications and approvals.=>followup special 301 report revision note for GS2-IR-Economy.
2. Industrial design: registration for 10 years. Renewed again for 5 years.
3. Trademarks: Automated registration of trade marks. Can be renewed for infinite time.
4. GI: Statutory GI registry body @Chennai. Foreign companies can register GI in India under WTO-TRIPS agreement.
5. Copyright: HRD ministry

Side note: to counter us, China too launched "Made in China" scheme to give R&D, Tax sops to Mfg-Sectors: aviation, bio—medicine production, railway and ships, IT-electronics

LABOR FACTORY REFORMS

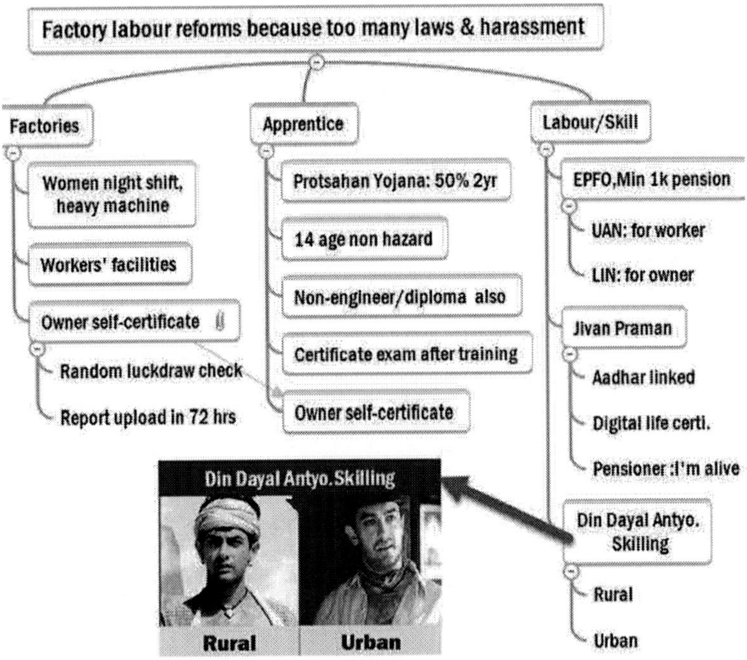

AGAIN FIFTY DOZEN TOPICS BUT THESE ONES HELPFUL FOR GENERIC QUESTIONS

Why need factory/labour reforms

- 44 union + >150 state acts=> conflicts, bribery, inspector raj
- Industrial disputes act: >100 workers=need Government permission before firing => contractual labour without social security benefits (SSB).
- Apprentice made to work like regular employee yet no SSB.
- Owner can be arrested for petty issues like no spittoon.
- Foreigners won't come to Make In India, unless these issues fixed.

Factory bill 2014

- On Narendra Jadav Committee (2010)
- Factory def: 20 workers if power used; 40 workers if not.
- Women: nightshift with safety-transport provisions; can work on heavy machinery unless pregnant/PH
- Worker: Reforms in Overtime, paid leaves; right to cool drinking water, spittoon, restrooms. Canteen depending on (#) of workers.
- Owner: self-certification, can decide workweek, can't be arrested on small issues like no restroom/cool water.
- Benefit: women empowerment, no more bribery inspector raj

Small factories bill 2014

- 2000: 2nd National labour commission recommends separate law for small factories.
- New bill 2014: for MSME with upto 40 workers.
- Women can work on heavy machines.
- Small one-room "factories" can't setup separate washroom, spitton etc. so they're allowed to have joint facilities with other small factories.
- Self-compliance features similar to (non-small) Factories bill 2014

Apprentice bill 2014

- Minimum age 14 years to join non-hazardous industry as an apprentice
- Government to decide quota and training syllabus in each industry
- Companies can accept non-engineer/diploma; fix workdays; multiple companies can join to give pre-training.
- Post-training a certification exam.
- Web portal for self-certification; reasonable fines.
- Benefit: flexibility to company, skilled youth to help make in India.

Additional topics:

#1: Modi scheme-Apprentice protstahan yojana: Government will contribute 50% of stipend for first two years of training

#2: Self-compliance/ Self certification: CRITICISM

- 2013 National crime report: >350 workers died in boiler explosion.
- Inspector-raj is necessary. Suppose Defective Boiler & other dangerous machines. Owner himself won't work/ check. May not hear complaints from workers & yet upload "everything tested OK" self-certificate on portal. (keep that in mind for Ethics case studies)

#3: random inspection

- Modi reform: labour/factory inspection will be done on random lucky draw by computers. (to ensure those self-compliance claims are right)
- Inspector to upload report within 72 hours. => less opportunities for manipulation and bribes.

Companies Act 2013

- Replaced '56
- 3 types: one person, private (2-200), public ltd. (7-unlimited).
- BoD reforms: min.15 directors in public ltd, 1/3rd independence, 1 woman, 1 Indian resident.
- Independent directors: performance review by AGM, 10 year term limits.
- Whistleblower protection, internal and external audit mechanism, limits on CA about how many firms they can audit per year.
- Quorum requirements for AGM and board meetings
- CSR: 2% of last 3 years' avg.profit. Selected companies only e.g. above 5 crore net profit /500 cr. Net worth, 1000 crore turnover.

Companies Act: 4 statutory bodies

1. Company law tribunal (NCLT) to reduce burden of HC. Directly approachable, 3 months deadline to solve case. Appeal @NCLAT
2. NFRA: Financial reporting authority. Set accounting standards, power of civil court, can punish CA and B.Com. ICAR doesn't like it.
3. Investor edu.+protection authority: financial literacy to prevent Saradha, sahara scams. Chaired by Secretary of corp.affairs ministry
4. SFIO: given statutory status, power to search-seize, other agencies need to handover witnesses and evidences.

Schemes: Skill / Social security

- Following block covers only labour / skilling related schemes.
- I'm not going into all those health-education schemes.
- Urban infra Development schemes=>under GS3 Economy revision note coming soon.

Din Dayal Antyodaya

- Why?: 57 million worker shortage in 1st world by 2020.
- Make in India useless without skilled workers. 10% of new workers skilled. (China 50%)

Rural component:

- SGSY=>NRLM=>Ajeevika=>skill components: Din Dayal Upa. Gramin Kaushalya Yoj.
- 15 age+; train 10 lakh youth in next 3 years;
- setup training centre; international syllabus; PH attention

Urban component:

- HUPA: train 5 lakh every year via Livelihood centres via NSDC Corop.
- vendor market training; shelter for homeless
- urban SHG: 10k loan; enterprise – loan interest subsidy

Jivan Praman

- Why? Pensioner need to submit physical life certificate every year-to show he's alive and claim pension.
- Jivan Praman = Aadhar-based Digital Life Certificate.
- DEITY (Dept. of Electro.&IT) designed software.
- Software reads pensioner's Aadhar card, biometric data=> uploaded to server=> digital life certificate generated.
- Pension giving babu can access online and release pension.
- Pensioner no need to physically visit office => less inconvenience and bribery harassment. Dignity to elderly.

EPFO

- UAN: Uniform account number for >4 crore subscribers: can view account, transaction data, grievances redressal. No need to get new number when changing jobs.
- LIN: Labour identification number for ~6 lakh employers. So they can file online provident contribution, annual returns. Less inspector raj and harassment.
- Assured Minimum Rs.1000 pension, compulsory EPS for upto 15k salary.

RSBY revamped (soon)

- Rashtriya Swasthya Bima yojana.
- Plans to merge Aam Admi Bima Yojana and India Gandhi old age pension with it
- Smart card for unorganized workers.
- 3rd party audit, call centre for grievances

Labour/Skill: Misc.Schemes

Udaan: Skilling J&K youth by MHA+NSDC

- SKill India Budget 2014.
- Employability + entrepreneurial skill. (get job and give job)
- Even traditional welder, carpenters, cobblers, masons be given training to become suitable to Make in India.(e.g.

pepperfry.com online furniture shopping site-after delivery carpenter assembles at your home)

USAAD

- Skilling minority artisans
- Kashmiri embroidery, bengali jardosi, sikh phulkari embroidary, buddhist thangka paintings

Nai Manzil: Skilling Madressa passouts to join main-stream (computer, english etc)

- Varistha pension bima 60 and above
- From 15th aug. 1 year validity

HR KhanCommittee on how to use unclaimed money from post-office, PPF etc. for elderly welfare.

NARENDRA MODI GOVT UNVEILS ITS FIRST TRADE POLICY

Aiming to nearly double India's exports of goods and services to $900 billion by 2020, Narendra Modigovernment announced several incentives in the five-year Foreign Trade Policy (FTP) for exporters and units in the Special Economic Zones.

Unveiling the first trade policy of the National Democratic Alliance (NDA) government, Commerce Minister Nirmala Sitharaman said the FTP (2015-20) will introduce Merchandise Exports from India Scheme (MEIS) and Services Exports from India Scheme (SEIS) to boost outward shipments.

Besides, higher level of incentives will be provided for export of agriculture products under the Foreign Trade Policy (FTP), which seeks to integrate with Make In India and Digital India initiatives of the government.

"FTP lays down a roadmap for India's global trade engagement in the coming years...India (will become) a significant participant in world trade by 2020," Sitharaman said.

"The government aims to increase India's exports of merchandise and services from USD 465.9 billion in 2013-14 to approximately USD 900 billion by 2019-20 and to raise India's share in world exports from 2 percent to 3.5 per cent," Commerce Secretary Rajeev Kher said.

Photo: Narendra Modi government aims to increase India's exports of merchandise and services from US dollar 465.9 billion in 2013-14 to approximately US dollar 900 billion by 2019-20.

The FTP also seeks to establish an Export Promotion Mission to provide an institutional framework to work with State Governments to boost India's exports.

"Senior officials have been appointed as designated focal points for exports and imports in several Central Government departments," said a release on the FTP.

Unlike the annual reviews of the past, the FTP will be reviewed after two-and-half years to ensure continuity in the trade policy.

Sitharaman said that export obligation would be reduced by 25 per cent and incentives available under the MEIS and SEIS would be extend to the units in the SEZs to make them more attractive for investors.

SEZs has lost their sheen after imposition of the minimum alternate tax (MAT) and dividend distribution tax (DDT) in 2012.

The duty credit scrips would be made freely transferable and usable for payment of customs duty, excise duty and service tax, she said, adding "debits against scrips would be eligible for CENVAT credit or drawback."

Further business services, hotel and restaurants would get rewards scrips under SEIS at the rate of 3 per cent and other specified services at the rate of 5 per cent.

SEIS would be applied to 'Service Providers located in India' instead of 'Indian Service Providers'. Served From India Scheme (SFIS) replaced with SEIS.

Under MEIS, the main sectors to be provided support includes processed, packaged agricultural and food items, agricultural and village industry goods.

"These schemes (MEIS and SEIS) replace multiple schemes earlier in place, each with different conditions for eligibility and usage. Benefits from both these schemes will be extended to units located in SEZs," the minister added

The nomenclature for export houses is being changed to 1, 2, 3, 4, 5 star export house.

Highlights

Following are the highlights of the Foreign Trade Policy 2015-20 announced by Commerce & Industry Minister Nirmala Sitharaman today:

Increase exports to USD 900 billion by 2019-20, from USD 466 billion in 2013-14.

Raise India's share in world exports from 2 per cent to 3.5 per cent.

Merchandise Export from India Scheme (MEIS) and Service.

Exports from India Scheme (SEIS) launched.

Higher level of rewards under MEIS for export items with high domestic content and value addition.

Export obligation under EPCG scheme reduced to 75% to promote domestic capital goods manufacturing.

FTP to be aligned to Make in India, Digital India and Skills India initiatives.

Duty credit scrips made freely transferable and usable for payment of custom duty, excise duty and service tax.

Export promotion mission to take on board state governments.

Unlike annual reviews, FTP will be reviewed after two-and-half years.

Higher level of support for export of defence, farm produce and eco-friendly products.

FTP to promote eCommerce cos focusing on job creation

Under the new five-year Foreign Trade Policy (FTP), the government will provide incentives to eCommerce companies exporting products from sectors that create jobs.

Presenting the policy, Commence and Industry Minister Nirmala Sitharaman said government will provide incentives to eCommerce firms that export products from sectors on which the government is focusing on job creation.

Under the new five-year Foreign Trade Policy (2015-20) the government has introduced two new schemes – Merchandise Exports from India Scheme (MEIS) and Services Exports from India Scheme (SEIS) to promote exports.

Firms that export goods through courier or foreign post office using e-commerce of FOB (Freight on Board) value up to Rs 25,000 per consignment will be entitled for rewards under MEIS.

The objective of MEIS is to offset infra inefficiencies and associated costs involved in export of goods, which are manufactured in India and especially those having high export intensity, employment potential and can enhance India's export competitiveness.

If the value of exports using e-commerce platform is more than Rs 25,000 per consignment then MEIS reward would be limited to FOB value of Rs 25,000 only.

The goods entitled for benefit under the scheme are handloom, books & periodicals, leather footwear, toys and customised fashion garments.

"Export of such goods under courier regulations shall be allowed manually on pilot basis through airports at New Delhi, Mumbai and Chennai...Department of Revenue shall fast track the implementation of EDI mode at courier terminals," the policy said.

FTP proposes new institutions to boost global trade

The new Foreign Trade Policy unveiled today proposed setting up of a host of institutions, including Trade Council and National Committee on Trade Facilitation, to improve India's share in global trade and implement of WTO obligations.

The country aims at increasing its share in world exports from 2 per cent to 3.5 per cent by 2020.

Pursuant to the WTO agreement on trade facilitation, the policy has proposed setting up National Committee on Trade Facilitation. That pact is aimed at easing customs procedure to reduce transactions cost for traders.

The policy said several initiatives are under way for the simplification of procedures and digitization of various processes involved in trade transactions.

Steps are being taken by various ministries and departments to simplify administrative procedures and reduce transaction costs based on the recommendations of two task forces constituted by the Directorate General of Foreign Trade.

The implementation of these recommendations is being actively pursued, the policy said.

Commerce Secretary Rajeev Kher said that India is committed to implement the WTO's Trade Facilitation Agreement (TFA).

A National Committee on Trade Facilitation is being constituted for domestic coordination and implementation of the TFA, he said.

The Secretary also said an important consideration while framing the policy was aligning FTP with both India's interests as well its obligations and commitments under various WTO agreements has

In the ongoing Doha Round of trade negotiations, he said, India will continue to work towards fulfilling its objectives and to work with like-minded members to remove any asymmetries in the multilateral trade rules which place a developing country at a disadvantage, such as the rules relating to public stock-holding for food security purposes.

"The current WTO rules as well as those under negotiation envisage the eventual phasing out of export subsidies.

This is a pointer to the direction that export promotion efforts will have to take in future, i.e. towards more fundamental systemic measures rather than incentives and subsidies alone," he said.

He also said that specific measures will be taken to facilitate the entry of new entrepreneurs and manufacturers in global trade through extensive training programmes.

"The Niryat Bandhu scheme will be revamped to achieve these objectives and also further dovetailed with the ongoing outreach programmes," Kher said, adding capacity development efforts will focus on export promotion councils and commercial missions.

Further, a new institution – Centre for Research in International Trade – is being established not only to strengthen India's research capabilities in the area of international trade, but also to enable developing countries to articulate their views and concerns from a well-informed position of strength.

The policy also said that two institutional mechanisms are being put in place for regular communication with stakeholders – the Board of Trade and the Council for Trade Development (CTD) and Promotion.

While the Board of Trade will have an advisory role, the CTD would have representation from State and UT governments.

"The CTD will be an institution between the Centre and the states with the objective of internalising the thinking and the processes and the participation of state government into central government policy making, implementation and monitoring," Kher said.

'India needs to gear up to face challenges of mega trade pacts'

Expressing concerns over two mega free trade agreements TPP and TTIP, the government today said the Indian industry needs to gear up to meet challenges that would emerge from these pacts.

While India is participating in the Regional Comprehensive Economic Partnership (RCEP) agreement, it is not part of Trans Pacific Partnership (TPP) and Trans-Atlantic Trade and Investment Partnership (TTIP).

Commerce Secretary Rajeev Kher said that these pacts would add a completely new dimension to the global trading system.

"The mega agreements are bound to challenge India's industry in many ways, for instance, by eroding existing preferences for Indian products in established traditional markets such as the US and EU and establishing a more stringent and demanding framework of rules.

"Indian industry needs to gear up to meet these challenges for which the government will have to create an enabling environment," Kher said.

He said India's future bilateral and regional trade engagements will be with regions and countries that are not only promising markets, but also major suppliers of critical inputs and have complementarities with the Indian economy.

"The focus of India's future trade relationship with its traditional markets in the developed world would be on exporting products with a higher value addition, supplying high quality inputs for the manufacturing sector in these markets and optimising applied customs duties on inputs for India's manufacturing sector," he added.

The TPP is a proposed trade agreement under negotiation among 12 countries — Australia, Brunei, Chile, Canada, Japan, Malaysia, Mexico, New Zealand, Peru, Singapore, the US and Vietnam. TTIP is between the European Union and the US.

The 16-member RCEP comprises 10 Asean members and its six FTA partners namely India, China, Japan, Korea, Australia and New Zealand.

The Secretary said signing an FTA is just a beginning and not the end of the process as it would give benefit to traders.

"Recognising that it is important to review whether the concessions under these agreements are being gainfully utilised and have resulted in meaningful market access gains, an 'Impact Analysis' of FTAs has been instituted," he said.

There is a need to simplify and ease rules of origin criteria to position India effectively in global and regional value chains.

"The likelihood of duty inversions will continue to be closely monitored to ensure that industry is not put to any disadvantage. A system for capturing preferential data will be put in place at the earliest," he said.

Indian industry has raised concerns over these FTAs saying that it is benefiting more to the partner countries with which India has implemented such pacts.

The lack of information about India's FTAs was also a common complaint flagged by industry. To address this, an intensive FTA outreach programme has been launched.

INDIA: THE ECONOMY AFTER FOUR MONTHS OF MODI GOVERNMENT

Economic growth has moderately rebounded, capital inflows have increased, exports have accelerated and helped the trade balance, confidence has increased, bond yields have declined, and equity prices have risen. However, inflation, the budget, and a lack of policy response introduce challenges and uncertainty.

India's economy is probably showing early signs of recovery. The economy expanded at its fastest pace in two-and-a-half years at 5.7 percent year over year in Q1 FY 2014–15. External sector performance improved, the equity market reached an all-time high, and domestic investments improved significantly. Increased economic activity also improved consumer and business sentiment.

However, the Q1 numbers are not conclusive because a few challenges still continue to persist. Poor growth in the last two years has pushed the economy far below its potential, which implies that the economy has to strive harder to compensate for the loss in growth. That, in turn, will require a big push in the form of policy reforms, fiscal consolidation, coordinated monetary policy, and improved industrial performance. The question is whether the economy can sustain this turnaround going forward. The latest political and policy issues indicate that the government is serious about its commitment to bring back the country's prosperous years. However, there is much to be done before economic growth accelerates at a sustainable pace, and this might be just the beginning.

Improved economic outlook

Real economy: After disappointing GDP growth of 4.6 percent in the past two quarters of FY 2013–14, the new fiscal year began with stronger growth, primarily due to a boost from government spending and higher business investment. Government consumption expenditures grew 8.8 percent; they were expected to be high in Q1 because of the general elections that were held in April and May. However, a more sustainable driver of growth, that is, total fixed investment, also grew 7 percent after showing dismal performance for over a year. Negative stock building throughout the past year led to robust investment growth. Investment is expected to remain strong in the coming quarters as businesses expand their operations to cater to growing demand. Improved availability of financial resources to the private sector, fiscal consolidation, improved external demand, and stabilizing global commodity prices will further provide impetus to economic recovery. Private final consumption expenditure growth remained modest at 5.6 percent, though it fell on a quarterly basis. On the external front, exports of goods and services grew at a healthy rate of 11.5 percent, while imports fell 0.4 percent.

Figure 1. Strong domestic demand helps economy grow in Q1 FY 2014–15

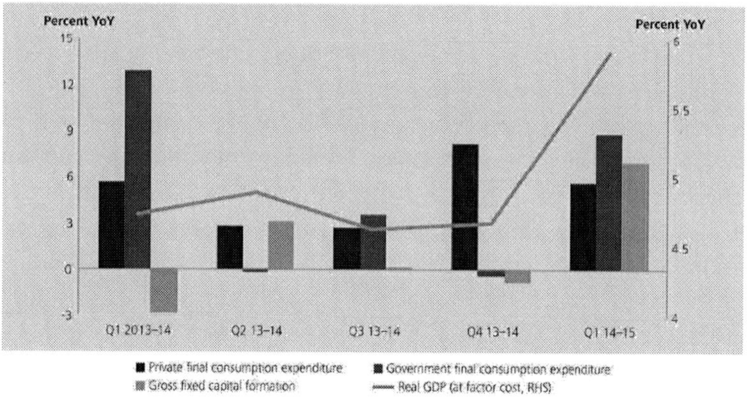

Note: Q1 refers to the fiscal year, which begins in April and ends in March of the following year.
Source: Reserve Bank of India, August 2014; Press Information Bureau, August 2014; Bloomberg, August 2014.

External sector: The balance of payment situation has improved significantly in the past year due to substantial improvements in both the current and capital account balance. The trade balance improved due to strong exports as global demand firmed and imports fell, owing to controls on imports of non-essential goods. Consequently, the current account deficit improved from 5.1 percent in Q1 FY 2013-14 to 1.7 percent a year later.

Though the current account deficit was slightly higher in Q1 FY 2014–15 relative to past three quarters due to a higher trade deficit, it was tracking below 2 percent of GDP and is still within the comfort zone. However, what is noteworthy is that the widening of the trade deficit was on account of an increase in oil and non-oil, non-gold imports during April–June 2014. Poor exports too have contributed to higher trade deficit lately. There could be an upward pressure on the current account deficit going forward, if economic activities improve further.

Figure 2. Improved balance of payments

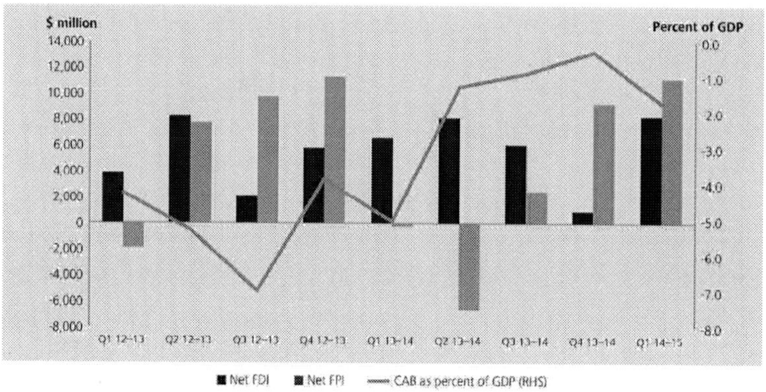

Source: Reserve Bank of India, September 2014; Bloomberg, September, 2014.

Capital inflows too improved in the last few quarters. Foreign portfolio investment started improving as early as Q4 FY 2013–14 as uncertainty with respect to the impact of the Federal Reserve's tapering of the US monetary policy on emerging economies, including India, decreased. In addition, there was growing optimism among investors who expected the current Prime Minister Narendra Modi to win the general elections. However, foreign direct investment (FDI) inflows reversed only after Modi's win. Net FDI picked up markedly in Q1 FY 2014–15 to levels not seen in the past three years.

Figure 3. Equity market at an all-time high

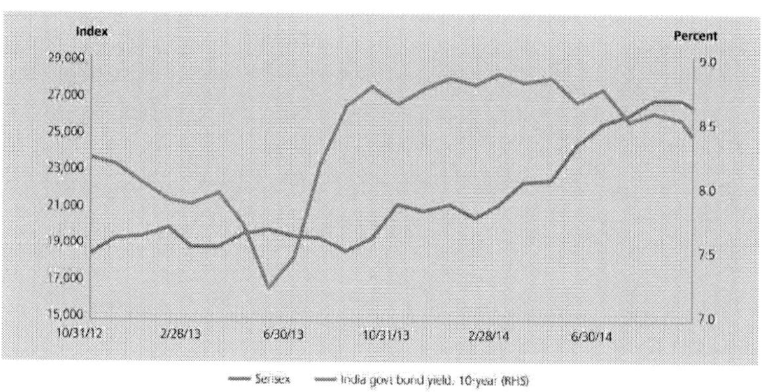

Source: Bloomberg, October 2014.

Financial market and sentiments: Optimism about an improving economy and expectations that the new government will likely usher in a period of significant fiscal and economic reforms are also reflected in the equity and bond markets. The equity market rose 20 percent since April 2014, and it touched a record-high level of above 27,000 in September. Government bond yields too fell 0.4 percentage points during this period. However, the impact on government bond yields has not been great due to the economy's high fiscal deficit concerns.

Consumer confidence and business sentiment have been on a rise since the elections. There has been a significant improvement in consumer confidence with respect to future expectations. The future expectations index improved due to an increase in positive perceptions of factors such as economic conditions, household circumstances, income, and employment. The business outlook for the Indian manufacturing sector—the business expectation index—improved in Q2 FY 2014–15 due to greater optimism on the overall business situation, production, order books, capacity utilization, imports, and exports. In addition, pessimism on the cost of finance, cost of raw material, and profit margins decreased among manufacturing companies.

Figure 4. Economic sentiments are improving

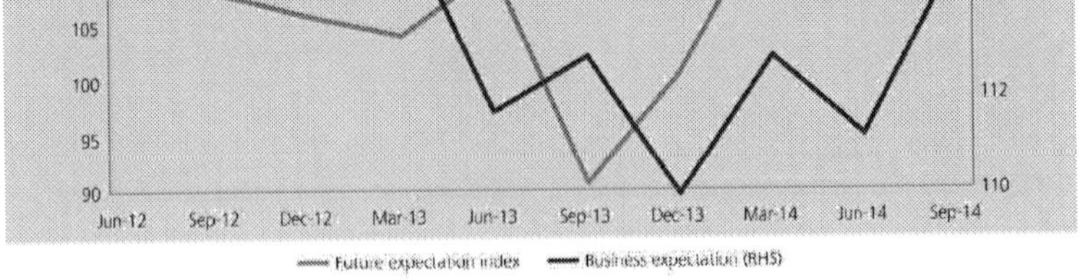

Source: Reserve Bank of India, September 2014.

Future outlook: India's economic growth is expected to improve in the forthcoming quarters. Some of the rating agencies have projected a better growth outlook against the backdrop of a new government coming to power with a single-party majority for the first time in three decades. The various policy initiatives by the new government to attract investments and to improve industry sector performance, among others, have helped improve sentiment and expectations. The Reserve Bank of India projects an annual growth of 5.3 percent in FY 2014–15 and 6.4 percent in the following year. As mentioned earlier, there could be a rise in the trade account deficit because of rising demand, but the capital account is likely to remain healthy. Expectations on interest rate movements in the United States and economic reforms in India will continue to drive growth in the financial market in the coming quarters. Overall, economic and market sentiment is expected to remain optimistic.

However, projected growth rates will likely remain below the levels seen earlier for a year or more. This is because the economy continues to struggle with persistent economic challenges that may weigh on the growth outlook of the economy.

Challenges

Manufacturing sector still unstable: The latest monthly data on the index of industrial production (IIP) indicate that the manufacturing sector remains highly vulnerable. After a promising growth rate of 5 percent in May, the IIP fell for the next three consecutive months. Strong growth in capital goods, which grew at the highest rate in three years at 23 percent in June, turned negative in the subsequent months. The manufacturing index fell over a percent in July and August after a strong 5.1 percent growth in May.

Growth in the consumer durables index has been the biggest drag; although it had turned positive in May after falling for the past 17 consecutive months, it resumed its falling trend post that month. The HSBC India manufacturing purchasing managers' index (PMI), which provides a more recent overview of business conditions in the manufacturing sector, suggests further moderation in manufacturing activity in September. The index fell to 51 in September from 52.4 in August. The poor IIP numbers indicate that industrial growth will remain a drag on economic performance in Q2.

Inflation still a concern: While there has been some relief with respect to inflation in 2014 relative to 2013, when it was hovering in the double digits, inflation still remains high. The latest data suggest that consumer price inflation (CPI) fell below 7 percent, yet remains more than the Reserve Bank of India's (RBI's) target range for inflation. Wholesale price inflation (WPI) has eased considerably from 3.7 percent in August to 2.4 percent in September, primarily due to favourable base effect.

With growing concerns about an uneven rainfall across the country, it is expected that poor crop output will likely push inflation up in the coming months. Supply constraints—particularly in food and infrastructure—and high dependence on fuel imports will likely keep inflationary pressures high. However, the continuing fall in oil and commodity prices will ease inflation. According to a survey conducted by the RBI, the proportion of respondents expecting double-digit inflation in the next three-month period has declined. Similarly, fewer respondents expect higher prices a year from now.

Figure 5. Inflation has eased down lately, though inflationary pressures remain high

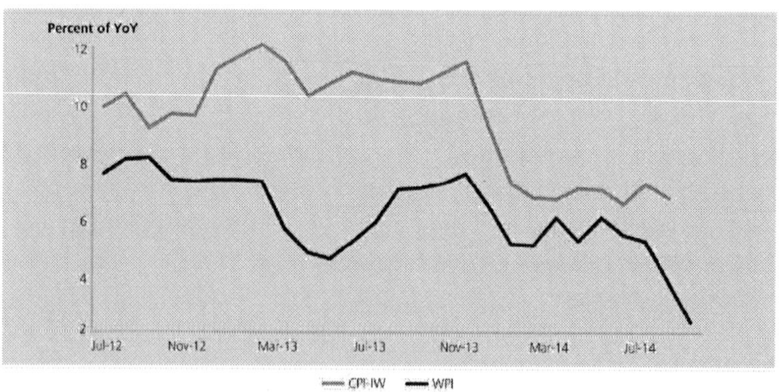

Source: CSO India, Ministry of Statistics and Programme Implementation, August 2014.

High fiscal deficit: The government's strategy of fiscal consolidation has repeatedly gone off course since 2008 due to a series of unfavorable developments. Faced with prospects of a sovereign rate cut and the crowding out of private investments in the economy, the government undertook a series of reforms, including fuel subsidies and rail fares, starting in September 2012. However, the momentum of fiscal consolidation slowed due to the general elections in May 2014. In addition, the continuing slowdown in economic growth, static industrial growth, a moderate increase in indirect taxes, the subsidy burden, and not-so-encouraging tax buoyancy made it difficult for the government to improve the deficit. The fiscal deficit for Q1 FY 2014–15 increased sharply to 11 percent after recording a marginal surplus in Q4 FY 2013–14. Part of the rise in the deficit was also due to higher government expenses from the general elections held in May.

The new government announced that it would strive to achieve a fiscal deficit of 4.1 percent in FY 2014–15 in the union budget. In addition, the finance minister announced a fiscal deficit trajectory of 3.6 percent in FY 2016 and 3.0 percent in FY 2017. However, the government has not laid down any specific roadmap on how it will achieve the target deficit. More importantly, no specific proposals to reduce subsidies were announced apart from expressing the need for more effective implementation of subsidies. While the explicit confirmation that the government will adhere to the fiscal plan is a positive step and may instill confidence, investors are awaiting concrete measures to be taken in this direction.

THE FIRST FOUR MONTHS OF THE GOVERNMENT'S ACTIONS

Since the new government has come into power, there have been a few changes in the functioning of the administration. The government has emphasized "less government and more governance," and efforts are being made toward making ministries more accountable and streamlined. One favourable outcome of these actions has been speedy decision making in clearing some stalled projects. About 17 infrastructure projects, which had been pending since the previous government's tenure, have been cleared in the last three months. In addition, initiatives such as making online environmental and forest clearances for industrial projects available, focusing on skill development, amending labor laws, and allocating funds to the manufacturing sector, among others, have generated a lot of enthusiasm among the corporate sector and investors.

Improving farm productivity, building quality infrastructure, and boosting manufacturing in India are some of the other areas on which the government is currently focusing. Measures such as setting up farm credit, prize stabilization funds, and agriculture-tech infrastructure funds have been proposed to boost agricultural sector output and productivity. Strategies such as public-private partnerships and tax holidays in the transport sector, providing custom duty relief to the energy sector, digitalizing rural India, and building smart cities and metro infrastructure in some cities are expected to improve infrastructure. Policy strategies such as the revival of special economic zones, tax breaks for manufacturing units investing over INR 250 million, the revival of medium and small scale enterprises, and the building of an industrial corridor will likely provide much needed thrust to the manufacturing sector. The prime minister emphasized the need to strengthen the manufacturing sector and indigenize production by appealing "Come, make in India" to investors in his first Independence Day speech.

The government has also prioritized improving international trade and investment relations. The prime minister's recent meetings with the leaders of the three largest economies (the United States, China, and Japan) is being seen as a big step in that direction. In addition, during his US visit, Modi met a galaxy of top American corporate executives and nonresident Indians. The intention was to reinvigorate their interest in investing in the government's new initiatives related to smart cities, infrastructure, digitalization, education, and health. These diplomatic drives are expected to improve India's ties with other nations in the coming years and boost investment in the economy.

That said, the government has had limited success in resolving issues such as land acquisition and structural bottlenecks, which have impact on inflation and input prices.. Policies and plans laid out by the government are encouraging, but implementation has been very limited, with no clear roadmap to delivery. The fiscal deficit remains a concern, and no concrete actions have been taken to tackle subsidies. There has been criticism that, in order to expedite environmental clearances for industrial projects, the government is compromising justice and the well-being of the environment, natural resources, and communities.

So far, the performance of the new government has been a mixed bag. Although the government's approach to various issues have encouraged investors and improved optimism about economic outlook, actual measures have been incremental with limited consequences. There is much more to be done. That said, it has been only four months since the new government has taken up its responsibilities. The government is taking small steps toward fundamental changes. Once these policy changes start being reflected in action, they may have much more far-reaching effects on the economy.

RAGHURAM RAJAN'S CORRECT TO DOUBT MODI'S 'MAKE IN INDIA'

Reserve Bank of India (RBI) governor Raghuram Rajan is good at asking the right questions. A distinguished economist with exceptional foresight—he was one of the few to predict the 2008 financial crisis—he's now triggered a debate within India over Prime Minister Narendra Modi's flagship 'Make in India' campaign: an effort to boost India's manufacturing sector to China-like levels.

In a speech last week, Rajan questioned whether that should be India's goal at all. The conventional wisdom is that the only way to find jobs for a young and growing population, and to move workers off the farm and into cities, is to expand India's export-focused industries. That's the same route Japan, China and the so-called Asian Tigers all pursued successfully. Yet, Rajan asked, does the world really need another export powerhouse?

With demand in developed nations slowing, there simply may not be enough customers for Indian-made goods, no matter how cheap. The alternative—stimulating domestic demand artificially, by raising tariffs on imports—has been tried and failed spectacularly under previous socialist governments.

What Rajan's questions really expose is the fact that so far, Modi's much-hyped campaign offers more rhetoric than substance. Even if one agrees with the goal of boosting manufacturing, the government has yet to offer any convincing strategies for achieving it. Modi has placed great emphasis on raising India's ranking in the World Bank's ease-of-doing-business survey from 142 to 50. That would require taking an ax to India's tangle of red tape: simplifying processes for opening a business and for registering property; improving the enforcement of contracts and collection of taxes; making it easier to acquire permits.

Yet while businesses would happily embrace such changes, they're unlikely to unleash a manufacturing revolution. Like China, India's already tried to implement several of these reforms in special economic zones that advertise lower taxes and looser land and labour regulations. These efforts have yet to amount to much, at least partly for the reasons Rajan has laid out—weak demand in advanced countries.

These policies focus too much on symptoms of India's malaise. The real problem is that markets for four critical inputs for manufacturing, or indeed any business—land, labour, power and capital—are badly distorted. Until the government resolves those distortions, 'Make in India' will remain nothing but a slogan.

Consider land. A new land-acquisition law, passed in the dying months of the previous government in 2013, makes buying farmland on which to build factories tremendously complicated and expensive; by law, companies have to pay four times the market price in rural areas. There's simply no free market for land in India.

On labour, India should have a cost advantage over China, whose labour-intensive goods now flood the Indian market. Chinese wages have risen rapidly over three decades of double-digit growth. India's haven't, and almost half the population is still engaged in unproductive agriculture. Yet tough labour laws mean that the opportunity costs of hiring workers remain cripplingly high. While the government has started a debate on reforming those laws, few changes are evident yet.

Unreliable and expensive power supplies hamper all of India's businesses. Indian governments have long subsidized agriculture and regular consumers by charging higher rates to industry. China and other emerging nations have followed the opposite strategy. India need not reverse course completely, but it needs at least to even out prices for everyone while boosting overall supply.

The issue of expensive capital is one that should particularly exercise Rajan. He knows that India's closed financial system artificially raises the cost of capital. He's stuck with a tight monetary policy for the moment because of high inflation. But compared to the rest of the world, Indian interest rates tend to be too high even when monetary policy is more accommodative. There's also plenty more room for India to open up its financial system, even if it remains wary of the kind of cowboy capitalism that led to the 2008 crash.

The government can help manufacturers by following through on pledges to invest in roads, ports and connectivity. But only when India's markets for land, labour, power and capital work efficiently will the foundations for a true cost-competitive manufacturing revolution exist. Rajan might then find himself a bit more optimistic: Indian companies shouldn't need any special protections to compete with cheap Chinese goods at home. And when the advanced economies finally recover, there will be other markets to conquer.

TOP FIVE PROGRAMMES LAUNCHED BY MODI IN 2014

Digital India

On August 21, 2014, the "Digital India" campaign was launched. The idea is to change India into an electronically empowered economy. According to this programme, the Government of India wants all Government departments and the people of India to connect with each other digitally or electronically, so that there is effective governance. It also aims at reducing paperwork by making all the Government services available to the people electronically. There is also a plan to connect all villages and rural areas through internet networks.

There are three major components of Digital India: Digital infrastructure, digital literacy and digital delivery of services. The Government plans to complete this project in five years. That is, by 2019, the Digital India project is expected to be fully functional.

Pradhan Mantri Jan Dhan Yojana

On August 28, 2014, Prime Minister Narendra Modi launched the Pradhan Mantri Jan Dhan Yojana. This scheme was announced when he gave his first Independence Day speech on August 15 , 2014. This is a prestigious financial inclusion programme. On the very first day of the launch of the programme, 15 million bank accounts were opened and each of the account holders was given Rs 1,00,000 insurance cover. By September 2014, 3.02 crore accounts were opened and around Rs 1,500 crore were deposited. According to the yojana, anyone can open new bank accounts with zero balance too.

Swachh Bharat Abhiyan

On 24 September 2014, Prime Minister approved the Swachh Bharat campaign, which was a modification of the Nirmal Bharat Programme, launched by the previous Government. The Swachh Bharat Abhiyan was launched formally on October 2, 2014, the birth anniversary of Mahatma Gandhi. The objective is to make India a clean India by 2019, the 150th birth anniversary of Mahatma Gandhi. The plan is to provide toilet and sanitation facilities in all rural and remote areas, to create public awareness of cleanliness, to clean roads, streets, encroachments and make India one of the cleanest countries of the world.

Make in India

This was basically a slogan, coined by Narendra Modi on September 25, 2014 to attract the global world to invest and manufacture in India. It then became an international marketing campaign. "Make in India" campaign was initiated so that India has ample job opportunities and the economy gets a boost. 'Make in India' seeks to make India a self-reliant country. It also aims to allow FDI in the country as well as bring back to health the loss-making Government firms. The Make in India campaign is completely under the Central Government, in which the Government has identified 25 major sectors which have the potential of becoming a global leader.

Saansad Adarsh Gram Yojana

On October 11, 2014, Prime Minister Narendra Modi launched the Saansad Adarsh Gram Yojana. According to this yojana, each MP will take the responsibility of developing three villages by 2019. The idea is to make India's villages to be fully developed with physical and institutional infrastructure. There are certain guidelines for this scheme, which has been formulated by the Department of Rural Development. The Prime Minister released the guidelines on October 11, 2014 and requested all MPs to develop one model village by year 2016 in their constituency and two more by 2019.

'MAKE IN INDIA' CALL GETS SMART RESPONSE FROM ABROAD

Make in India has been the NDA government's flagship campaign to boost manufacturing in India. In a mega launch ceremony, Indian Prime Minister Narendra Modi threw open the doors of the Indian manufacturing sector to foreign investors with a promise to enhance the ease of doing business in the country. The Government's vision to craft out a manufacturing hub in the nation is the first step to enhancing the contribution of the manufacturing sector towards the GDP. Twentyfive key sectors were marked out as priority sectors and foreign investors have been promised all assistance and information required to set up businesses in India.

The Prime Minister followed up on the Make in India campaign with a series of labour reforms that were long overdue. The response to Make in India call has been quite promising, domestic as well as foreign, although it's not time yet to see the impact of these reforms. Tying it up with Digital India and the expansion targets of the economy, the Government is certainly working on what seems to be a comprehensive plan to rope in foreign investments to boost the economy and growth.

MAKE IN INDIA TO STRENGTHEN INDIA-OMAN TIES

The President of India, Pranab Mukherjee, extended an invitation to all the private and public sector companies of Oman to set up manufacturing units in India and enter into close ties with the 25 priority sectors. The hope of lucrative returns and the plethora of opportunities for investment in the country were the highlights of President Mukherjee's message to Dr. Ali Bin Masoud Al Sunaidy, Commerce and Industry Minister of the Sultanate of Oman. Dr. Masoud Al Sunaidy called on the President at the Rashtrapati Bhawan on Monday. "Bilateral trade between India and Oman has increased from USD 4.6 billion in 2012-13 to USD 5.77 billion in 2013-14. However, trade remains much below its potential and both sides need to bring it to a higher level commensurate with the depth of the bilateral relationship," President Mukherjee told the visiting Omani Minister.

The soon to be held seventh joint commission meeting between India and Oman is likely to provide both the nations a perfect platform to strengthen trade ties and for investors from Oman to explore investment opportunities in our country. The Omani Minister welcomed the Indian President's suggestions and expressed the hope that the two countries could further strengthen traditional ties in the years to come with more companies deciding to manufacture in India.

Fiat plans for 'Make in India'

Modi's call to Make in India has had things moving in the automobile sector. Fiat Chrysler Automobiles has come up with a plan to manufacture a range of C-segment Jeep brand premium sports utility vehicles in India and export these SUVs to countries such as Australia, South Africa, and the United Kingdom. This manufacturing (export) unit is likely to be up and running within two years and shall bring in an investment of about INR 1,500-2,500 cr. The project has been called M6 or 556 and will see the production of the first SUVs in the country. Fiat Chrysler has hitherto been sustaining losses due to low sales numbers in their Indian operations and the exports are likely to reverse this trend. A formal announcement is still awaited, though.

The Fiat-Chrysler merger has enabled the company to look at various new investment options and the automobile manufacturing sector of India looks rather promising. Fiat is likely to produce the new Jeep line at its Ranjangaon plant in Maharashtra. Almost 20,000 such C-segment SUVs are likely to be produced every year and they will be priced between INR 20 and 25 lakh in domestic markets.

Defence boost to Indian manufacturers

In a major boost to the Indian defence manufacturing sector, the Indian Government has cleared INR 80,000 cr worth of defence deals including the construction of six submarines. On October 26 last, the Defence Acquisition Council (DAC) approved the manufacturing of these diesel-electric submarines in a single domestic shipyard. The entire project is likely to cost the Government INR 50,000 crore. Defense manufacturing is one of the core sectors identified by the Make In India campaign. This acquisition is also likely to boost the morale of the Indian Navy which has been hurt due to a series of accidents over the past year.

Sweden praises 'Make In India'

The NDA Government's Make In India campaign has become the key highlight at the Sweden India Nobel Memorial Week which is currently being held across 10 different Indian cities – Ahmedabad, Bangalore, Chennai, Delhi, Guwahati, Hyderabad, Indore, Kolkata, Mumbai and Pune.

This is the eighth such memorial week being held by the Swedish Embassy in India. Swedish companies such as Tetrapak, Scania, Ericsson, and Volvo India have committed to successfully participating in Make in India and strengthening their decade old relationship with the Indian manufacturing sector.

The Swedish Ambassador, H E Harald Sandberg praised Modi's initiative to boost the manufacturing, automobile, infrastructure and other sectors of the Indian economy drawing upon the traditional strengths of the country. The Sweden India Nobel Memorial Week is being held between October 26 and November 1 and apart from the campaign is also focusing on Nobel Peace Laureate Kailash Satyarthi.

Healthcare through 'Make in India'

Make in India is not only for foreign investors, says Modi. The Indian healthcare industry must utilize the full potential of India's burgeoning manufacturing industry and produce world class medical devices indigenously. This will bring quality healthcare to the doorstep of the poor masses of the nation, he said at the inaugural ceremony of the HN Reliance Foundation Hospital in Mumbai. Want of affordable primary healthcare is of primary importance in a populous country like India, said the PM. The only means to achieving this end is by cutting costs and manufacturing in domestic units. With the help of technology and Digital India, the quality standards of such products can be raised as well.

MODI'S VISION OF 'SMART CITIES' TAKES SHAPE AS GOVERNMENT COMMITS

Smart cities is the catchphrase as Prime Minister Narendra Modi's government lays the groundwork for his ambitious program aimed at setting up 100 such urban settlements nationwide.

Modi's vision for advanced cities that benefit from the latest technology has finally begun to take shape with the Ministry of Urban Development identifying almost all the locations where they will be built as well as existing cities that are to be remodelled on these lines.

This done, the ministry has asked the 22 states where the programme will be implemented to send detailed project reports so a final blueprint can be outlined.

Describing the scheme, officials of the urban development ministry say they plan to set up seven smart cities each in Gujarat, Kerala, Rajasthan and Karnataka.

Modi's constituency Varanasi, they added, is among the six cities identified in Uttar Pradesh for the smart makeover.

Five years A senior ministry official said the government has set 2019 as the deadline to deliver the first three smart cities, all of which will be built as part of the Delhi-Mumbai Industrial Corridor (DMIC).

The DMIC is a project the government aims to build as a 'global manufacturing and trading hub'. These smart cities are Dholera, Shendra-Bidkin and Global City.

Overall, seven smart cities will be set up between Delhi and Mumbai under the DMIC project, which is being built in partnership with the government of Japan.

There are at least three more industrial corridors along which new cities are being built: Amritsar-Kolkata, Bangalore-Chennai and Chennai-Visakhapatnam. Besides, states have been asked to identify cities along the Amritsar-Kolkata corridor.

Intelligent: Prime Minister Narendra Modi's vision for advanced cities that benefit from the latest technology has finally begun to take shape.

Pictured, a Delhi Metro train passes over Gurgaon Rapid Metro trains in the satellite city

A master plan is ready for three cities-Punderi, Krishnapatnam and Tumkur-along the Bangalore-Chennai corridor, said an official of the ministry, adding that the Asian Development Bank (ADB) had concluded a feasibility study for cities along Chennai-Vizag corridor.

The Centre will also invite bids for another project, Shendra-Bidkin industrial zone in Maharashtra, by mid-2015.

Much like in the DMIC, the official said foreign assistance would be crucial to the implementation of the project.

Several countries, including Singapore, Germany, the UK, US and South Korea have expressed interest in these projects.

In fact, during his visit to Japan from August 30 to September 3, Prime Minister Modi is hoping to seal a deal on infrastructural investment for the smart cities initiative, with Japan proposing project development agreements on high-speed railways, more industrial corridors, and road-and rail-links.

In the NDA government's maiden Union Budget, Finance Minister Arun Jaitley set aside Rs 500 crore for the setting up of an institution called '3P India'.

Apart from other areas, the institution is expected to help streamline public-private partnerships (PPPs) in the smart cities segment, for which the Budget exclusively allocated a Rs 7,060 crore sum.

Integrated: Smart cities have an integrated transit system where BRT corridors, such as the one in Delhi (pictured), as well as suburban train networks are linked with pedestrian and cycle lanes for easier travel

Smart cities, in the most basic terms, are urban settlements that exploit technology to offer more structured and hospitable living conditions for residents.

The infrastructure of a smart city should be equipped with systems aimed at better management of energy resources, water, transport and traffic, safety and security.

Information and communication technology (ICT) forms the backbone of such cities.

A master plan for ICT infrastructure implementation has been developed by Cisco Systems specifically for Dholera Special Investment Region.

Naidu pegs heritage vision on Varanasi

Attraction: Varanasi is among India's biggest tourist hotspots, thanks to its image as a hub of tradition and spirituality

Union Urban Development Minister Venkaiah Naidu on Friday made a presentation to Prime Minister Narendra Modi on developing Varanasi as part of a scheme aimed at bolstering the heritage status of cities known as hubs of tradition and culture.

In popular imagination, Varanasi is synonymous with temples and spirituality, and is for this reason a big draw for foreign tourists.

Varanasi, Modi's political constituency, is one of several similar towns and cities-namely, Mathura, Gaya, Ajmer, Amritsar and Kanchipuram-shortlisted by the ministry as heritage cities it seeks to develop in a way that allows them to better showcase their historicity, art and culture.

The plan also involves organising events aimed at attracting more tourists to these places.

The strategy is an upshot of the severe criticism the poor management of these places often evokes.

Despite the fact that hold pride of place among India's popular tourist destinations, these cities and towns grapple with security problems as well as poor hygiene conditions.

The scheme is aimed at the preservation and revitalisation of India's rich heritage.

It also seeks to enhance the quality of urban life in such cities, apart from improving their physical, social and economic structures, sources close to minister Naidu said. Finance Minister Arun Jaitley had in his budget proposal for 2014-15 made a provision of Rs 100 crore in the current financial year for the development of heritage cities.

With its presentation to Modi on Friday, the urban development ministry unveiled a general template for development of heritage cities and an action plan with reference to Varanasi.

Besides the plan to set up 100 smart cities, which has been touted as the urban development ministry's flagship programme which will replace the UPA's JNNURM, developing religious places of high historic significance has been high on the agenda of Naidu.

INDIA'S MODI ARTICULATES VISION FOR ECONOMIC CHANGE

India's government is moving away from the populist approach of previous administrations that used handouts to win over different groups and generate voter support, Prime Minister Narendra Modi said.

"This has become an almost settled way of doing politics in India," Mr. Modi said in a speech at the Council on Foreign Relations on Monday. "But India's young people don't want to live on dole-outs anymore. They want to be treated differently."

Mr. Modi, who came to power in a landslide victory in May, articulated a broad vision for economic change, saying he was determined to rise above "small interests to focus on good governance."

His statements point to a shift in political thinking in a country governed for most of its post-independence history by the Congress party, which in the past decade expanded entitlements for the poor and farmers.

It is unclear how far Mr. Modi will be willing to go to reorient economic policies. He is unlikely, for instance, to reduce food subsidies,which benefit a majority of Indians. Nor has he indicated how quickly he wants to enact change.

While saying he didn't subscribe to a "populist approach to economic management," Mr. Modi underscored the limits of reform in a country that is still plagued by abject poverty. When asked about his government's widely criticized blocking of a trade agreement at the World Trade Organization over a separate discussion on food security, Mr. Modi said, "I can't keep my people hungry."

India told the WTO in July that it won't sign on to a trade-facilitation agreement unless a deal is reached on the issue of stockpiling food grains. Steps like this and an underwhelming budget have led critics to accuse Mr. Modi's four-month-old government of sending mixed messages about reform and not moving boldly enough to retool India's sputtering economy.

Government ministers say they don't want to push policies bound to be opposed or get stuck in Parliament. Their approach, they say, is to gradually create consensus and support for economic change. Mr. Modi said his government had already started working on some politically difficult decisions, such as amending labor laws blamed for restraining the manufacturing sector. He said the federal government welcomes initiatives by state-level administrations to start amending the laws that burden companies with many regulations, including those that make it difficult to fire workers. He must also tackle a land-acquisition law that has been a major concern among businesses.

"We are moving forward with responsibility on even those issues that may not be seen as politically expedient," Mr. Modi said. "Ultimately, those steps will benefit everyone."

He is seeking to woo U.S. businesses to invest in India to help kick-start growth. Before speaking at the Council on Foreign Relations, Mr. Modi had meetings with executives of U.S. businesses, including Boeing , IBM and MasterCard , in which he promised to get rid of bureaucratic delays and make tax policies more stable.

In a number of speeches on his U.S. visit, he has pitched India as a provider of labor for an aging world and a potential manufacturing hub, saying India was uniquely positioned for exponential growth.

"India has three D's: democracy, demographic dividend and demand," Mr. Modi said. "No other country in the world has all these three things."

NARENDRA MODI'S ECONOMIC 'VISION': IS BJP SELLING WHAT UPA MADE?

With much anticipation, I awaited the rolling out of the BJP's proposed economic policies for India. According to some TV pundits, Narendra Modi would conjure up a vision that would catch the nation's collective fancy and propel the BJP to power. All this talk may have worried his opponents; it shouldn't have. Modi's "vision" and "plan" for the economy, as shared in recent speeches, fell woefully short of expectations; a damp squib, if you will.

Conjurer of the vision thing

In speeches at FICCI and the BJP's national council meeting, Modi rolled out his "vision" for India's economy. Before regaling the audience with his ideas, he launched into a customary bashing of the UPA for the "despair" prevailing in India and how ours had become a country of "underachievers". While there can be no disagreement that we can do more and better, Modi does disservice to the nation by talking it down, and by not showing pride in all that has been achieved. Perhaps he is not aware or would rather that people forgot the following: India is now a middle-income country; there are 140 million fewer extremely poor Indians; we have had a stable, if not sexy, government that ensured, for the most part, very high growth rates that will be tough for future governments to match. The UPA managed all this "underachievement" in an exceedingly difficult global economic climate and challenging domestic coalition politics.

So, what is this ModiVision? The main planks of Modi's programme are education, healthcare, urbanisation, and infrastructure, apart from tackling inflation and black money. He also mentioned good governance, agriculture, and services. It was an all encompassing "vision" that left many observers, well, underwhelmed. The general criticism has been that his ideas are either not original or provide little in terms of specifics, or any description of trade-offs necessary to deal with competing priorities. I will take a somewhat down-to-earth view of his high flying ideas: is Modi selling what the UPA has already made?

Of dreamers and doers

Let's start with Modi's concern for education. He said the BJP's dream was "to have an IIM, an IIT and an AIIMS in all states." While he and the BJP have been dreaming, the UPA has been doing. The number of central universities has gone up from 17 in 2004 to 44 in 2013, IIMs from six to 16, IITs from seven to 16. The gross enrolment ratio has increased from 12% to 18% in higher education, within striking distance of the international average of 20%. For a country of India's size, that is a huge change.

But in emphasizing higher education, Modi let slip his tendency to focus on grand things, neglecting the building blocks that make modern economies click. I refer to school education. Under the UPA, there has been a tenfold increase in expenditures on the Sarva Shiksha Abhiyan to improve rural literacy. Along with this, an expanded mid-day meal scheme benefiting 10 crore children is keeping kids in school for much longer. Having said that, and as a recent report by the Annual Status of Education Report indicated, the learning aspect has not kept pace with enrolment and that is where we must focus in future. For example, in Modi's Gujarat, fewer than 27% of students in grades VI-VII can do division (among the worst ratios in the country). We must consolidate our gains by sharpening our focus on learning in schools, and simultaneously promote higher education and skill development opportunities.

On health, Modi's big idea is a still-to-be-defined insurance programme. Meanwhile, not only has the UPA increased public investment in health almost threefold since 2004, progress is being made in exactly the areas he talked about. For instance, the UPA has revamped the Rashtriya Swasthya Bima Yojana, a health insurance scheme for patients below the poverty line. Almost four crore smart cards for RSBY beneficiaries have already been issued. With the conversion of the National Rural Health Mission to a National Health Mission, urban poor and middle class families will now benefit from increased investments in healthcare as well. Most importantly, health outcomes are improving. Infant and maternal mortality are decreasing, and life expectancy has increased by 5 years during the UPA's tenure. These are no mean achievements.

Command and control in 21st century India

With an eye on middle-class voters, Modi talked up infrastructure and urbanisation as if anybody is against such things. True to his rhetorical style, he spoke of building a hundred smart cities and bullet trains. How do we get there? He will tell us later; trust him.

But, what does the UPA's record suggest? Infrastructure, especially in the road and power sectors has seen phenomenal growth. Rural roads have grown by 2 lakh km; investments under the Pradhan Mantri Gram Sadak Yojana went up tenfold. A scheme envisioned by Atal Bihari Vajpayee was put on steroids by the UPA. Power lines have been drawn to 4.6 lakh villages; India has added more power capacity in the last 9 years than in the preceding period since independence. Per capita consumption of electricity has gone up from 559 kWh to 813 kWh since the NDA's "Shining India" campaign. Towns are transforming into cities, modern airports are coming up, Metros and rail links are unclogging urban streets. The great Indian middle class, almost the size of the United States, has come of age in the last 10 years. To keep up with this growth, we must ensure a smooth transition from a largely rural to a more urban economy. But that will require more than a rhetorician-in-chief.

I should have seen this coming. The BJP talked about tax reforms and proposed a laughable bank transactions tax; Modi hid behind states' rights to stall the much-needed Goods and Services Tax reform and then has the cheek to propose a national agricultural market; the BJP loves to talk about poor investor sentiment but plays vote bank politics over FDI in retail; they rail against inflation, then propose a command-and-control, overarching price stabilisation fund; they cry hoarse over corruption but rehabilitate smugglers of illegal raw material to China. The BJP's rhetorical packaging is good; the underlying product is a dud. I don't want to say "I told you so" after it is too late. I would rather we all pay attention now.

MODI'S BIG IDEAS TO TRANSFORM INDIA

Partial dismantling of subsidies, move towards a more transparent policy on natural resources and efforts to make India more inviting for foreign investors are some of Modi government's big achievements.

Image: Prime Minister Narendra Modi

The Narendra Modi-led National Democratic Alliance government is poised to complete six months. It is an alliance because it chooses to be one and has no coalition compulsions to speak of.

In part because the global and domestic economic environment has been extraordinarily supportive – low commodity prices and; lowest levels of inflation in nine years and record food stocks – the government in India has faced fewer challenges. But has it maximised its opportunities?

Is it spending too much time congratulating itself and its Prime Minister and not thinking enough about how to restructure policy? Has it been weighed down by internal doubts and differences on future direction?

It has had many achievements as well: a partial dismantling of subsidies; movement towards a more transparent policy on natural resources; and moves to make India more inviting for foreign investors.

In its foreign policy, the substance may be the continuation of past policy but the style has changed dramatically. But the government continues to struggle with collective inexperience which has tended to centralise decision-making, curbing individual initiative.

The BJP fancies itself as a bold, swashbuckling government: but in some of the decisions it has taken, it has been inexplicably tentative.

Many of the initiatives it had announced: more power to the states; the revamping of the Planning Commission are yet to get off the ground.

Business Standard examines and evaluates six months of policy, decision-making, political management and the style of the new government.

It trains the spotlight on the individuals who make the government run and identifies the six biggest ideas, achievements, strengths and weaknesses so far.

SMART CITIES

One of the ideas from the BJP poll manifesto, this saw early action. In its first Budget in July, this government allocated Rs 7,060 crore (Rs 70.60 billion) for smart cities, though the initial estimate for the project was Rs 35,000 crore per annum.

The plan is to build 100 smart cities in India over a period of time. Smart cities are broadly defined as urban spaces that are technologically integrated, well-planned and environment-friendly.

It's a long-term project and could well be spread over 10 years or more, officials say. A flexible PPP (public-private partnership) model is being worked out; many countries including the US, Japan and Singapore, have committed to play a role.

Critics say power outages, poor infrastructure and dearth of clean drinking water may play spoilsport.

6

"Make in India": Manufacturing Innovation and Policy Initiative

The study will suggest the urgent need for enterprise-oriented technology transfer from public funded R&D institutions to link the Science and technology system with small and medium enterprises production units. Similarly, the SMEs associations should be strengthened to provide opportunities for their members to continuously learn about new technology developments and opportunities to enhance the competitiveness of enterprises in the sector. Lab to industry Initiative aims at achieving improvement in the quality of life of people by bringing into fruition provisions of the programmes for the development and growth of manufacturing industry. R&D is the spinal cord for the futuristic growth of industrial growth and to fulfil the demand of upcoming consumer demands. However, there exist many challenges in making this industry truly attain its potential. Labour reform that will boost the employment and provide social security benefits to labourers.

These include the inadequate infrastructure, limited focus on value addition and exports, changing tax structure, limited focus on R&D and availability of funding mechanism.

As per, The Organisation for Economic Co-operation and Development OECD "Better policies " series India's economy has grown at an impressive pace over the last two decades as a result of wide-ranging structural reforms to open up the economy and make it more competitive. A study on productivity trends in Indian manufacturing undertaken by Unel(2003) has concluded that total factor productivity (TFP) growth in aggregate manufacturing and many sub-sectors accelerated after the 1991 reforms.

MAKE IN INDIA

The development of the industry has been identified as a prime requirement for exploiting backward linkages to agriculture and forward linkages to overall economy. Thus, for regional development in India, a need of developing manufacturing or industrial base of each state has been identified. For balance growth, the concentration of industrial activities must decline over a period of time and industrially backward states must attract good share in total output of the nation. The analysis will help to identify the effectiveness of balanced growth strategy of Indian policy planners. In present paper, an attempt has been made to analyse the level of manufacturing development with the innovation in mind. At the same time regional disparity should be declined by doing installations with cultural lenses. An attempt has been made to analyse the 'Make in India' trends in industrial activities specially manufacturing sector among Indian states.

NEW GOI INIITIATIVES

As per the policy initiatives GOI has taken few steps to facilitate investments, foster innovation, protect intellectual property and build best-in-class manufacturing infrastructure. Presently India place 142nd among 189 countries in ease of business in 2015 so it requires. This picture will summarize Doing business 2015 data for India.

ROLE OF SERVICES AS INPUT TO MANUFACTURING SECTOR

It has been observed that India's growth is been fuelled up due to service sector. And also it has been seen that by cross country analysis has shown that service sector has contributed output and employment in India's GDP. So in the 'Make in India' program, services sectors are very essential part to boost the manufacturing innovations.

Indian Economy is full of pool of talent in IT/ITES industry and has contributed more than 56 percent in economic development. It, not only proved in India but taken the workload of developed nations and helping them in intellectual marathon. They become the world leader in giving IT/ITES support to various MNC's.

During the global economic crisis, the services sector's share in real GDP increased from 63% in 2007–08 to 64.5% in 2008–09, while that of the agricultural and industrial sectors decreased. The services sector experienced the smallest decline in growth rate compared to the other two sectors. The growth rate of the services sector fell from 10.8% in 2007–08 to 9.3% in 2008–09, a decline of 1.5 percentage points, compared to declines of 3.3 and 4.7 percentage points in the agricultural and industrial sectors, respectively.

INFRASTRUTURE PROJECTS

Creation of new smart cities and industrial clusters in identified corridors having connectivity will initiate new infrastructural projects. National Industrial Corridor created to coordinate, integrate, monitor and supervise development of all Industrial corridors. Development Authority Delhi-Mumbai Industrial corridor, Chennai-Bengluru Industrial corridor. It is also planning to connect North Eastern states with other Industrial corridors in cooperation with Japanese Government. New Industrial cluster are being created for advance practice in Manufacturing. Modified Industrial infrastructure up gradation scheme with an emphasis on use of recycled water through liquid discharging system and Central Effluent Treatment Plants. The intellectual property regime, further up-gradation of IT facilities; compliance with Global standards and online Application process. Major impetus is required to give skill development.

OPENING OF SECTOR

Various areas are still not open for market players, which can play an important role in succeeding the Make in India campaign. With easing of investment caps and controls in India's High value industrial sectors-Defence, Construction and Railways. Like FDI cap rose from 26 per cent to 49 per cent in Defence sector. In Railways dedicated freight corridors can help in this particular development, through PPP, High speed Trains, Dedicated freight lines, Rolling stocks including train sets and locomotive/coaches manufacturing and maintenance facilities, Railway electrification, signalling system, Freight terminals, passenger terminals, Infrastructure in industrial park, Mass Rapid Transit System.

Make in India program represents an attitudinal shift in how India relates to investors, not as a permit issuing authority, but as a true business partner. True assistance and guide to first time investors, from time of arrival and there will be focused targeting of companies across sectors.

MANUFATURING POLICY OF INDIA

The National Manufacturing policy is set to achieve a manufacturing target of 25 per cent from 16 per cent, in countries Gross Domestic Product by 2022; creation of 100 million additional jobs by 2022 in manufacturing sector as also appropriate skills sets among rural migration and the urban poor for inclusive growth.

Manufacturing policy,

- Employment-intensive industries like textiles and garments, lather and footwear, gems and jewellery and food processing equipment.
- Capital goods industries like machine tools. Heavy electrical equipment, heavy transport, earthmoving & mining equipment.
- Industries with strategic significance like aerospace, shipping, IT hardware & electronics, telecommunication equipment, defence equipment and solar energy.

- Industries where India enjoys a competitive advantage such as automobiles, pharmaceuticals medical equipment.
- Small & medium enterprises.
- Public sector enterprises.

The policy intends to leverage the existing incentives/ schemes of government. A technology acquisition and development fund has been proposed for the acquisition of appropriate technologies, the creation of a patent pool and the development of domestic manufacturing of equipment used for controlling pollution and reducing energy consumption.

INCENTIVES TO MANUFACTURING UNITS

- Transfer of Assets-Transfer of assets will be facilitated by NIMZ.
- Green Technology & Practices-5 per cent interest in reimbursement & 10 per cent capital subsidy for the production of equipment/ machines/ devices for controlling pollution, reducing energy consumption and water conservation.
- Technology Development-Incentives for the production of equipment/ machines/ devices for controlling pollution, reducing energy consumption and water conservation; SME's will be given access patent pool for reimbursement of technology.
- Special benefits to SME's-Rollover relief from long term capital gains tax to individuals on sale of residential property in case of reinvestment of sale consideration; Venture capital funds with a focus on SME's.
- Government procurement-public procurement with stipulation of local value addition in specific sectors.
- Industrial training & Skill up gradation measures-The creation of a multiple tier structure for skill development.
- Exit mechanism –It envisages an alternate exit mechanism through job loss policy and sinking fund or a combination of both.

JOBLESS GROWTH IN MANUFACTURING SECTOR

Despite the notable economic performance of Indian industry in the last two and a half decades with an annual growth of 5.3 percent, organized manufacturing employment growth was less than 0.5 percent.

Since a strong productivity growth could generate job loss when aggregate demand is insufficient, rising rural incomes unleash a multiplier effect, increasing demand for farm and non-farm products and services, thereby stimulating rapid growth of employment opportunities in other sectors.

CONCLUSION

The development of the purchasing power of manufacturing sector, in fact, is essential to stimulate the effective demand for industrial goods and to sustain industrial production in the long run. Make in India program will boost the economy by innovations in technological up gradation, supported by new policies. Need of labour reform that will boost the employment and provide social security benefits to labourers.

The fact that implications of deregulation for concentration differ across Indian manufacturing states, strongly supports the need for a state-specific approach to competition policy. While this is quite common practice in developed countries, developing economies like India has started developing this approach. Recent discussions suggest that India is taking the right path. And with hope India will soon achieve the sustaining high and inclusive growth with an aspiring idea of Make in India program.

MANUFACTURING SECTOR IN INDIA

With launch of the 'Make in India' initiative, Mr Narendra Modi, the Prime Minister of India, aims to give global recognition to the Indian economy and also place India on the world map as a manufacturing hub.

India has also set for itself an ambitious target of increasing the contribution of manufacturing output to 25 per cent of gross domestic product (GDP) by 2025, from 16 per cent currently.

India's economy is expected to grow at 7.4 per cent in 2014-15 as per a Government forecast. According to a new formula which uses 2011-12 as the new 'base year', the revised statistics showed inflation-adjusted economic growth rate for October-December 2014 at 7.5 per cent, making India the fastest growing major economy in the world.

Market Size

Business conditions in the Indian manufacturing sector continued to improve in January 2015 fuelled by accelerated growth of output, marking the third straight month of expansion on the HSBC Services Purchasing Managers' Index (PMI). The PMI rose to 52.4 points in January 2015 from 51.1 in December 2014. The composite PMI that combines both services and manufacturing sectors rose to 53.3 points in January 2015 from 52.9 in the previous month.

India's manufacturing sector could touch US$ 1 trillion by 2025, according to a report by Mckinsey and Company. There is potential for the sector to account for 25-30 per cent of the country's GDP and create up to 90 million domestic jobs by 2025.

In a major boost to the 'Make in India' initiative, the Government has received confirmation from top technology firms such as GE, Bosch, Tejas and Panasonic regarding their decision to invest in the electronic, medical, automotive and telecom manufacturing clusters in India. "We have received 57 investment proposals of over Rs 19,000 crore (US$ 3.05 billion) of which 30 proposals worth Rs 6,500 crore (US$ 1.04 billion) have been approved," said Mr Ravi Shankar Prasad, Union Minister for Communications and Information Technology, Government of India.

The domestic market size of the chemical industry is around US$ 118 billion and it is approximately 3 per cent of the global chemical market, according to a report by Tata Strategic Management Group. It is highly diversified with more than 80,000 chemicals and currently accounts for 15 per cent of manufacturing GDP which makes it very crucial for the economic development of the country.

Investments

The Government of India has received investment proposals for electronics manufacturing worth Rs 18,000 crore (US$ 2.89 billion) for 2015-16 and expects the figure to double in another two years.

India has become one of the most attractive destinations for investments in the manufacturing sector. Some of the major investments and developments in this sector in the recent past are:

- US-based First Solar Inc and China's Trina Solar have plans to set up manufacturing facilities in India. Clean energy investments in India increased to US$ 7.9 billion in 2014, helping the country maintain its position as the seventh largest clean energy investor in the world.
- Samsung Electronics Co Ltd has invested Rs 517 crore (US$ 83.11 million) towards the expansion of its manufacturing plant in Noida, Uttar Pradesh (UP) under the UP Mega Policy. "Samsung India Electronics is committed to strengthen its manufacturing infrastructure and will gradually expand capacity at this plant to meet the growing domestic demand for mobile handsets, as per the company.
- India is currently among the top 10 sourcing countries for IKEA. The plan is to double sourcing from India to €630 million (US$ 688.61 million) by 2020.
- Shantha Biotechnics Pvt Ltd has started building a facility to manufacture Insuman, an insulin product to treat diabetes. Sanofi SA, which acquired Shantha Biotechnics, will invest Rs 460 crore (US$ 73.93 million) to build the facility.
- BMW and Mercedes-Benz have intensified their localisation efforts to be part of 'Make in India' initiative. "The localisation efforts will reduce the waiting period

and accelerate the servicing process of our cars as we had to (previously) depend on our plants overseas for supply and will help us on the pricing front."

- Suzuki Motor Corp plans to make automobiles for Africa, the company's next big bet, as well as for India at its upcoming factory in Hansalpur, near Ahmedabad, Gujarat, as per Mr Toshihiro Suzuki, Executive Vice-President, Suzuki.

Government Initiatives

In a bid to push the 'Make in India' initiative to the global level, Mr Narendra Modi, Prime Minister of India, plans to pitch India as a manufacturing destination at the World International Fair in Germany's Hannover. Mr Modi is likely to showcase India as a business friendly destination to attract foreign businesses to invest and manufacture in the country.

The Government of India has taken several initiatives to promote a healthy environment for the growth of manufacturing sector in the country. Some of the notable initiatives and developments are:

- The government has asked New Delhi's envoys in over 160 countries to focus on economic diplomacy to help government attract investment and transform the 'Make In India' campaign a success to boost growth during the annual heads of missions conference. Prime Minister Mr Modi has also utilised the opportunity to brief New Delhi's envoys about the Government's foreign policy priority and immediate focus on restoring confidence of foreign investors and augmenting foreign capital inflow to increase growth in manufacturing sector.
- The Government of Uttar Pradesh (UP) has secured investment deals valued at Rs 5,000 crore (US$ 803.77 million) for setting up mobile manufacturing units in the state.
- The Government of Maharashtra has cleared land allotment for 130 industrial units across the state with an investment of Rs 6,266 crore (US$ 1.01 billion)

- Dr Jitendra Singh, Union Minister of State (Independent Charge) of the Ministry of Development of North Eastern Region (DoNER), MoS PMO, Personnel, Public Grievances & Pensions, Atomic Energy and Space, Government of India, has announced the 'Make in Northeast' initiative beginning with a comprehensive tourism plan for the region.

Road Ahead

The Government of India has an ambitious plan to locally manufacture as many as 181 products. The move could help infrastructure sectors such as power, oil and gas, and automobile manufacturing that require large capital expenditure and revive the Rs 1.85 trillion (US$ 29.74 billion) Indian capital goods business.

India is an attractive hub for foreign investments in manufacturing sector. Several mobile phone, luxury and automobile brands, among others, have set up or are looking to establish their manufacturing bases in the country.

With impetus on developing industrial corridors and smart cities, the government aims to ensure holistic development of the nation. The corridors would further assist in integrating, monitoring and developing a conducive environment for the industrial development and will promote advance practices in manufacturing.

INDIA'S RECENT DEVELOPMENT PERFORMANCE AND ITS CHALLENGES

India's economic performance since the start of the 21st century provides grounds for both optimism and concern; which assessment prevails will likely turn on the policy choices made today and in the next few years.

India experienced the most sustained period of rapid growth in its economic history during the 2000s – an average of close to 9% a year between 2003/04 and 2010/11 – even taking into account a brief but sharp slowdown in 2008/09, during the global economic crisis. Rapid growth in the 2000s contributed to an unprecedented fall in poverty. The poverty headcount rate (using the national poverty line) fell from 37% in 2004/05 to 22% in 2011/12, an extraordinary decline over so short a period.

More recently growth slowed to only around 5% in 2012/13 and 2013/14. While it has recovered modestly to about 5.5% in the first half of 2014/15, it is uncertain whether this represents the start of a sustained recovery. Cross-country evidence suggests that, while many countries enjoy temporary growth booms, this is nearly always followed by a "reversion to the mean" and more mediocre growth. For India to join the select group of countries that achieve sustained rapid growth over several decades will require policy-makers to provide a relentless focus on finding and unblocking the critical obstacles and constraints to structural change and inclusive growth.

A second, broader concern is that the benefits of faster GDP growth in recent years are being undermined by unplanned harmful spill-overs from the current growth model – severe local air pollution and damage to health, rising energy insecurity due to an increasing share of coal and other energy imports, excessive drawdown of groundwater in agriculture, and the costs of a rapid but problematic urbanisation, such as urban sprawl, congestion, pollution and reduced urban productivity. Thus, even as it grapples with the problems of how to achieve rapid and inclusive economic growth, India is also necessarily grappling with how to ensure that growth is sustainable – that its natural assets are able to continue providing the resources and environmental services on which the well-being of present and future generations depends.

Some 2 million (or over 20%) of all premature deaths in India in 2010 were related to some type of environmental risk. Of these, the most important is *household air pollution* from burning solid fuels, which is estimated to be responsible for just over 1 million premature deaths. Some 49% of households in India rely on firewood for cooking, especially in rural areas. In poorly ventilated buildings, indoor smoke can be 100 times higher than acceptable levels for small particles. The health risks are especially great for women and girls who do most of the cooking. A major push to expand access to electricity and provide improved cleaner cookstoves will therefore have a significant co-benefit in terms of reduced illness and deaths from household air pollution.

Outdoor (ambient) particulate matter (PM) pollution caused an estimated 630,000 premature deaths in India in 2010. Of the 30 cities with the worst ambient $PM_{2.5}$ pollution worldwide, 15 are in India, including the top four. Estimates place a statistical value of lives prematurely lost annually in India due to ambient $PM_{2.5}$ pollution at 5.5–7.5% of GDP. Since $PM_{2.5}$ pollution and CO_2 emissions both come largely from the same source – the burning of fossil fuels – it is important to consider the large health benefits from reduced air pollution associated with abatement of CO_2 emissions. For India these benefits are estimated at US$55 per tonne of CO_2 abated, close to double the US government's estimate of US$32 per tonne for the climate change benefits of reducing CO_2emissions. Importantly from the perspective of Indian policy-makers, the air quality benefits are not only larger, they are enjoyed in the near term; accrue locally, mostly to the country itself; and are more certain compared with climate change benefits.

In the remainder of this paper we argue that key reforms in energy, urban and agricultural policies and institutions can unlock more rapid economic growth and improved welfare for the Indian public while tackling many of the unwanted national side-effects of the existing model of growth, such as severe air pollution and growing energy insecurity. Such reforms also provide substantial avenues for India to make its due contribution to cooperative global efforts to mitigate greenhouse gas (GHG) emissions, and climate risks.

KEY DEVELOPMENT CHALLENGES AND OPPORTUNITIES IN THE ENERGY SECTOR

India consumes a relatively small amount of energy in both absolute and per capita terms compared with other major economies such as the OECD (Organisation for Economic Co-operation and Development) countries or China. But energy consumption is growing rapidly, at 4.6% per year in 2000–13, which represents a doubling in 15 years. This growth can be broken down into 6.8% annual GDP growth, minus a 2.2% annual decline in the energy intensity of GDP.

Growth in energy demand in India is likely to remain robust, not only because of fast economic growth but also because of structural trends, such as increasing industrialisation and urbanisation, which tend to boost demand. Unlike China, much of India's manufacturing development still lies in the future.

Domestic energy production has not kept pace with quickly rising consumption, so that energy imports have surged. Energy has become central to the country's chronic trade imbalance, with rising energy insecurity an important concern for policy-makers. India's international trade deficit for fuels averaged an annual 6.4% of GDP over 2008–12 – twice the size of its current account deficit, which averaged 3.2% of GDP annually in this period. The current account deficit has fallen recently, in part because of lower world oil prices. The country's external position nevertheless remains vulnerable to volatility in energy prices. These trends underline the importance of reforms to reduce unnecessary existing inefficiencies and waste in energy use.

Alongside fast growth in energy demand, India's energy supply has also become steadily more carbon intensive as the share of fossil fuels has risen, in particular with growing use of coal for electricity generation, and diesel and gasoline for transport. The combination of fast growth in energy demand and the rising carbon intensity of energy has resulted in the rapid increase of CO_2 emissions from energy use, averaging a little over 5.5% a year, as well as severe outdoor air pollution. Indeed, the increase in CO_2 emissions appears to have accelerated in recent years (2007–13). As a result, the long-term decline in the ratio of CO_2 to GDP appears to have slowed or halted recently. This is important because India's voluntary international commitments for emissions are couched in terms of a long-term decline in the ratio of emissions to GDP.

There are several directions in which India's mission to enhance energy efficiency and achieve a cleaner fuel mix can be intensified and broadened in scope.

As in a number of other countries, fuel and power subsidies in India originated from a desire to protect consumers, and the poor in particular, from high and volatile energy costs. But there is growing recognition that energy subsidies are an inefficient way of providing social protection, while also imposing significant costs on the economy and harm to the environment.

Fuel subsidies are estimated to have averaged 1.4% of GDP since 2007/08. Recognising their costs, the Government of India has recently moved to scale back fuel subsidies using a number of fuel-specific measures.

The fiscal burden of fuel subsidies will also decline because of the steep fall in world oil prices in the second half of 2014, although, in the absence of reforms, the fiscal burden would also increase again when oil prices rebound in future.

The present oil price decline provides an excellent opportunity to accelerate the removal of the remaining fuel subsidies and to place the ad hoc reforms of recent years on a permanent basis at a time when the impact on consumers will be limited.

India's electricity sector is rife with inefficiencies and supply bottlenecks that result in huge unmet demand, hamper economic growth, restrict access by the poor, stimulate inefficient energy consumption and worsen both local air pollution and carbon emissions. Extremely low subsidised electricity prices for agricultural users do little for agricultural productivity while stimulating excessive groundwater use and GHG emissions in agriculture.

The electricity sector also suffers from extraordinary transmission and distribution losses, some 21% of electricity output in 2011, compared with just 6–7% in China and the USA. Financial losses in the electricity sector have snowballed since 2003, reaching 0.7% of GDP and 17% of the gross fiscal deficit in 2011. Losses have been met by state subsidies and, increasingly, debt borrowings, which have reached more than 10% of state GDP in several northern states. Mounting power sector debts now pose a threat to the balance sheets of financial institutions. Worsening finances in the power sector have, in turn, led to increased rationing of power supplies and a squeeze on new investment, further reducing the quality of power infrastructure and services – a vicious circle.

The 2005 World Bank Enterprise Survey for India found that one-third of firms saw power shortages as the single most important constraint on their growth. Power subsidy reform, while difficult, is not impossible. In Gujarat, for example, large farmers were recently willing to accept higher power prices in return for a more reliable power supply.

India's energy fuel mix is also far from socially optimal, once the harmful spill-overs from coal and other fossil fuels are taken into account. For example, air pollution damages and growing energy insecurity. One recent estimate suggests that the price of coal in India would need to at least double if it were to fully reflect the health and other damages associated with coal use. Yet the share of coal in total primary energy has increased from 33% in 1990 to 45% in 2012, accompanied by a rising share of expensive, foreign currency denominated coal imports for power generation.

As in the rest of the world, the cost of renewable energy has seen an unexpectedly rapid decline in recent years, some 65% over the last three years by one estimate. The price of imported coal could be 30–50% higher than the cost of wind and solar by 2030. Replacing the marginal unit of energy supply from imported coal with a marginal unit from financially competitive renewable energy would allow India to secure substantial additional social benefits, such as greater energy security and a cleaner environment. Wind and solar capacity is small but rising fast. Government targets for renewable capacity are being sharply increased but still remain far below estimates of the physical potential for solar and wind in the country.

KEY DEVELOPMENT CHALLENGES AND OPPORTUNITIES IN AGRICULTURE AND LAND USE

Agriculture remains an important sector of the Indian economy, providing almost half of all employment, with over two-thirds of the population still living in rural areas. From a heavy dependence on foreign food aid in the early decades after Independence, agricultural development has advanced sufficiently for India to become first self-sufficient and then a net exporter of food.

However, while there has been substantial progress in improving the productive capacity of Indian agriculture over the decades since Independence, the rate of improvement has been relatively modest by international standards.

There has been some acceleration in growth of the overall agricultural sector since the mid-2000s but, among other reasons for caution, productivity performance for traditional crops is lagging.

Agriculture remains vulnerable to existing climatic variability and future climate change, while also driving rapid growth in groundwater extraction, something that threatens the long-term economic sustainability of the sector. Through direct and indirect channels, agriculture also generates about 30% of India's GHG emissions.

Given this backdrop, we argue that there are significant reform opportunities to achieve "triple wins" – that is, to raise farmers' incomes, to strengthen resilience to climate change and to abate GHG emissions – in particular by improving the orientation of public spending on agriculture. While there is no single, comprehensive source of information, studies suggest that the total volume of public spending on agriculture is significant and growing.

The largest category of spending is on subsidies for fertiliser, power, irrigation and credit, significantly exceeding spending on rural infrastructure and agricultural research and development (R&D). Yet evidence suggests that the economic returns on agricultural subsidies are close to zero, while those for rural infrastructure and agricultural R&D are very high. Public R&D spending and investment are also much more powerful than subsidies for the purpose of rural poverty reduction.

Not only is the present orientation of public expenditure in agriculture unhelpful for economic productivity, but it also discourages environmental sustainability. This is because agricultural subsidies tend to promote both excessive use of water as well as GHG emissions through a number of related channels. Power subsidies, for example, stimulate both high power consumption and high GHG emissions, as well as lift irrigation using tube wells, which causes excessive drawdown of groundwater and depletion of water tables.

Agriculture accounts for 90% of annual freshwater withdrawals, a proportion that is unusually high by international standards and that has hardly fallen over recent decades, despite the gradual decline in the relative importance of agriculture in the economy. Overall, freshwater withdrawals now absorb over 50% of internal renewable water resources, a proportion that has risen from about one-quarter in the later 1970s.

Livestock is another agricultural sector with significant potential economic and environmental gains. India has one of the largest livestock herds in the world. Productivity is generally low, however, with average milk yields about half of the world average for example.

Meanwhile, methane emissions from livestock are the largest source of agricultural GHGs in India, an outcome made worse by poor diet. There appear to be significant opportunities to boost economic returns and curb emissions by promoting better feeding and animal reproduction management to bring about a smaller, more productive herd. Opportunities to expand forest cover also offer significant opportunities for increased carbon sequestration, groundwater recharge and employment opportunities for forest communities.

DEVELOPMENT CHALLENGES AND OPPORTUNITIES IN BUILDING MORE PRODUCTIVE AND INCLUSIVE CITIES

The Government of India has rightly focused on the potential of "smart cities" as an important driver of development. The New Climate Economy report provides evidence for this proposition by detailing how more compact, connected and well-coordinated cities promote both development and greater energy and pollution efficiency, for example through agglomeration economies: the forces through which a more dense clustering of individuals and firms in urban areas promotes more innovation and faster productivity growth. Unfortunately, there are few automatic guarantees that urban development will necessarily evolve in this way. Market failures, policies and weak institutions can lead to much less productive and less clean outcomes.

India's urban population almost doubled from 222 million in 1990 to an estimated 410 million in 2014 and is expected to reach 800 million by 2050. Cities now contribute over two-thirds of GDP, bring in over 90% of government revenue and contribute the majority of jobs. But the pattern of urbanisation is also one rife with numerous stresses and dysfunctions: rapidly expanding urban sprawl, inadequate and unreliable urban infrastructure, high land prices, proliferating slums, growing congestion and travel times, reduced agglomeration economies, intense local air pollution and rising GHG emissions.

Rapid urban growth is occurring on many different margins and frontiers. Some of the most explosive growth is occurring in peri-urban areas, on the periphery of existing big cities. Restrictions on building per unit of land reduce the intensity with which city land is used, pushing up land prices, reducing average floor space and pushing businesses and households to seek cheaper land further and further away from city centres. Mumbai homes have only about 30 square feet per person, compared with 140 square feet per person in urban China, for example.

The dysfunctional patterns of urbanisation in India arise from a number of long-standing, deeply ingrown and mutually interlocking policy distortions and institutional weaknesses. Highly restrictive land regulations cause intense pressures for urban sprawl. Floor space indexes, which regulate the maximum allowable ratio of the gross built-up floor area to the area of a plot, are generally far lower than in many of the most economically dynamic and prosperous cities in the world, such as Shanghai, Hong Kong, New York and Tokyo. Rent control laws and the lack of a well-developed housing finance system also constrain the supply of new housing stock. Efficient functioning of land markets is also hampered by weak systems for appraising land values, determining property rights and conducting public land acquisitions.

Yet proposals to build more compact cities are countered by concerns that greater densities in urban cores would overwhelm the rickety and inadequate existing infrastructure of urban areas in terms of water supply, sewerage and sanitation, access to electricity and public transport. In 2011 only 61% of urban households had access to treated tap water. Among major Asian cities, Chennai and Delhi were ranked the two worst cities for hours of water availability. Clearly, a vast upgrading in the scale and quality of urban infrastructure is needed if India is to fully tap the potential of its cities.

Efforts to strengthen urban infrastructure and planning are in turn hampered by the weaknesses of urban governance and institutions. The Constitution defines 18 functions for devolution to the local government level. In practice, however, the allocation of responsibilities between various levels of government remains muddled. Local governments' administrative capacity and accountability to residents is limited at best, while their fiscal resources remain far below the levels needed to accomplish their tasks.

The government's intention to massively expand urban investment on "smart cities" provides a tremendous opportunity to simultaneously tackle these interlinked issues. In recent years the Jawaharlal Nehru National Urban Renewal Mission (JnNURM) has represented a major effort by central government to significantly increase the volume of resources for urban infrastructure development, while also encouraging policy and institutional reforms to improve the effectiveness with which such resources are used at both the state and urban local government level. A thorough impact evaluation of the JnNURM can help to lay the basis for a renewed and comprehensive urbanisation strategy in India.

"MAKE IN INDIA"-A BOOST TO THE MANUFACTURING SECTOR

The Prime Minister Narendra Modi, prior to the commencement of his maiden US visit, last month launched 'Make in India', a major national initiative which focuses on making India a global manufacturing hub.

Key thrust of the programme would be on cutting down in delays in manufacturing projects clearance, develop adequate infrastructure and make it easier for companies to do business in India. The 25 key sectors identified under the programme include automobiles, auto components, biotechnology, chemicals, defence manufacturing, electronic systems, food processing, leather, mining, oil & gas, ports, railways, ports and textile.

The national progamme aims at time-bound project clearances through a single online portal which will be further supported by the eight-member team dedicated to answering investor queries within 48 hours and addressing key issues including labor laws, skill development and infrastructure.

The objective of the mega programme is to ensure that manufacturing sector which contributes around 15% of the country's Gross Domestic Products is increased to 25% in next few years.

Speaking to more than 500 top global CEOs along with captains of Indian industry at the event in Vigyan Bhawan, New Delhi on September 25th, Prime Minister termed 'Make in India' initiative a lion step to usher in increased manufacturing in the country, which will ultimately generate more employment opportunities for the poor and give greater purchasing power in their hands. The mega even was watched live in several cities in India and abroad through video conferencing,

He urged the domestic as well as global investors not to look at India merely as a market, but instead see it as an opportunity. "When we talk of Make in India, we are not just offering a competitive situation and we give you an opportunity to create a huge market for your product. After all, handsome buyer is equally important as cost effective manufacturing.," Modi told a packed audience.

Cutting down on procedural delay

However, for making India an investment hub, the first and foremost importance step would be to create a efficient administrative machinery which would cut down on delays in project clearances. Economists say that India has been very stringent when it comes to giving procedural and regulatory clearances. Besides a time bound clearance from all regulatory authority would create a conducive environment for business.

The Prime Minister acknowledged that India being ranked low on the 'ease of doing business' ranking by World Bank and added that he has started to sensitize the Government officials in this regard. On his recent meeting with World Bank President Jim Yong Kim, Modi said "World Bank President was also expressing this worry. Probably we were 135th in the world at that time. If we have to come to 50 from 135 then Government alone can do this. If Government brings transparency in its decisions and rules, pushes works with simplicity we can occupy number 50 from 135 in ease of doing business,".

Delay in getting regulatory clearances lead to rise in cost of production. A leading multinational automobile major said "costs of production in India increase because of various government policies, procedures, regulations and the way some of the laws are implemented,". The quicker the government addresses these challenges its better for the industry to set up facilities in the country.

For providing better infrastructure for the industry, there has been a big constraint in term of land acquisition. Often land acquisition for the industrial purpose run into trouble at the local level.

Tax sops & focus on innovation

Economists have noted that with the globalization becoming a reality, Indian manufacturers will have to compete with the best and cheapest the rest of the world has to offer even in the domestic market.

They urged for providing tax concessions to any industry which would set up manufacturing facility in the country. Besides a critical aspect is the country's huge small and medium-sized industries which could play a big role in making the country take the next big leap in manufacturing.

"India should be more focused towards novelty and innovation for the sectors indentified and integration with the country's premier institute for carrying out research and development would be critical to the success of the make in India programme," a leading industrialist said.

Skill development & thrust on education

Stressing that his government has given top priority to skill development, Prime Minister had said the government is currently doing mapping for assessing skill manpower demand for specific sectors. He noted that there has to be synchronization between the objectives of the government, academic world, industry and job seekers for ensuring that industry specific skills are imparted.

Experts argue that the country needs to focus on quality education not just skill development. "In the emerging economy, people will need to continuously learn new skills to meet the economy's changing requirements," an official with an industry association observed.

Prime Minister also promised that specific sectors would be asked to access Industrial Training Institutes (ITIs) located across the country to train manpower locally as per their needs. "You will get a good worker for your industry and our ITI will start running. Our youngsters will get employment, his family will be strengthened and better purchasing power will help the economy. ," Modi told top industrialists.

In the last couple of years, National Skill Development Agency (NSDA) initiated work on creating a labour market information system which would help industry sourcing their manpower requirement.

After getting information on labour market, the government would provide accredition to manpower agencies so that the industry can access information on the manpower requirement.

Reforms in the labour laws

Besides the skill development, labour law flexibility is a key element for the success of this campaign for increasing manufacturing in the country. Economists say that "labour law flexibility does not imply 'hire and fire' policy, it's about providing a sound social safety net to workers."

Experts say that the country has some of the most comprehensive labour laws at the same time a large parts of working population do not have access to social security net.

Prime Minister had stressed the faster the bulk of Indian middle class increases, the faster people move from poverty to middle class, the faster will be their conversion into a favourable market for the world. He said his government's focus will be on physical infrastructure creation as well as creating a digital network for making India a hub for global manufacturing of goods ranging from cars to softwares, satellites to submarines and paper to power.

A leading Economist said the big challenge for 'Make in India' campaign would face constant comparison with China's 'Made in China' campaign. The China launched the campaign at the same day as India seeking to retain its manufacturing prowess. "India should constantly keep up its strength so as to outpace China's supremacy in the manufacturing sector," he noted.

Categorically stating that there is a need for some fundamental changes in Indian economy so that the country emerges as global manufacturing base, Modi explained "on the one hand, manufacturing growth is to be promoted, at the same time we need to ensure that direct benefit goes to the youngsters of India. He should get employment so that there is improvement in the economic situation of even the poorest family. These poor should move towards middle class and there purchasing power should improve. This will lead to manufacturing growth and growth of the market,".

Demographic dividend

Notwithstanding the challenges faced in making India a manufacturing hub, the country is poised to reap rich dividend for being one of the youngest nations in the world.

According to reports by 2020, India is set to become the world's youngest country with 64% of its population in the working age group.

With the Western countries, Japan and even China aging, this demographic potential offers India and its growing economy an edge that economists believe could add a significant 2% to the GDP growth rate annually.

Prime Minister also had said that India is the only country in the world which offers the unique combination of democracy, demography, and demand from a rising middle class.

Besides, the campaign would ensure closer centre and states relations for promoting India as a global manufacturing hub. "If investment comes in the States, it comes in India also. States and Centre should work collectively, shoulder to shoulder as a team. they should find solution together and things move forward,". Modi urged.

Although a sound beginning has been made for the Make in India campaign, now the ball is in the government's court to ensure its success.

FULFILLING THE PROMISE OF INDIA'S MANUFACTURING SECTOR

India's manufacturers have a golden chance to emerge from the shadow of the country's services sector and seize more of the global market. McKinsey analysis finds that rising demand in India, together with the multinationals' desire to diversify their production to include low-cost plants in countries other than China, could together help India's manufacturing sector to grow sixfold by 2025, to $1 trillion, while creating up to 90 million domestic jobs.

Capturing this opportunity will require India's manufacturers to improve their productivity dramatically—in some cases, by up to five times current levels. The country's central and state governments can help by dismantling barriers in markets for land, labor, infrastructure, and some products. But the lion's share of the improvement must come from India's manufacturers themselves.

Recognizing this, a few leading ones are upgrading their competitiveness by bolstering their operations to improve the productivity of labor and capital, while launching targeted programs to train the plant operators, managers, maintenance engineers, and other professionals the country needs to reach its manufacturing potential. A closer look at the experiences of these companies offers lessons for other Indian manufacturers and for global product makers considering opportunities in India.

Made in India?

India's manufacturers have long performed below their potential. Although the country's manufacturing exports are growing (particularly in skill-intensive sectors such as auto components, engineered goods, generic pharmaceuticals, and small cars) its manufacturing sector generates just 16 percent of India's GDP—much less than the 55 percent from services. Moreover, a majority of India's largest manufacturers don't return their cost of capital, a factor that dampens investment in the sector and makes it less attractive than its counterparts in competing economies, such as China and Thailand. Indeed, China's manufacturers captured nearly 45 percent of the global growth in manufacturing exports from low-cost countries between 2001 and 2010, whereas India accounted for a paltry 5 percent.

Nonetheless, India's rapidly expanding economy, which has grown by 7 percent a year over the past decade, gives the country's manufacturers a huge opportunity to reverse the tide. History shows that as incomes rise, the demand for consumer goods skyrockets. And many of India's consumption sectors—including food and beverages, textiles and apparel, and electrical equipment and machinery—have reached this inflection point. In fact, our research suggests that these sectors will grow from 12 to 20 percent annually over the next 15 years.

To be sure, global economic growth is poised to create opportunities for low-cost manufacturers everywhere: by 2015 the market for manufactured goods from low-cost countries will more than double, to nearly $8 trillion a year. China will probably capture much of the growth. Still, we estimate that up to $5 trillion a year will be up for grabs as global companies seek to diversify production and sources of supply beyond China, both to address rising factor costs there and to chase domestic demand in other countries.

India has a massive workforce, an emerging supply base, and access to natural resources needed in production—notably, iron ore and aluminum for engineered goods, cotton for textiles, and coal for power generation. The country could become a viable manufacturing alternative to China in industries ranging from apparel to auto components and might even dominate some skill-intensive manufacturing sectors.

If India's manufacturing sector realized its full potential, it could generate 25 to 30 percent of GDP by 2025, thus propelling the country into the manufacturing big leagues, along with China, Germany, Japan, and the United States. Along the way, we estimate that India could create 60 million to 90 million new manufacturing jobs and become an attractive investment destination for its own entrepreneurs and multinational companies.

India's product makers must embrace global best practices in operations—while tailoring them to India's unique environment—to improve the efficiency and effectiveness of the country's manufacturing investments dramatically. A look at how some Indian companies are making inroads in these areas suggests a path that others can follow.

Bolster operations

India's legacy of industrial protectionism has left many of the country's manufacturers uncompetitive. To seize the opportunities now available to them, they must dramatically increase the productivity of their labor and capital. The rewards could be significant: a McKinsey benchmarking study of 75 Indian manufacturers found that for an average company, the potential productivity improvements represented about seven percentage points in additional returns on sales.

Improve labor productivity

Indian manufacturers lag behind their global peers in production planning, supply chain management, quality, and maintenance—areas that contribute to their lower productivity. Consequently, workers in India's manufacturing sector are almost four and five times less productive, on average, than their counterparts in Thailand and China, respectively.

Nonetheless, some Indian companies are making strides. Tata Steel, for instance, improved its output per worker by a factor of eight between 1998 and 2011, largely by adapting its operational and management practices to India's unique conditions. The company dramatically improved the output of its blast furnaces, for example, by learning to adjust them continually to account for the large variations in the ash content of Indian coal from shipment to shipment. In this way, the steelmaker can burn coal with a high ash content more efficiently than would otherwise be possible.

The company has also made significant organizational changes to support the new ways of working. To make employees more accountable, for example, Tata Steel reduced the number of managerial layers to 5, from 13. It also began investing heavily in building analytical and interpersonal skills among frontline managers and staff to ensure access to scarce competencies. Today, the company's Shavak Nanavati Technical Institute trains more than 2,000 employees a year in both "hard" skills as well as "soft" ones, such as conflict resolution. Together, these moves strengthened the company's focus on continuous improvement—Tata Steel won the coveted Deming Prize in 2008 for advances in process excellence and quality improvements—and helped it become one of the world's lowest-cost steel producers.

Improve capital productivity

India's manufacturers must also improve the productivity of their capital, in some cases by 50 percent or more. While such improvements are challenging, they are possible if companies set bold targets and adopt an "owner–entrepreneur" mind-set when tackling large capital projects or making other big investments.

For example, a global mining and metals company that was setting up aluminum smelter operations in India set a capital cost target 50 percent lower than the industry's global average. The company then empowered its project teams to reach the goal—for example, by giving them greater freedom to make decisions about capital specifications and which low-cost equipment suppliers to use.

Moreover, the company did not give the contract out on an EPC basis. Instead, it brought together a mix of Chinese and European companies to finalize the design and to supply the equipment needed, and the integration and commissioning work was done in-house, thus saving much of the margin that would otherwise have been given away. Together, these moves helped the company to launch its Indian smelter operations at a capital cost 50 percent below industry averages (and 20 percent less than other players in the same market spent).

Many Indian companies are also assessing the technical design of their capital equipment to make trade-offs between capital expenditures and life cycle expectations for reliability—essentially "Indianizing" the specifications. Tata Power, for example, has lowered its capital expenditures in a drive to identify relatively inexpensive designs and specifications for big projects. During the planning stages of a new 4,000-megawatt facility, for instance, the company brought together customers, suppliers, and Tata engineers to make a number of Indianized design decisions. These included using cheaper welded tubes instead of seamless ones in feedwater heaters and redesigning the layout of the turbine-generator building to make it more compact. Together, such trade-offs saved the company more than $100 million in capital outlays while preserving the plant's core capabilities and meeting standards for safety and reliability.

Meanwhile, some Indian companies are working to raise the productivity of their*existing* assets—for example, by focusing on the reliability of equipment. In our experience, throughput improvements from 40 to 100 percent are possible when Indian companies apply traditional lean-management techniques to keep machines running longer and to reduce time wasted during retooling and production line changeovers.

Tata Steel, for instance, focused on standardized tasks throughout its mills and trained workers to uncover the root causes of equipment problems. One of the company's melting shops we studied raised its production dramatically over two years by standardizing jobs and empowering its operations and maintenance employees to identify potential problems of key machines that had previously been prone to creating production bottlenecks.

Targeted skill development

India's manufacturers could learn a lot from the IT sector's experience in promoting the large-scale development of skills. India's IT services and business-process-outsourcing sectors together hire nearly a million new recruits a year and bring them up to speed in just months.

A key factor in this success was the early recognition among Indian IT companies, back in the 1990s, that the number of engineering graduates in computer sciences wouldn't meet the needs of the country's burgeoning IT sector. In response, Infosys, Wipro, and other companies began hiring graduates from all engineering disciplines and using in-house curricula and faculties to build skills among new hires. That approach ultimately led to the formation of a successful network of independent, privately owned computer-training institutes, such as Aptech and NIIT.

India's manufacturers should follow a similar path by establishing in-house training centers to promote vital manufacturing roles, including those of fitters, machinists, maintenance engineers, and welders. Some Indian companies are already taking matters into their own hands. For example, to impart vocational skills, India's largest automaker, Maruti Suzuki, has adopted six technical institutes across the country, some in regions with little manufacturing presence. By using the company's own managers as faculty for some classes, Maruti Suzuki inculcates trainees with a strong feel for its culture as well. The automaker is now expanding its training programs to include employees of key suppliers.

Although training programs make good business sense, they are also increasingly necessary to get local populations to accept the establishment of a manufacturing footprint in India. Tata Motors' partnership with the Gujarat state government to improve the skills of local workers, for example, helped the company to ameliorate concerns about the displacement of residents by the construction of a Tata Nano car factory, while giving the company access to new workers. Today, nearly 1,000 people who live within a 10-kilometer radius of this Sanand factory make Nanos. Similarly, Tata Steel has agreed with the Orissa state government to train and improve the skills of workers living near a planned steel plant in Kalinganagar. The company has pledged to give local villagers jobs in the project's execution and operations.

Frontline workers aren't the only ones whose skills need upgrading; India's manufacturers must also improve those of managers. Consider the experience of the cement maker Holcim, where executives set—and achieved—such goals as significantly improving the reliability and energy efficiency of the production process, as well as other important operating metrics at the company's Indian subsidiaries.

At the heart of this initiative is an academy the company set up in its Indian plant to help future leaders bolster their skills through a "field and forum" approach that intersperses class work with hands-on fieldwork in the form of operational-improvement projects. Similarly, Holcim trains its managers to focus performance dialogues with frontline employees on the importance of identifying the root causes of problems and of finding potential solutions through cross-functional teams. The company uses operational "war rooms" in its Indian plants to serve as a clearinghouse for the best ideas and to uncover the best contributions. In parallel, Holcim created an ambitious leadership program to support the personal development of up-and-coming manufacturing leaders.

The combination of rocketing domestic demand and the multinationals' desire to diversify their manufacturing footprint offers Indian product makers a once-in-a-generation opportunity to emerge from the shadow of the country's services sector. By improving their productivity and bolstering operations, they could become an engine of economic prosperity for the whole country.

HOW CAN THE NEW GOVERNMENT MAKE INDIA A GLOBAL MANUFACTURING HUB?

The recent launch of the "Make in India" campaign by Prime Minister Mr. Narendra Modi where leading businessmen and CEOs of about 3000 companies from 30 countries were present is an impressive effort on the part of the new Government to boost investor confidence in the country. Moreover, Mr. Modi's recent US visit and meeting with CEOs of some of the top global firms like Goldman Sachs, Google, General Electric, Cargill, Boeing and many others definitely set the ground for investment in India.

But at the ground level, there are a lot of challenges that the government has to overcome in order to turn the vision of achieving a sustainable 10% growth in the manufacturing sector into reality. This research paper aims to analyse the key issues facing the "Make in India" vision and recommend possible strategies to deal with the same.

Topics	**DB 2014 Rank**
Starting a Business	156
Dealing with Construction Permits	183
Getting Electricity	134
Registering Property	115
Getting Credit	30
Protecting Minority Investors	21
Paying Taxes	154
Trading Across Borders	122
Enforcing Contracts	186
Resolving Insolvency	135

Source: Doing Business report, World Bank Group

Below are highlighted some of the issues which the new Government has to take care of for turning the "Make in India" vision into a reality:

Improving the ease of doing business in India: According to World Bank report, India ranks 142 out of 189 countries in the category for ease of doing business based on surveys conducted in the two major cities of India, Mumbai and Delhi prior to the new Government came to power. To increase investor sentiment, it is necessary that the Government works to improve the various components of Doing Business indicators like starting a business, dealing with construction permits, getting electricity, registering property, getting credit, protecting minority investors, paying taxes, trading across borders, enforcing contracts and resolving insolvency because it is these indicators that a firm looks at before going forward with an investment decision in a country. The Ease of Doing Business score is obtained by conducting surveys of start ups in the largest business cities of India. While calculating scores for each parameter the Doing Business (DB) group takes into consideration the time taken and the cost incurred by a company to complete the various legal formalities for each parameter. The break-up of the Ease of Doing Business score parameter wise is given below for Mumbai:

Thus, as seen from the figures in the red, it is primarily in the areas of starting a business, dealing with construction permits, paying taxes and enforcing contracts among the other indicators that the Government needs to focus on. Some of the suggested reforms for the above mentioned areas of concern are mentioned below:

Starting a Business: Rapidly developing economies around the world have taken steps to make it easier for starting a business, like streamlining procedures by setting up a one-stop shop, making procedures simpler or faster by introducing information technology and reducing or eliminating minimum capital requirements. India should therefore implement similar reforms to reap benefits like greater firm satisfaction and savings and more registered businesses, more financial resources and job opportunities.

Dealing with construction permits: Regulation of the construction sector is critical to protect the public. However excessive constraints on the construction sector may compel companies to pay bribes to pass inspections or simply build illegally to avoid the excessive costs in time and money incurred for compliance to regulations leading to hazardous constructions that put public safety at risk. Therefore, smart regulations ensure that standards are met while making compliance easy and accessible to all. In an effort to ensure building safety while keeping compliance costs reasonable, governments around the world have adopted coherent and transparent rules, efficient processes, stricter deadlines and adequate allocation of resources.

Paying taxes: Taxes are essential sources of revenue for the Government. However, the power of taxation should be exercised with extreme caution and judiciousness so that it does not negatively impact the economy and the investment climate. Policies like retrospective taxation which negatively impact investor confidence must be done away with. Online tax filing and payment should be introduced in as many tax parameters as possible. Also, taxes on essential and elastic goods and services should be kept low so that there is not a heavy tax burden on either the consumer or the producer. The implementation of the Goods and Services Tax will foster a climate of investment and growth by bringing about myriad benefits like broadening the tax base, eliminating indirect taxes, central sales tax, state-level sales tax, entry tax, stamp duty, taxes on transportation of goods and services ,et cetera. It is expected to help build a transparent and corruption-free tax administration. GST will be levied only at the destination point and not at various points unlike the current tax system where a manufacturer needs to pay tax when a finished product moves out from the factory and it is again taxed at the retail outlet when sold. It is estimated that India will gain $15 billion a year by implementing GST as it would promote exports, raise employment and boost growth.

Enforcing Contracts: In India, settling commercial disputes is an extremely costly and time consuming process. According to data collected by Doing Business, contract enforcement takes on the average 1420 days, costs 39.6 % of the value of the claim and requires 46 procedures. The Supreme court should enforce short and strict deadlines for dispute settlement and reduce the number of unnecessary formalities associated with dispute settlements.

LAND ACQUISITION CHALLENGES:

One of the very important initial steps for establishment of manufacturing facilities by a firm is acquiring land. Under the new Land acquisition act, developers would require the consent of up to 80 per cent of people whose land is acquired for private projects and of 70 per cent of land owners in the case of public-private partnership projects. But the greatest concern in acquiring such land is the proper rehabilitation and resettlement of affected inhabitants of those lands. The government has to identify and devise strategies for the rehabilitation and resettlement of the displaced people failing which the result can be serious conflicts. Moreover, the rehabilitation and resettlement also becomes a costly venture.

Land acquisitions for factories, roads and housing projects in states like Haryana and UP have sparked clashes between farmers and state authorities, resulting in huge project delays. One alternative for the government is to acquire only wasteland for industrialisation purposes. This will eliminate the requirement of the consents and the costs of rehabilitation and resettlement and therefore lead to speedier execution of projects. The following categories of land have been classified as wasteland as per the Wasteland Atlas of India in association with National Remote Sensing Centre, Indian Space Research Organisation:

- Barren
- Degraded forest
- Gullied land
- Ravenous land
- Salt affected land
- Salt encrustation
- Shifting cultivation
- Snow covered area
- Steep sloping area
- Waterlogged area
- Upland without scrub
- Land with scrub.

According to data available in Wasteland atlas of India as per 2003 figures, a total of 552692.26 square kilometres of wasteland exist in India out of the total geographical area of 3287263 square kilometres.

This vast amount of wasteland presents a huge potential for setting up manufacturing facilities after appropriate engineering and geographical assessments of these areas. Moreover, acquisition of these wastelands is unlikely to invite any criticism and hence we can look at speedier execution of development projects.

IMPROVING THE EMPLOYABILITY OF GENERAL AND ENGINEERING GRADUATES:

The greatest asset of any firm is its human resource. Companies will set up manufacturing facilities in India only if it is able to find requisite amount of good quality skilled labour in the country. Around 51% of the workforce is employed in the agricultural sector which contributes to only about 17% of the GDP and around 22% of the workforce is employed in the manufacturing sector which contributes to around 26% of GDP.

However, various surveys conducted on employability reveals a vast skills gap between graduate skills and market needs. According to Higher Education in India: Vision 2030 , a report produced by international consultants Ernst and Young for the Federation of Indian Chambers of Commerce and Industry (FICCI), 75% of IT graduates, 55% of manufacturing, 55% of healthcare and 50% of Banking and Insurance graduates are deemed unemployable. Moreover, the National Association of Software and Services Companies (NASSCOM) maintains that of around 3 million graduates each year, less than a third of graduates of engineering colleges and only 10% to 15% of regular graduates are employable. It is therefore important to dwell upon the possible reasons which cause low employability of Indian graduates in general and engineering graduates in particular.

In most of the engineering institutions the course curriculum is by and large, theoretical in nature and students are not made aware of the applications of the theories in industry. The programmes and their course content reflect lack of interaction among academic institutions and industries. In the process, the curriculum quite often fails to meet the needs of the industries. Not many structural changes have taken place in the curriculum even though rapid developments have been taking place continuously in the field of science and technology.

Moreover, the evaluation system has not been made robust enough to find out the knowledge level of the students. The philosophy of the semester system and the continuous evaluation process are not being understood by the students and also by the faculty members. Thus they are applied in a routine manner and the students concentrate only on the grades and not on learning. Since there is a lack of interaction between academic learnings and industries, graduates coming out of technical institutions do not have the adequate knowledge to implement projects or carry out research independently. This creates a severe mismatch between employer needs and the skills of the graduates. Since job requirements are continuously changing it is quite difficult to produce tailor made engineers unless there is regular and structured interaction between academia and industries.

In this regard, to facilitate technical institutions to respond to the need of providing state of art Telecom equipment based operational skill to engineering graduates to enhance their qualification, competence and employability by enhanced skill up-gradation, AICTE has signed an MoU with BSNL to use the training facilities and faculty of BSNL for the benefit of students of AICTE approved institutions under its Employability Enhancement Training Programme (EETP). Likewise, similar enhancement programmes can be carried out by MoUs with companies in various other sectors like automobile, power, consumer electronics, heavy machinery, construction as well as defence.

Similar measures already exist in some of the top of the world universities like MIT, Harvard and Stanford. Also, since most of the future processes are going to be integrated through Information Technology, Government should make computer education compulsory starting from the school level itself so that the country is able to produce enough computer educated labour to cater to the demand in IT and ITES BPOs. Such measures on the part of the Government will go a long way in bridging the gap between graduate skills and market needs.

However all above mentioned points sound relevant when we look at higher education in isolation only. If we see the whole education system starting from the elementary level we find that the problems lie at every stage of our education system. At the school level we find that the present day syllabus does not stress simple and subtle concepts, but involves tiresome details.

Most entrance tests for admission to better known institutions emphasise speed and memory and not calm and collected thinking. Thus an all out effort is needed to produce readily-employable technical man power in the country. The improvement of infrastructure, redesign of curricula, improvement of teaching-learning methods and attracting well qualified teachers, along with the above mentioned measures to bring in industry interaction along with academices ,are only a few steps that could be initiated by individual institutions.

Infrastructure development of major roads and highways in the country:

It is needless to say that well developed and well maintained infrastructure, particularly, roads and highways is vital for an efficient inbound and outbound logistics of a manufacturing firm to ensure efficient movement of raw materials and finished goods across the country as roads carry 65% of its freight in the country. India has a total of 48.65 lakh kilometre of road network comprising National Highways (92,851 Km), State Highways (1,38,489 Km), Major District Roads, Rural roads and Urban roads (All together 46.34 Lakh kilometre) as per figures from website of Ministry of Road Transport and Highways as on 31st March, 2014. National Highways comprise 1.7% of India's total road network but carry 40% of road traffic.

Most of these highways are two lane highways. Only 10,000 Km of highways have been widened to four lanes with two lanes in each direction as of August, 2011. Moreover, as of 2010, 19064 Km of NH were still single-laned roads. With increase in vehicular traffic and congestion in the major cities of India and for smooth movement of large container trucks, it is imperative that the Government in association with private parties through public-private partnerships convert the single-lane or double-lane national and state highways to four or six lane roads to cater to the growing congestion problem in India.

However, most of these conversion projects are stuck at various stages of bureaucratic delays. With the new government at the centre, we can hope for faster execution of projects by removal of unnecessary approval stages and thereby leading faster clearances.

Moreover, to improve the flow of traffic, Government should work to introduce smart traffic control systems whereby real time data on vehicular traffic flow can be obtained through sources like traffic cameras and can be used to control the sequence and duration of traffic signals at major junctions across India. With these initiatives, the manufacturing sector will receive a shot in the arm to tread the path of development.

CAPACITY ADDITION IN THE POWER SECTOR TO MEET INDUSTRIAL ENERGY DEMAND:

Without the power industry, no other industry would survive. India has an installed capacity of 253.389 GW as of August 2014.

In a May 2014 report by India's Central Electricity Authority, India had an energy requirement of 1048672 Million Units (MU) of energy out of which only 995157 MU of energy were available and out of a peak demand of 147815 MW, 144788 MW was the supply. Also, the 17th electric power survey of India report claims that over 2010-11, India's industrial demand accounted for 35% of electrical power requirement which will further grow significantly as more and more manufacturing facilities come up.

As per the 12th five year plan, the Government had targeted a capacity addition of 88,537 MW out of which only 46,766 MW have been achieved so far as of August,2014. Delay in environmental clearances and shortage of fuel supply are some of the major challenges faced by the Indian power sector. The

Supreme Court's decision to deallocate 204 coal mines is further going to add to the woes of the power sector. To meet the fuel shortage and avoid importing coal in order to prevent increasing cost of power production, the Government must focus on raising domestic coal production and improving quality of the existing mines by ensuring efficient and transparent allocation of coal blocks. Moreover, the Government should also work on scaling up other renewable sources of power like Hydro by focusing on resource rich states like Arunachal Pradesh, J&K and Himachal Pradesh after accurate and proper assessment of the environmental impact of setting up power plants in these states.

All environmental and safety factors must be considered in total before execution of any power project so that the local people and various other stakeholders are assured of safety and minimal environmental impact due to operation of the proposed power projects in order to avoid situations similar to those against Kundankulam Nuclear Power Plant of NPCIL and Lower Subansiri Hydro-electric project of NHPC limited.

Above all, there must be sufficient cooperation between the Center and the State in this regard so that the funds allocated by the Center are properly utilized by the State towards planning and development of power projects.

Strengthening the capabilities of the CISF to meet growing demand for industrial security:

It is highly probable that most of the future manufacturing facilities will have to be set up in remote areas of India, some of which are infested with insurgency and terrorism.

Major industrial installations in India like oil refineries, nuclear installations, space installations and other heavy engineering industries have always been on terror radar. Currently, the Central Industrial Security Force (CISF) is the elite security force which provides security cover to 300 industrial units and other establishments located all over India. With rise in establishment of manufacturing facilities and the growing threat of internal as well as external terrorism, the demand for industrial security cover will rise manifold.

Earlier the CISF used to protect installations set up only by wholly owned subsidiaries of the Central Government but the CISF Act has been amended after 26/11 Mumbai attacks to provide dirrect security cover to private installations which will be a great benefit for the private companies who were earlier employing poorly trained security personnel to guard their establishments. Further capacity addition of the CISF in terms of personnel, military gear and logistics needs to be effected to increase the strength from the current strength of 165000 personnel and training to be provided in line with other elite counter insurgency units like NSG and Marine Commandos so that they are able to provide the best of security even in the most hostile of terror infected regions.

Conclusion

Although the ease of doing business score went down to 142 from 134 last year, the World Bank has taken care to distance this downslide from the NDA government which took charge barely a week earlier and World Bank has used data till May 2014 whereas most measures to improve doing business were undertaken subsequent to that. The various measures undertaken by the NDA Government to address issues related to economic growth, delay in Government decisions and reforms in the Labour law, Land law and taxation have kick started the manufacturing sector and shot the GDP growth by 5.7 % in the last quarter. The Modi Government has also signed a staggering USD 35 Billion investment deal with Japan for infrastructure development. If governance continues in the current manner, we can definitely hope to see significant and sustainable growth in the manufacturing sector and progress tow ards India becoming a global manufacturing hub.

OUTLOOK FOR INDIAN MANUFACTURING IN THE 21ST CENTURY

The outlook for the manufacturing component, of the industry sector, of the Indian economy will, naturally depend on the prospects for the total economy. So, we begin the analysis in this paper with a possible total vision for India. From that we derive the requisite vision for manufacturing, in order to power the economy and the nation towards her vision.

However, visions are not just wishes, like horses, which beggars could ride, in their fantasy. The actualisation of the manufacturing vision will depend on the ability of Indian industry and its partners to meet the exacting demands of competitiveness.

Indian manufacturing could ride on two legs — the strength of domestic demand; and competitiveness in the world market. The outlook also depends on how well certain public policy issues surrounding manufacturing are resolved. In the end, the shape of Indian manufacturing in the 21st century will be the net result of actions by the concerned stakeholders. The paper ends with suggestions for their actions.

INDIA VISION

What are the prospects for India? The answer to this question has tended to oscillate over the last seven years, since the 1991 paradigm shift of the policy frame of the Indian state from the earlier licence-permit raj towards liberalisation and globalisation.

i. Independent Indian agencies like the NCAER and CMIE believed by 1993 that the economy may have been re-positioned from the earlier 4% trend average growth p.a. to about 7% growth.
ii. Multilateral institutions like the World Bank, IMF and ADB also came to share this view.
iii. Bilaterally, countries like the U.S., Germany and Australia had identified India as a major, among the top ten etc. trading partner.
iv. Many MNCs were discovering and rediscovering India as an emerging market.
v. Merchant and investment bankers were recommending India to their global clients.
vi. Indian infrastructure — power, telecom, roads and ports

—-needing about 200 billions US dollars, — considered a major investment opportunity.

vii. Foreign institutional investors seeing the scope for higher returns, from portfolio investment.

viii. A series of socio-political events such as the demolition of the Babri mosque in December 1992, scams in the stock market in 1994, in telecom tenders, the fall of two coalition governments after the 1996 elections, and another coalition after the 1998 elections, the nuclear explosions, sanctions, etc. have been casting shadows on the above prospects.

ix. There has been a domestic down turn since 1995.

x. This has been worsened by the S.E. Asian currency crisis; the recessions of Japan and Korea; currency devaluations, etc.

The fundamentals of the Indian economy still appear strong enough to go by the core philosophy of mathematical statistics, namely that beyond

a. Random fluctuations;
b. Seasonal variations; and
c. Cyclical factors; there is the
d. Secular, long term trend.

The trend for India may be an upward trend for the next twenty years, averaging the following kinds of growth rates per annum –

i. GNP growth of 7% plus;
ii. Industry growth of 10% plus; and
iii. Export growth of 15%.

I have been advocating a three dimensional Vision for India in the 21st century.

a. An *Economic Vision* of emerging as the third largest economy, next only to the U.S. and China, based on a sustained average 8% p.a. GNP growth, 12% industrial growth and 15% export growth, for about two decades.

b. A *Social Vision* of improving the quality of life of all the people, reducing inequalities and inequities based on region, class, growth, gender, age, etc.

c. A *Spiritual Vision* of practising and sharing with humanity the ageless wisdom and guidance of Indian philosophy and heritage, in achieving material prosperity, without damaging the individual psyche, family, community and ecology.

INDIA MANUFACTURING VISION

The vision of manufacturing is, naturally, intimately connected to the national vision.

i. The *direct* relationship is with the Economic Vision.

ii. But the *process* of how we go about actualising the Manufacturing and Economic Visions has an *indirect* bearing on the Social and Spiritual Visions.

The relationship is a two-way interactive one.

a. The Manufacturing Vision is broadly a *derivative* of the India Vision.

b. It can also be one of the significant *drivers* of the India Vision.

I propose, to begin with, a two part Vision for Indian Manufacturing.

i. To be a mighty *locomotive* for expanding and catering to a huge *domestic* market.

ii. To make India a *power house* of supply to the *global* market. In due course, additional dimensions can be added to the Vision. E.g.:-

iii. To carry Indian manufacturing capabilities overseas, based on strategic considerations, with linkages to Indian technology, capital and management.

iv. To fulfill deep social purposes through multiplier job creation, protection of the ecology, and *daanam*, philanthropy to health, education, art and spiritual pursuits.

MANUFACTURING COMPETITIVENESS FRAMEWORK

The future of Indian manufacturing will, understandably, depend primarily on the degree of its competitiveness. The competitiveness, in turn, rests on the following factors.

i. Indigenous sources of quality raw materials at low relative cost.

ii. Cost effective technologies for conversion into products, packaging, transportation, storage, delivery and service.

iii. Adequate size of domestic market to allow for economies of scale and scope.

iv. Sufficient ex-factory cost advantage, to absorb the costs of movement and distribution in export markets.

v. Intense domestic competition, which serves to prepare the players for foreign competition, both through imports, and in export markets.

vi. Visionary and competent management, which can formulate and implement robust business strategies, including especially marketing and manufacturing strategies; and mobilise the necessary physical, financial and human resources.

vii. Supportive physical and social infrastructure and work culture.

MANUFACTURING FOR THE HOME MARKET

There are many industries where manufacturing has high potential, given the country comparative advantages, such as raw materials and local demand. However, the growth is not, naturally, guaranteed. It is contingent upon competent management, infrastructure, industry structure and other supportive factors.

i. Industrial Raw Materials-Substantial deposits of iron ore, non-ferrous ores, coal, lignite, limestone, granite etc. offer scope for expansion of steel, aluminium, zinc, copper, power, cement and building materials. The necessary restructuring and consolidation towards a few viable players seem to have begun. In steel, the main players may be Tisco, Ispat, Jindal and SAIL. In cement L&T, India Cements, ACC, Gujarat Ambuja, Birla and JK.

ii. Agricultural Raw Materials:

   a. India has already been, for some years now, the world's second largest producer of milk. It is expected to become the largest by 2000 AD. While ensuring adequate consumption of milk by the poor, there will be a rising surplus for processing, packaging, branding, local marketing and even exports. Amul, SmithKline Beecham Consumer Healthcare, Cadbury, Nestle, Vadilal, Hindustan Lever and others are expanding their capacities. This is to be expected, with the world's largest bovine population. According to the Indian Dairy Association, India has a 15% share of world milk – 70 million tonnes, out of 460. At a growth rate of 5.5% p.a., it could reach 230 million tonnes by 2020, more than one third of the global output of 630 millions. The current dairy business volume is estimated at Rs. 80,000 crores. There is still scope for improvement. The milk share of 15% is less than the livestock share of 19% — 272 mn. out of 1.4 billion. India has even greater dominance in buffaloes – home to more than half. Dairy products are helped by the fact that buffaloes yield, higher fat content, 55% of India's total milk output. There is also a growing infrastructure for logistics management, especially on the milk procurement side, with 90,000 village cooperatives, 170 district unions and 23 state federations. There is also a critical mass knowledge network, with 31 veterinary colleges and 80 agricultural research institutes.

   We elaborated somewhat on dairy, as a case study, with which many urban educated Indians may not be familiar, to illustrate its potential for manufacturing growth. Much still remains to be done. For example, the milk yield per animal in India is 522 kg. p.a. compared to 5,000 kg. In the U.S., Australia and the Netherlands.

b. Perhaps not quite so spectacular as the dairy industry, there is scope for manufacturing in several other agri-businesses.

- Edible oils
- Fruits
- Cotton
- Vegetables
- Tea
- Flowers
- Coffee
- Spices
- Rubber
- Herbs.

iii. FMCG -A variety of factors will also create immense scope for manufacture of fast moving consumer goods.

a. The progressive fall in the percentage of the population below the poverty line. A lower middle class of about 400 million and an underclass of about 200 million.

b. Rising levels of literacy.

c. Assertion of women, including in the rural areas.

d. Spread of ideas and life styles, especially through TV.

e. Changing life styles, such as in the use of tooth powder/pastes, bathing soaps, washing suds, processed and packed foods, beverages and snacks.

The rising volumes for a potentially huge domestic market, will lead to falling unit cost and relative price, making import less of a threat. It is possible that some or more of these goods may be made by MNC controlled or JV plants in India. That would still be *Indian* manufacturing, although not controlled by Indian *promoters*. It will have the potential for high value addition in India, to the benefit of many stakeholders —- customers, dealers, vendors, employees, FI and retail investors.

iv. Durables-Although initially smaller than FMCG, this segment of manufacturing also has the potential to grow, for the following kinds of reasons.

   a. Rising middle class of about 250 million, including the urban middle income groups and the relative rural rich.

   b. An upper class, high income group of about 50 million.

   c. International travel, study, work, stay and exposure to contemporary, higher technology, premium durables for

      - the kitchen,
      - bedroom,
      - living areas,
      - transportation, and
      - entertainment.

   In this category, local manufacture by MNCs is even more likely, compared to the FMCG, because of their historical lead in product and process technology, brand equity and on-going high investments in R&D. Initially and in the medium term, even imports are possible. However as the volumes build up, the ubiquitous MNC product manufacturing life cycle will apply —-CKD, SKD, local assembly, local procurement, total production and even exports.

v. Industrial Intermediates-In many of these, Indian manufacturing is vulnerable to low growth, downsizing and even closure.

a. Where the economies of scale and scope are very large; and that industry is tending towards a global oligopoly of three to five players, such as –
   - Chemicals.
   - Ferrous and non-ferrous –
   - Ingots,
   - Blooms,
   - Billets; and even Sections.

b. Where there is a severe raw material shortage, such as-
   - Paper.
   - Coking Coal.

vi. Capital Goods-This sector tends to be even more dominated globally by a few players.
   - Computer, Telecom, IT hardware – in all the segments-
   - the basic infrastructure;
   - the service providers;
   - the customers' premises.
   - Production Equipment such as-
   - Flexible manufacturing systems,
   - CNC, CAD, CAM
   - Transfer lines, and
   - Heavy machine tools.

In these cases also, domestic manufacturing has some scope in the following ways –

a. As the volumes build up, the importing MNC may start local assembly, and gradual value addition.
b. Local suppliers of components and sub-assemblies.
c. Small, niche segments.

MANUFACTURING FOR EXPORT

There are products for which India is already a significant

export base. In many of these, and in some new ones, she can emerge as a major powerhouse and global source of manufacturing.

i. Commodity Exports

   These include –

   -Iron Ore

   -Tea

   -Manganese and other ores

   -Coffee

   -Raw hides and skins

   -Spices.

   But it is necessary and possible to move towards more value addition, packaging, branding and global distribution, to enhance the net revenues and margins.

ii. Agri Exports: The McKinsey study on the Indian Food Chain, had projected the possibility of the processed food sector tripling from 20 billion U.S. dollars to 60 billion, if it is modernised. While this may not happen by the original target date of 2000 AD, it could by 2005. The recent Food Expo in Atlanta, Georgia, USA, at the annual meeting of the Institute of Food, noted the spread of vegetarianism in the US, as part of a health concern, promoted and endorsed by celebrities. US Basic, Inc. has pioneered a range of organic foods, with global inputs, including from Asia. The British Vegetarian Society has adults only TV advertisement campaign, with the slogan "Vegetarians are better lovers"!

iii. Manufactured Exports: There are several sectoral export promotion councils, advocating and supporting manufacture for exports among their member firms. The industry exports range from over 7 billion dollars in 97-98 by textiles to less than a billion in some sectors. But several are aiming at high growth rates. For example, the chemical sector is targeting a 30% p.a. growth rate upto 2001, to go from 2.9 billion to 6.3 billion dollars.

Many sectors seem to have promise. Among them

a. Gems and jewellery,

b. Auto components, and

c. Software.

Asianisation and Internationalisation

While bulk of the Indian exports will take place from India-based plants for quite some time, there may also be scope for some overseas investment by Indian firms. Such plants will continue to have supply linkages with the mother plants in India. Some examples are –

a. Ranbaxy's pharma formulation plants abroad, including one in China.

b. A.V. Birla Group's old investments in South East Asia.

c. Nagarjuna Group's and Godrej investments in Vietnam.

A recent study by Ernst & Young identifies possible opportunities, in the depressed Asian market for acquisition of assets, sourcing, backward integration and marketing. Beyond Asianisation, the more competitive Indian firms have to also internationalise their business. The government, FIs and other agencies should support Indian business in this process.

The main point is that Indian manufacturing can not and need not depend entirely on the domestic market. Her share of world trade can be raised from the present 0.6% to about 2% by 2005. This may mean that about 20% of the manufacturing output is exported.

PUBLIC POLICY

To strengthen Indian manufacturing in the 21st century, we need to address a number of issues in public policy, besides, of course dynamic corporate management action, which we shall take up in the next and including section.

i. Competitiveness-India's ranking for competitiveness by the World Economic Forum has been hovering at a low of around 40 out of 50 important trading nations. This needs improvement through the following kinds of action at the macro level.

ii. Infrastructure-Having embarked on liberalisation, perhaps the single most important area for improvement is in the physical infrastructure. Massive investments are needed in Power, Telecom, Roads, Ports, Airports and Railways. Estimates vary from a minimum of Rs. 100,000 crores to about 200 billion U.S. dollars or Rs. 800,000 crores. A study by A.F. Ferguson & Co. for the CII Logistics 97 conference has particularly documented the high cost of logistics, exceeding the employee and financing costs in many industries. The World Bank sees an inverse correlation between freight costs and share of world trade.

iii. Government Restructuring-A substantial part of the above investment has to come from domestic and foreign private sector. To raise investor confidence and attract such funds, government at central and state levels need to be restructured on the following model-

   a. Government to have only the *policy* role.

   b. An independent, quasi-judicial regulator in each sector, such as the

      - Telecom Regulatory Authority of India (TRAI);
      - Central Electricity Regulatory Commission (CERC) and SERCs; and the
      - Insurance Regulatory Authority.

   c. All techno-commercial operations to be corporatised and marketised, such as

      - the power plants of the State Electricity Boards;
      - the telecom service operation of the Ministry of Telecom;
      - Ports and Airports.

iv. Bureaucratic Reform-Percolating the spirit of liberalisation in all government departments and agencies, at central, state and field levels; and ending the harassment, delays, petty corruption and *inspector raj* of the lower bureaucracy.

v. Legal Amendments-Pushing quickly through the Parliament and state assemblies all the necessary amendments to old, obsolete, obstructive laws, so as to enable Indian business to proceed with speed as manufacturing investment, location, relocation, expansion, modernisation and other decisions, without any handicap in comparison to their overseas competitors.

vi. Downsizing Government-Transfer scarce resources from unproductive, fixed, inflationary, establishment expenditure to the market, available at lower cost to industry.

vii. PSU Divestment-Proceed rapidly in the direction indicated by the Finance Minister in his 1998 Budget, namely of closing sick units and bringing government holding in non-strategic units to 26%. Use the proceeds for the following kinds of constructive applications –

   a. Reduction in the mounting public debt, so as to cut the interest payments.

   b. Investment in that part of infrastructure that may not attract private investment, such as

      - Non-toll roads;
      - Rural telephony;
      - Less attractive, but necessary, ports and airports.
      - Targeted, bare minimum subsidies,

   c. Social capital investment in health, literacy, education, retraining etc.

viii. Finance Sector Reform-Do not crowd out the private sector from the capital market. Adopt the concept of Private Equity Funds, using parts of Insurance, Provident, Pension and other Institutional Funds for the private sector. Also revive confidence in Primary issues for the retail investor. People are estimated to have lost about

Rs. 20,000 crores in failed new issues between 1992 and 95.

ix. Supportive Trade Framework-Negotiate with the WTO, trade blocks, agencies and countries to ensure a reasonable period of adjustment for Indian industry to become fully competitive. Where necessary, take quick and adequately punitive anti-dumping action. Protect against threats like the "terminator" seed. Ensure food security. There is no home market growth, without food assurance, not to speak of stability for exports. Act fast on dumping complaints. Strengthen the Anti Dumping Authority. It has less than 10 staff, compared to 300 in US and 185 in EU.

x. Regional Competitiveness-Each state government should attempt to improve its infrastructure and attract appropriate industries. An example is the targeting of the IT industry by the Andhra Pradesh Government, with the Chief Minister himself acting as a *champion*.

xi. Work Culture-Raise the national work culture, by necessary amendments to the old labour laws and procedures, and enact appropriate new laws, including the provision for plant closure and exit, under specified, severe business conditions.

xii. Partnership-Strengthen and sustain the partnership between government and business, so that India, Inc. can become and remain a global manufacturing power in the 21st century.

MANAGEMENT ACTION

Indian entrepreneurs and executives must take the following kinds of actions to ensure a bright future for Indian manufacturing.

i. Corporate Manufacturing Vision-Evolve for their own groups, companies and divisions, a long term manufacturing vision, worthy of the India Country and Manufacturing Vision offered earlier in this paper.

Communicate, discuss, amend and enrich it as a *shared vision* with all their employees and business partners.

ii. Manufacturing Strategies-Formulate competitive strategies for successful manufacturing, as part of their overall business strategies, keeping in mind the India country comparative advantages of their products; domestic and export demand; and the required success factors. As far as possible, go for world scale and contemporary technology; and cost-competitive plants, as Reliance have done.

iii. Technology-Pursue an optimal mix of acquisition and development of competitive technologies in process, product, packaging and other relevant areas. Spend more on R&D. Reduce the huge gap with MNCs in patents. Hoechst 547, Hindustan Lever 435, Lucas 399,

Bayer 311 and Pfizer 253, against IPCL 4, Ranbaxy 4, SAIL 4, Kirloskar 28, Tata 31. Only Bajaj with 124, patents has leveraged innovation so far for a strong competitive position.

iv. Manufacturing Organisation-Strengthen the manufacturing organisation through competent leadership, necessary expertise, training, learning, incentives and values. Tone up organisational discipline and performance orientation. Take the tough, unpleasant, but necessary decision, such as the recent decision of the A.V. Birla group, requiring all to retire at 60, from 2000 AD, including 100 senior executives now at the level of Vice President and above.

v. Global Quality-Sustain the campaign to achieve and sustain international quality levels, through ISO, TQM and other relevant systems, skills, practices and culture.

vi. Cost Competitiveness-Exploit, retain and build on India's inherent labour and material cost advantages. Manage costs through a battery of steps –

   a. Cost consciousness, through information sharing;

b. Cost control against demanding *standards*; and cost reduction by using all promising techniques like
   - Interfirm comparisons,
   - Benchmarking,
   - Activity, Based Costing
   - Business Process Reengineering
   - Value Analysis
   - Value Engineering, etc.

vii. Optimal Investment Policies-Careful choice and phasing of manufacturing investments for expansion, modernisation, debottlenecking, retrofitting, diversification etc; and financing them through a competitive mix of equity, debt, domestic and foreign funds and instruments. Reengineer the capital structure and working capital, so as not to erode good manufacturing margins by high financial charges.

viii. Supportive Marketing Strategies-Including distribution reach; brand equity; segmented pricing in the home market; aggressive marginal cost pricing, where necessary, in the export markets; customer service, delight and surprise.

ix. Reinforcing Procurement Strategies-Similarly, in the upstream end, develop a local and/or virtual cluster of strategic vendors and assist them in enhancing the value chain for mutual benefits.

x. Contemporary Systems-Use the amazing power of information technology for better micro planning, operation, participation and contribution. Use e-mail, intranets, extranets, EDI, e-commerce and all emerging applications of e-business. One of the Indian oil majors HPCL has called for bids for a Rs. 100 crores Enterprise Resource Planning package.

xi. Sanctions into Opportunity-Inspire all the stakeholders of each business — customers, dealers, vendors, including SSI, employees, investors and the local community —-

to convert the post-Pokhran II sanctions into an opportunity for self-confidence and strengthening the foundations of Indian business. Tap the gold mine of internal cost saving potential to beat the temporary additional cost of sanctions.

xii. Vacated Areas-Compete and take up manufacturing in those sectors being vacated by the richer countries due to mature technologies, labour cost disadvantage and environmental hazards. While occupying such markets, take care to innovate for continuous cost reduction; avoid exploitation of adult, child and female labour; and damage to the local, Indian ecology. A recent A.C. Nielsen survey of Asian youngsters shows that the new generation considers saving the environment to be quite important. The study covered 5,700 young people, from 12 countries of the Asia Pacific, including 825 respondents from Mumbai, Delhi, Chennai, and Bangalore; alas, not Calcutta.

xiii. Joint Ventures-In areas where the technology is still unfolding, fast changing and in need of sustained, heavy investments, partner with a globally competitive MNC. Offer him the India manufacturing advantage. Bring an expertise in managing the local component of the value chain to the table. Engage in good governance to forestall his temptation for 100% ownership. Make the MNC work for mutual advantage. A recent study by an inter-institutional group of FIs on corporate governance concludes that firms led by professionals outperform those run by promoters. The answer may be a healthy partnership of dignity and mutual esteem between both.

xiv. Shake Outs-Participate proactively in your industry's restructuring, either as a stronger acquiror of weaker competitors; or as an acquiree, seeking to merge with the right partners, to the benefit of the stakeholders of both firms. Take advantage of the new M&A Funds being allocated by FIs and large banks.

xv. Multiplier Employment-While seeking to be lean and efficient in your own high value addition operations, ensure high indirect contribution to job creation through upstream vendor jobs and downstream dealer, fabricator and customer jobs.

CONCLUSION

The manufacturing sector as a whole has to, and will grow in India for the foreseeable future. Particular sectors, where India has no country advantage may, and should, decline. There are many areas in which India has significant potential advantages. The law of competition is that, alas, threats hit faster, by others' momentum. Opportunities need momentum to capture, from Indian industry and government. Their partnership is critical to actualising the immensely attractive Indian economic and manufacturing vision.

7

Make in India : Defence Sector

Achieving self-reliance and reducing dependence on foreign countries in defence is a necessity today rather than a choice, both for strategic and economic reasons. The Government in the past has created production capabilities in defence in form of Ordnance Factories and Public Sector Undertakings to cater to the requirements of our Armed Forces. However, there is a need to enlarge the role of Indian private sector as well to develop capabilities and capacities for production of various defence equipments.

Our Prime Minister has taken a very important initiative in form of 'Make in India' to promote and encourage domestic manufacturing of various items. The requirement for domestic production of defence equipment is more than for any other sector because it will not only save precious foreign exchange but will also address the national security concerns.

Government being the only consumer, 'Make in India' in defence sector will be driven by our procurement policy. The Government policy of promoting domestic defence industry is adequately reflected in the Defence Procurement Policy, wherein preferential treatment is given to 'Buy (Indian)' and 'Buy and Make (Indian)' categories of acquisition over 'Buy (Global)'. In the days to come, import is going to be the rarest of the rare option and first opportunity would be given to the Indian

Industry to develop and manufacture the required systems. As Indian companies presently may not have adequate capabilities in terms of technology, they are encouraged to partner with foreign companies for joint ventures, technology transfer arrangements and tie-ups.

If we look at the profile of Acceptance of Necessity (AONs) granted by Defence Acquisition Council (DAC) in the last couple of months after the new Government has come to power, proposals worth more than Rs.65,000 crores have been categorized under 'Buy (Indian)' and 'Buy and Make (Indian)'. The process of further orienting the Defence Procurement Procedure towards procurement from domestic industry will continue in future as well. The procurement process would be made more efficient, time bound and predictable so that the industry can plan its investment and R & D well in advance to meet the requirement of our armed forces.

Till now, there were many entry barriers for the domestic industry to enter into defence sector in terms of licensing, FDI policy restrictions etc. In the last six months, the Government has taken several policy initiatives to ease the process of entry into defence manufacturing. The most important is the liberalization of the FDI policy regime for Defence sector to encourage foreign investment in the sector. FDI up to 49% is allowed through Government route (with FIPB approval). FDI above 49% is also allowed on a case-to-case basis with the approval of Cabinet Committee on Security wherever the proposal is likely to result in access to modern and state-of-the-art technology in the country. Restrictions in earlier policy related to Foreign Institutional Investment (FII) and majority shareholding to be held by single Indian shareholder have been removed.

Even though private sector industry was allowed to enter in defence manufacturing since 2001, after obtaining industrial licence under IDR Act, the process of obtaining industrial licence was very cumbersome and used to act as a major road block for the industry, particularly small and medium industry, who were in the business of making part, components, sub systems and sub-assemblies. The Government liberalized the licensing policy and now most of the components, parts, raw materials, testing equipments, production machinery, castings, forgings etc. have been taken out from the purview of licensing. The companies desirous of manufacturing such items no longer require industrial licence and will also not be subjected to FDI ceiling of 49%. A comprehensive Security Manual indicating the security architecture to be followed by various class of industries has been put in public domain, so that companies could easily access the same and follow it accordingly. The initial validity of industrial licence has been increased from two to three years.

For the first time, a Defence Export Strategy has been formulated and has been put in public domain. The strategy outlines specific initiatives to be taken by the Government for encouraging the export of defence items. It is aimed at making the domestic industry more sustainable in the long run as the industry cannot sustain purely on domestic demand. A Standard Operating Procedure (SOP) for issue of NOC for export of military stores has been finalised and has also been put in public domain. Requirement of End User Certificate (EUC) to be signed and stamped by Government authorities has been dispensed with for most of the defence items, particularly parts, components, sub-systems and sub-assemblies. This will largely ease out the export by the domestic industry. A web-based online system to receive applications for NOC for export of military stores has been developed and has been put in place.

There is a big opportunity in the defence sector for both domestic and foreign investors. We have the third largest armed force in the world with an annual budget of about US$ 38 billion and 40% of this is used for capital acquisition. In the next 7-8 years, we would be investing more than US$ 130 billion in modernization of our armed forces and with the present policy of MAKE IN INDIA, the onus is now on the industry to make best use of this opportunity for the benefit of both the business as well as the nation. Besides, under offset more than Rs. 25000 crore obligations are to be discharged in next 7-8 years.

While on the one hand, Government is making necessary policy changes with regard to procurement, investment including FDI, licensing, export etc., the industry also needs to come up and accept the challenge of up-gradation in terms of technology and required investments. Defence is the sector which requires huge investments and technology and is driven by innovation. The industry, therefore, has also to change its mindset and think for long term rather than temporary gains. We need to focus more on Research and Development and state of the art manufacturing capabilities. The Government is fully committed to create an eco-system for the domestic industry to rise and to provide a level-playing field to all sectors of industry, both public and private.

DEFENCE AT HEART OF MODI'S 'MAKE IN INDIA' OFFENSIVE

Expressing confidence that India would emerge as a major global centre for the Defence industry, Prime Minister Narendra Modi today promised conducive business environment for domestic as well as foreign players, including a discrimination—free tax system. Inaugurating the 'Aero India' show, the Prime Minister said the country needs to increase its defence preparedness and modernise its forces due to security challenges that were well known and invited foreign firms to become India's strategic partners rather than remaining just sellers. He said government's focus is to reduce imports and develop the domestic defence industry with a sense of mission which "is at the heart of our Make in India programme".

"We will build an industry that will have room for everyone — public sector, private sector and foreign firms," he said, adding the intention of the government was to develop a dynamic defence industry. Modi said a strong defence industry would not only make the country more secure but also make it more prosperous. "We must ensure that our tax system does not discriminate against domestic manufacture in comparison to imports," he said at Asia's premier air show at the IAF Yelahanka air base on the city outskirts. The Prime Minister said India's defence industry will succeed more "if we can transform the manufacturing sector in the country". Stressing the need for reducing imports, Modi said, "If we could raise percentage of domestic procurement from 40 per cent to 70 per cent in the next five years, we would double the output in our defence industry".

He also said studies have shown that even a 20 to 25 per cent reduction in imports could directly create additional 100,000 to 120,000 highly skilled jobs in the country. Modi also spoke about involving the country's scientists soldiers, academia, industry and independent experts more closely in research and development. Modi said as a nation of one billion people India also has a huge requirement for managing internal security. "We are increasingly integrating technology and systems into it," he said. The Prime Minister also told the participating overseas delegations that for too many of them India is a major business opportunity with the reputation as the largest importer of defence equipment in the world.

"That may be music to the ears of some of you here but this is one area where we would not like to be number one," Modi said at the biennial event, being attended by more than 250 Indian companies and 300 foreign firms. Defence Ministers, senior officials, and hundreds of business leaders from around the world are also in attendance at the largest ever AeroIndia, where Modi government's "Make in India" programme is in the spotlight. "Our security challenges are well known, our international responsibilities are evident, and we too need to increase our defence preparedness. We do have to modernise our defence forces. We have to equip ourselves for the needs of the future where technology will play a major role," he said.

"MAKE IN INDIA" IN DEFENCE: EMBEDDING INDUSTRY-WIDE DIALOGUE AND CONSULTATION

The "Make In India" *mantra* requires a refreshingly new attitudinal change to India's policy-making processes—namely, fostering a culture of trust between government and industry/

business stakeholders.. It may, therefore, be useful to envision how India's Defence Procurement Procedure (DPP) could be retrofitted with this new vision by incorporating a culture of dialogue and consultations into the defence acquisition process itself, as a necessary prerequisite for building enhanced confidence and trust in MoD's procurement systems in the longer-run.

While the DPP mandates its own revision once every two years., the provision is silent on external consultation protocols for the same. To that extent, it may be useful to incorporate mechanisms for formal public consultations with the Indian defence industry on drafts of proposed changes before their adoption by the Defence Procurement Board (DPB)and the Defence Acquisition Council (DAC). The suggestion is not really new and has been practiced earlier on a few occasions by the MoD: present "Make" procedures were based on recommendations of an inter-disciplinary group closely involving the Indian defence industry.; and more recent changes relating to indigenous content determination and for streamlining of "Buy and Make (Indian)" category of defence acquisitions relied extensively on industry consultations for fine-tuning the initial drafts. In a more general context, the Committee of Secretaries (CoS) had also supported the idea of prior public consultations for important policy formulations; and these CoS recommendations, together with useful past experiences in the MoD, could therefore provide a ready basis for mandating circulation of proposed DPP changes for industry comments and suggestions prior to DPB and DAC consideration.

Such engagement would also ensure better alignment of the process of DPP amendment with international best practices: every single EU Directive related to public procurement, defence acquisitions and PPP contracts routinely undergoes multiple rounds of stakeholder discussions on proposed drafts. Similarly, under the US public procurement system—both defence and non-defence—initial drafts of proposed regulatory changes are mandatorily published. With a standard 30-day notice period; and the final regulations necessarily indicate how certain public suggestions have been incorporated therein, or why certain stakeholder suggestions have not been accepted in the final rules: indeed an exceedingly high degree of transparency and consultations for refinement of procurement regulations practiced worldwide. This spirit of openness in the US procurement rule-making system permeates in its task-force functioning as well: the Acquisition Advisory Panel for procurement reforms. In the US setup in the mid-2000s was mandated by the US Congress to conduct its proceedings in public, and the Panel invited suggestions from all stakeholders on its draft report before finalising its suggestions. In contrast, the report of the *Dhall Committee* on public procurement reforms in India, as well as the more recent suggestions on defence acquisition reforms made by the *Naresh Chandra Committee* and the *Rabindra Gupta Committee,* have remained unavailable to Indian industry stakeholders, virtually ignoring the latter's potential for contributing meaningfully to the important reforms process.

A critical decision-point very early in MoD's capital acquisition processes is the categorisation of procurement proposals into "global" versus "domestic" procurements, and "outright purchases" versus "Buy and Make" decisions. The DPP now mandates a preferred order of categorisation and the next set of DPP reforms could therefore focus on improved information-sharing protocols between MoD and the Indian industry, perhaps along the lines of the US system where security-vetted key management personnel from its domestic industry routinely enter into in-depth, wide-ranging discussions on planned capabilities with DoD's acquisition workforce right from very early stages of acquisition planning. In contrast, DPP's present system of industry meetings facilitated by HQIDS is rather ad-hoc, with unilateral presentations by industry associations based on "hearsay" information on user requirements: a situation that could be easily and substantially improved. Similarly, RFIs issued by MoD may need transformation from essentially requiring one-way responses from industry stakeholders, and the RFI process could itself easily be converted into a far-more useful and impactful tool for market research and decision-making on categorisation and on the capabilities planned for eventual acquisition by the MoD using formal, bilateral discussions. Recent DPP changes to "Make" already allow for *advance* planning and industry consultations and this core idea can therefore quickly be seeded into all categories of capital acquisitions permitted under the DPP, rather than being limited to only "Make" as at present.

Improved dialogue and consultations could eventually help MoD in more ways than one: the possibility of close analysis and unconstrained dissection of proposed drafts by public stakeholders will surely improve the quality of initial drafts in the first place; while traditional stakeholder distrust in defence acquisitions could safely be expected to reduce significantly, and perhaps even be eliminated altogether, if permanent platforms are made available to the Indian industry for aligning its capabilities and planned investments in infrastructure and R&D with MoD's technical and weapons requirements well in advance of actual initiation of procurement cases.

Foreign vendors are already able to showcase their wares to Indian armed forces during joint military exercises; and it is time that a level-playing field is provided to the Indian defence industry for being able to showcase its capabilities and manufacturing plans to users in the defence establishment in a much more structured and formal manner than is possible at present. In sum, even though MoD already interacts with the Indian defence industry is a number of small and ad-hoc ways; the challenge going forward for the "Make In India" *mantra*to become an all-pervasive reality in defence acquisitions in India will be to multiply manifold the *onset, frequency, range* and *depth* of its industry engagements.

'MAKE IN INDIA' FOR DEFENCE: A ROADMAP

India is probably the only large country in the world which is overwhelmingly dependent on external sources for its defence requirements. According to *Stockholm International Peace Research Institute* (SIPRI), India is the world's largest arms importer, accounting for 14 per cent of global arms import during 2009-13. Replying to a question in the Rajya Sabha, the Union Defence Minister stated that India spent a whopping Rs. 83,458.31 crore on arms imports in a matter of three years ending 2013-14. This dependency on arms import is a stark reminder of how far India is from the objective of substantive self-reliance in defence production that it has aspired to since the early days of independence. However all is not lost. The 'Make in India' (MII) initiative launched by the National Democratic Alliance (NDA) government of Prime Minister Narendra Modi offers a ray of hope. Under the initiative, 25 sectors including defence manufacturing have been identified to revive India's industrial growth and more importantly propel the nation as a global manufacturing hub. If the objectives of the MII are to be realised in the defence manufacturing sector, the government needs to address some pressing issues that have hindered India's drive for self-reliance.

INSTITUTIONAL MECHANISM FOR DEFENCE MANUFACTURING

The greatest weakness in India's defence manufacturing is the lack of a high-powered institution that can lay out a long term roadmap for the defence industry, set a target for the industry, monitor the progress, and more importantly bring all the stakeholders on one platform and commit to the common cause of MII or self-reliance. In the absence of such an institution, crucial decisions with far reaching implications are being pursued by various stakeholders in a piecemeal fashion, and often at cross-purposes. For instance, while the armed forces are interested in acquiring equipment in the shortest possible timeframe without being too concerned about where it is acquired from, the Defence Research and Development Organisation (DRDO), the premier R&D agency of the Ministry of Defence (MoD), seems content with endless design and development efforts, with scant respect to timelines and the sanctioned budget. For their part, the defence production agencies, major parts of which are owned by the government, appear to be happy manufacturing, while the technology for it is not in their control. Consequently, the focus of producing defence equipment in-house and achieving true self-reliance loses focus and India ultimately ends up importing.

Realising the importance of an institutional mechanism, the Group of Ministers (GOM) set up by the previous NDA government under Vajpayee, had recommended the creation of a Defence Minister's Council on Production (DMCP) under the leadership of the Defence Minister himself. To give the DCMP a dynamic outlook, and enable it to seek ideas and experience from other sectors, the GOM had recommended that the high powered body should draw members not only from the top leadership of the defence establishment but also from the departments of space, atomic energy and science and technology, as well as eminent industrialists from the private sector.

As per the GOM's recommendations, the DCMP would, among other things, "lay down the broad objectives of the long term equipment policies and planning on production, simplification of procedures."

However, as is the fate of key recommendations of many government-appointed committees, this crucial recommendation of creating a DMCP has so far been ignored. Interestingly, the government was quick to implement one of the GOM's recommendations that led to the creation of Defence Acquisition Council (DAC) under the chairmanship of the Defence Minister. However, as the name suggests, the DAC is geared towards addressing the short-term procurement-related hurdles rather than addressing the concerns of the domestic industry for achieving self-reliance in the long term. As a matter of fact, indigenisation is a mere by-product of the DAC's decisions rather than being the cornerstone. For the MII to become a reality in the defence manufacturing sector and more importantly for the initiative to become a self-sustaining drive, the long existing culture of apathy towards indigenous defence manufacturing needs to change. A key requirement in this regard is the establishment of the DMCP at the earliest.

Defence Manufacturing and R&D Plan

The apathy towards in-house production of defence equipment is perhaps best exemplified in the way various defence plans are prepared and pursued. True, India has a well-articulated, if not the best, system of drawing defence plans that covers three distinct time periods: 15-year Long Term Integrated Perspective Plan (LTIPP), five-year Services Capital Acquisition Plan (SCAP) and two-year roll-on Annual Acquisition Plan (AAP). All these plans are prepared with a focus on 'acquiring' the best possible equipment available in the world. The DRDO and domestic industry are completely ignored in the planning process. To make matters worse, there is no channel for the armed forces to provide advance information to the domestic industry so as to enable the latter to come up with detailed financial, technological and industrial plans to meet the requirements in a timeframe that is acceptable to the armed forces. The Technological Perspective and Capability Roadmap (TPCR), announced in April 2013 as a means to bridge this gap, has been disappointing and regarded as completely useless by both industry and analysts for its lack of specificities and absence of any commitment from the government.

Consequently, when the acquisition process begins, it is often too late for the R&D and production agencies to offer a solution. To overcome this difficulty, the Economic Advisory Council to the Prime Minister, in a report of September 2013, had recommended that it would be useful to "convert the LTIPP into a defence manufacturing and R&D plan". More significantly, the advisory council had suggested that the conversion should be undertaken by a joint working group involving all important stakeholders including the Indian industry and R&D establishments. This vital recommendation does not seem to have received the required attention of the policy makers. Since much of the success of MII lies in translating the long term requirement of the armed forces into technological and industrial outputs, it is high time that the government comes out with a detailed plan for the industry and R&D agencies at the earliest.

The plan, in order to be successful, must identify specific projects that would be executed by local agencies.

Research and Development: Looking beyond the DRDO

One of the unique features of India's defence industrialisation process has been the near monopoly enjoyed by the DRDO over defence research and development. This began with the establishment of the DRDO in 1958 and has been perpetuated ever since. The dependence on DRDO for technology has however not yielded the desired results. Despite having a large pool of scientists/engineers and over 50 labs and establishments, the DRDO has been beset with many a problem leading to failures and cost and time overruns in the projects undertaken. This, combined with lack of R&D in industry and academia, has compelled the country to source technology from outside, leading to a vicious cycle where initial imports lead to further imports.

Compared to India, other advanced defence manufacturing countries encourage R&D at diverse sources that include dedicated research institutes, universities and industry. The model followed by many counties is one of R&D management, rather than limiting it to one agency. For instance, the *Defence Advanced Research Projects Agency* (DARPA) of the US, which has been at the heart of the several radical innovations including in the areas of stealth, internet, *Global Positioning System* (GPS) and Unmanned Aerial Vehicle (UAV), does not do R&D on its own. In fact, DARPA does not own a single lab of its own! Rather, it identifies talent and ideas from industry, academia, government laboratories and individuals, and awards R&D contracts to be executed in typical time scales of three-to-five years. DARPA's role is limited to shortlisting of projects and managing the programmes, which it does through 140-odd programme managers.

Among other counties which are successful in cutting-edge innovation, Israel offers another test case worth emulating. The giant strides that this small country has made are attributed to the Office of the Chief Scientist (OCS), which was set up in 1974 under the Ministry Industry, Trade and Labour. The OCS is responsible for executing the government's R&D policy to foster innovation and promote technological entrepreneurship. Like the DARPA, the OCS also awards R&D contracts to diverse sources and manages them with a small team that comprises of 30 full-time employees. OCA's core principle of R&D funding is not to subsidise R&D but to partially mitigate risks through government financial assistance. Interestingly, nearly one-fourth of the OCS budget (in 2011) came from the royalties paid back by companies that had successfully converted R&D funding into marketable products.

In order to expand its R&D base, India also needs to have an institution similar to DARPA or OCS. For this to happen there is need to look beyond the DRDO. The Scientific Advisor to Raksha Mantri (SA to RM) who is also Secretary, Defence Research & Development and Director General DRDO, should be relieved of his daily duties at the DRDO and given a role like that of the head of DARPA or OCS with a dedicated R&D fund at his disposal. This will not only create a healthy competition between DRDO labs and other agencies, but also lead to more innovation.

Human Resource Development

Unlike in most other sectors, defence industry requires a highly skilled labour force. Currently, there is hardly any thinking on how to create a robust human resource base both in terms of number and quality. Clear evidence to this effect is visible in the DRDO, which is the premier institution for India's defence innovation. The number of scientists at DRDO has not increased since 2001, although the number of projects has increased exponentially, with the organisation currently pursing 44 major projects (each costing over Rs 100 crore) worth Rs. 39,560 crore.

Another equally disturbing facet of most of the scientific organisations like the DRDO is the low educational profile of the scientific workforce. The Rama Rao Committee, which reviewed the functioning of the DRDO and submitted a report to the government in February 2008, was greatly perturbed to see the predominance of first degree holders in the DRDO's scientific cadre. It had noted that only 10 per cent of the scientific manpower had higher qualification of Ph.D. To make matters worse, majority of the workforce was not trained in research, observed the Committee.

Low education and lack of training is also an aspect that is common to other high-end R&D organisations like the ISRO and atomic energy department, and even to manufacturing establishments such as Hindustan Aeronautics Ltd (HAL). A major reason for this is the class room teaching orientation of most Indian universities, which themselves are far behind their global peers (as per the *Times Higher Education* World University Rankings 2013-2014, not a single Indian university figures in the top 200). However, to overcome the quality constraints, organisations like ISRO and Atomic energy have devised their own methods. ISRO, for instance, runs a dedicated university, the Indian Institute of Space Science and Technology (IIST), that taps talent at a very early age and provides graduate, post-graduate and doctoral programmes in the areas of space science and technology. There is no such dedicated university for defence. According to one estimate, the aerospace industry in its three verticals – R&D, manufacturing, and maintenance, repair and overhaul (MRO) – alone will require an additional manpower of over 185,500 by 2022, justifying the necessity to set up a dedicated defence technology university.

PRIVATE SECTOR AS EQUAL PARTNER

Although the Indian defence industry was opened to the private sector in 2001, the latter is yet to contribute in any meaningful manner. The biggest hindrance in the private sector's participation so far has been mistrust. When it comes to big contracts, procedural hurdles come in the way, making it virtually impossible for the private sector to get into complex defence manufacturing. Moreover, single source procurement from the private sector is still considered a taboo, whereas import without competition is greatly admired.

For the MII to succeed, there is a need to change the mind-set and treat the private sector as an equal partner. This can only be demonstrated by awarding big contracts, preferably through the 'Make' and 'Buy and Make (Indian)' procurement categories, which hold the key to the success of the private sector's participation in defence production. For the government, it is imperative to announce a list of contracts which can be awarded under these two categories.

A Conducive Financial Framework

Defence is undoubtedly a strategic sector and countries all over the world accord special treatment to nurture and develop this vital sector. For instance, in the early phase of defence industrialisation in South Korea, the government provided a wide range of financial and fiscal incentives besides raising funds for the industry through a special defence tax (a 10 per cent income and surcharge tax) which remained in force for 15 years till 1990. Israel, a country which boasts of an advanced defence industry, continues to incentivise local enterprises through a 15 per cent price preference.

The Indian defence industry, however, operates in a hostile financial framework that tends to render it less competitive vis-à-vis foreign manufactures. It operates in a double-digit interest regime compared to the nearly zero interest rate system prevalent in Europe, US and many other countries. This increases the cost of working capital for the Indian industry which is reflected in the final products, making them uncompetitive vis-à-vis the products offered by foreign manufactures. The Indian industry also suffers on account of the variation in exchange rates. As per the MoD's Defence Procurement Procedures (DPP), local private companies winning contracts under the 'Buy (Indian)' category are required to bear all the risks associated with exchange rate variation (ERV). Non-protection against ERV has, however, led several companies to virtual bankruptcy due to a wide variation in exchange rates as has been witnessed in the recent past.

Apart from the above, Indian industry also suffers from prevailing taxes and duties, which offer virtually no incentive for any local company to undertake defence production. In fact,

India follows an 'inverted structure' by which direct import is allowed free of duties whereas manufacturing the same product at home attracts several taxes and duties.

What is surprising is that there is no realisation by the concerned authority that taxes and duties can make or mar the local industry. As per several estimates, taxes and duties can raise the cost of local products by as much as 20 to 25 per cent. Considering that MII seriously seeks to promote local manufacturing, it is time to create a conducive financial framework for the local industry.

Among others, the government may accord 'infrastructure status' to defence industry, which would not only take care of the taxes and duties concerns of industry but also incentivise new investments. It is also highly desirable that certain sales of the local industry may be given 'deemed export status' whenever such sales are likely to substitute direct import.

Reform DRDO, DPSUs and OFs

It is a fact that much of India's defence industrial woes are attributable to the inefficiency of the three major players - – DRDO, the Defence Public Sector Undertakings (DPSUs) and the Ordnance Factories (OFs) -- which, despite having a long presence in the sector, are yet to become globally competitive. Several efforts have been made in the past to reform these organisations but all have failed due to vested interests and lack of political will.

Given that these are major players and their functioning will have a direct impact on the MII initiative, it is imperative to examine afresh the recommendations given by several past committees. Among others, the OFs should be corporatized and made more accountable for their functioning. All the unlisted DPSUs need to be listed in the stock exchanges to bring in transparency and enhance their corporate governance. The recommendations of the Rama Rao Committee on DRDO, especially the one for creation of a defence technology commission, should also be implemented at the earliest.

Conclusion

As per the official estimate of the MoD, India is likely to spend around $130 billion on defence modernisation in the coming seven-to-eight years. While this makes India one of the largest defence markets in the world, the opportunity it offers should be fully exploited for the benefit of local industry. This will not only improve India's self-reliance in defence production but will have a multiplier effect on the wider economy. The government must ensure that the local industry is geared and incentivised enough to rise up to the expectations and make the government's 'Make in India' initiative a success story.

8

Come and Invest in India

- 3rd largest armed forces in the world.
- 40% of budget spent on capital acquisitions.
- 60% of requirements met by imports.
- INR 250 Billion to be invested in 7-8 years.
- India's current requirements on defence are catered largely by imports.

The opening of the strategic defence sector for private sector participation will help foreign original equipment manufacturers to enter into strategic partnerships with Indian companies and leverage the domestic markets and also aim at global business. Besides helping build domestic capabilities, this will bolster exports in the long term.

- Opportunities to avail defence offset obligations to the tune of approximately INR 250 Billion during the next 7-8 years.
- The offset policy (which stipulates the mandatory offset requirement of a minimum 30% for procurement of defence equipment in excess of INR 3 Billion) introduced in the capital purchase agreements with foreign defence players would ensure that an eco-system of suppliers is built domestically.
- The government policy of promoting self-reliance, indigenization, technology upgradation and achieving economies of scale and developing capabilities for exports in the defence sector.

- The country's extensive modernization plans, an increased focus on homeland security and India's growing attractiveness as a defence sourcing hub. High government allocation for defence expenditure.
- India has the third largest armed forces in the world.
- India is one of the largest importers of conventional defence equipment and spends about 40% of its total defence budget on capital acquisitions.
- About 60% of its defence requirements are met through imports.
- The allocation for defence in the last budget was approximate USD 37.3 Billion.
- Defence Production Policy, 2011 to encourage indigenous manufacture _of defence equipment. Defence Procurement Procedure (DPP) has been amended to provide for the following :
    1. Preference to 'Buy (Indian)' and 'Buy and Make (Indian)' over 'Buy (Global)'.
    2. Simplification of the procedure for 'Buy and Make (Indian)'.
    3. Clear and unambiguous definition of indigenous content.
    4. Provision for Maintenance TOT to Indian Industry partners.
- Defence products list for industrial licensing, has been articulated in June 2014, wherein large numbers of parts/ components, castings/forgings etc. have been excluded from the purview of industrial licensing. The same is available at the DIPP's website, www.dipp.gov.in.
- The defence security manual for the private sector defence manufacturing units have been finalized and put in public domain by the Department of Defence Production. The manual clarifies the security architecture required to be put in place by the industry while undertaking sensitive defence equipments.

- The MAKE procedure, which aims to promote R&D in the industry with support from the government and the placement of orders (if R&D effort is successful), is also being revised to make it more attractive and unambiguous for the private sector.
- Up to 49% investment is allowed under the government route, above 49% on a case-to-case basis on approval by the Cabinet Committee on Security, wherever it is likely to result in access to modern and state-of-the-art technology.
- Investments by foreign portfolio investors/FIIs (through portfolio investment) are permitted up to 24% under automatic route.
- The defence industry is subject to industrial licenses under the Industries (Development and Regulation) Act, 1951.
- The requirement of single largest Indian ownership of 51% of equity removed.
- A lock-in period of 3 years on equity transfer has been done-away with in FDI for defence.

FDI in the defence sector is subject to other security conditions.

Procurement Policy

The defence procurement is governed by the Defence Procurement Procedure (DPP). The government has now decided to revise the DPP every year.

Offset Policy

The key objectives of the defence offset policy is to leverage capital acquisitions to develop the Indian defence industry.

Mandatory offset requirements of a minimum of 30% for procurement of defence equipment in excess of INR 3 Billion have been envisaged.

Guidelines for Establishing Joint Venture (JV) Companies By Defence Psus

A well laid out policy for formulation of joint venture between Defence PSUs and private sector keeping in view the objective of Defence Production Policy.

Procedures for the Grant of Industrial Licenses have been Streamlined

- The initial validity period of industrial licenses has been increased to three years from the present two years.
- Guidelines for the extension of validity of industrial licenses have been issued.
- Partial commencement of production is treated as commencement of production of all the items included in the license.

Financial Supportkey Provisions of the 2014-2015 Union Budget

- Provision of INR 2,290 Billion for defence services.
- Capital outlay for defence increased by INR 50 Billion including a sum of INR 10 Billion for accelerating the development of the railway system in the border areas.
- INR 1 Billion is provided to set up a Technology Development Fund for defence.
- INR 22.5 Billion has been provided to strengthen and moderniseborder infrastructure.
- The scope of exemption for granting full exemption from Basic Custom Duty (BCD) and Countervailing Duty (CVD) on goods imported for use in the manufacture of aircraft for the Ministry of Defence is being clarified to the effect that the exemption is available to all materials in any form _and articles thereof, subject to the overall condition that they conform to aeronautical specifications accompanied with a certificate of conformance and/or a release note.

- Either of the following two deductions can be availed:
  1. Investment allowance (additional depreciation) at the rate of 15% to manufacturing companies that invest more than INR 1 Billion in plants and machinery acquired and installed between 01.04.2013 to 31.03.2015 provided the aggregate amount of investment in the new plants and machinery during the said period exceeds INR 1 Billion.
  2. In order to provide a further fillip to companies engaged in the manufacture of an article or thing, the said benefit of additional deduction of 15% of the cost of new plants and machinery, exceeding INR 250 Million, acquired and installed during any previous year until 31.3.2017.

Tax Incentives

- R&D Incentives – Industry/private sponsored research programmes.
- A weighted tax deduction is given under Section 35 (2AA) of the Income Tax Act.
- A weighted deduction of 200% is granted to assessees for any sums paid to a national laboratory, university or institute of technology, or specified persons with a specific direction that the said sum would be used for scientific research within a programme approved by the prescribed authority.
- For companies engaged in the manufacture of an in-house R&D centre, a weighted tax deduction of 200% under Section 35 (2AB) of the Income Tax Act for both capital and revenue expenditure incurred on scientific research and development. Expenditure on land and buildings are not eligible for deduction.

State Incentives

Apart from the above, each state in India offers additional incentives for industrial projects.

Incentives are in areas like subsidised land cost, relaxation in stamp duty exemption on sale/lease of land, power tariff incentives, concessional rates of interest on loans, investment subsidies/tax incentives, backward areas subsidies, special incentive packages for mega projects.

Export Incentives

- Export promotion capital goods scheme.
- Duty remission scheme.
- Focus product scheme, special focus product scheme, focus market scheme.

Area Based Incentives

Incentives for units in SEZ/NIMZ as specified in respective Acts or for the setting up of projects in special areas such as the North-east, Jammu & Kashmir, Himachal Pradesh and Uttarakhand.

Investment Opportunities

- Defence products manufacturing.
- Supply chain sourcing opportunity.
- Defence offsets.

Foreign Investors

- BAE India Systems (UK)
- Pilatus (Switzerland)
- Lockheed Martin (USA)
- Finmeccanica (Italy)
- Boeing India (USA)
- Raytheon (USA)
- MBDA (France)
- Raffel (France)
- IAI (Israel)
- Rafael (Israel).

FOREIGN DIRECT INVESTMENT: IMPACT ON INDIAN ECONOMY

When a firm controls (or have a strong say in) another firm located abroad, e.g. by owing more than 10% of its equity, the former is said "parent enterprise" (or "investor") and the latter "foreign affiliate". For a country, attracting an inflow of FDI strengthen the connection to world trade networks and finance its development path. However, unilateral substantial FDI to a country can make it dependent on the external pressure that foreign owners might exert on it. Foreign investment plays a significant role in development of Indian economy. Many countries provide many incentives for attracting the foreign direct investment (FDI). Need of FDI depends on saving and investment rate in any country. Foreign Direct investment acts as a bridge to fulfill the gap between investment and saving. In the process of economic development foreign capital helps to cover the domestic saving constraint and provide access to the superior technology that promotes efficiency and productivity of the existing production capacity and generate new production opportunity.

FOREIGN DIRECT INVESTMENT IN INDIA: FDI AND ECONOMIC GROWTH

The historical background of FDI in India can be traced back with the establishment of East India Company of Britain. British capital came to India during the colonial era of Britain in India. After Second World War, Japanese companies entered Indian market and enhanced their trade with India, yet U.K. remained the most dominant investor in India. Further, after Independence issues relating to foreign capital, operations of MNCs, gained attention of the policy makers. Keeping in mind the national interests the policy makers designed the FDI policy which aims FDI as a medium for acquiring advanced technology and to mobilize foreign exchange resources. With time and as per economic and political regimes there have been changes in the FDI policy too. The industrial policy of 1965, allowed MNCs to venture through technical collaboration in India. Therefore, the government adopted a liberal attitude by allowing more frequent equity.

In the critical face of Indian economy the government of India with the help of World Bank and IMF introduced the macro-economic stabilization and structural adjustment program. As a result of these reforms India open its door to FDI inflows and adopted a more liberal foreign policy in order to restore the confidence of foreign investors. Further, under the new foreign investment policy Government of India constituted FIPB (Foreign Investment Promotion Board) whose main function was to invite and facilitate foreign investment Starting from a baseline of less than USD 1 billion in 1990, a recent UNCTAD survey projected India as the second most important FDI destination (after China) for transnational corporations during 2010-2012. As per the data, the sectors which attracted higher inflows were services, telecommunication, construction activities and computer software and hardware. Mauritius, Singapore, the US and the UK were among the leading sources of FDI to the country.

In 2013, the government relaxed FDI norms in several sectors, including telecom, defence, PSU oil refineries, power exchanges and stock exchanges, among others. In retail, UK-based Tesco submitted its application to initially invest US$ 110 million to start a supermarket chain in collaboration with Tata Group's Trent. In civil aviation, Malaysia-based Air Asia and Singapore Airlines teamed up with Tata Group to launch two new airline services. Also, Abu Dhabi-based Etihad picked up a 24 per cent stake in Jet Airways that was worth over Rs 2, 000 crore (US$ 319.39 million).

India has received total foreign investment of US$ 306.88 billion since 2000 with 94 per cent of the amount coming during the last nine years.

In the period 1999–2004, India received US$ 19.52 billion of foreign investment. In the period 2004–09, foreign investment in the country touched US$ 114.55 billion, further increasing to US$ 172.82 billion between 2009–September, 2013.

During FY 2012–13, India attracted FDI worth US$ 22.42 billion. Tourism, pharmaceuticals, services, chemicals and construction were among the biggest beneficiaries.

The January–November period in 2013 witnessed mergers and acquisitions deals worth US $ 26.76 billion in India, according to a survey by tax advisory firm Grant Thornton.

Recent Developments

New Zealand is looking to establish an office in Mumbai to broaden its education footprint in India. It plans to set up an education promotion and market development role within the New Zealand Consulate General, Mumbai. There was an increase of more than 10 per cent in student visas issued to Indian nationals in 2013, making India among the fastest growing student markets for New Zealand.

Korean South-East Power Company (KOSEP), part of South Korean state-owned power generator Korea Electric Power Corporation, has signed an initial agreement with Jinbhuvish Group, Mumbai, for technical support for its Rs 3, 450-crore (US$ 549.31 million) project in Maharashtra. The 600 megawatt (mw) power plant, which will be set up in Yavatmal district, is expected to be commissioned in 2016.

India and UAE have agreed to promote collaboration in renewable energy, focusing in the areas of wind power and solar energy. A Memorandum of Understanding (MoU) was signed by Dr Farooq Abdullah, Minister of New and Renewable Energy of India and Dr Sultan Ahmed Al Jaber, Minister of State of UAE in Abu Dhabi on January 18, 2014.

Luxury watch brand Jaeger-LeCoultre from Switzerland has filed for a 100 per cent single brand application to enter the Indian retail market. It thus became the first luxury company to apply for FDI through this route. Geneva-based Richemont SA that owns the luxury brand filed the application with the Department of Industrial Policy and Promotion (DIPP).

France's Lactalis, the biggest dairy products group in the world, will most likely buy out Hyderabad-based Tirumala

Milk Products for US $275–300 million. Lactalis has a yearly turnover of about US $21 billion. Tirumala had a turnover of Rs 1, 424 crore (US$ 226.71 million) for FY 2012–13. The Hyderabad-based company, which was founded in 1998, makes dairy products such as sweets, flavoured milk, curd, ice-cream, etc.

Recent policy initiatives

The Ministry of Home Affairs has finally given the approval to the proposal of allowing FDI in railways. The Cabinet Committee on Economic Affairs (CCEA) is expected to consider the proposal. Foreign investors can invest only in construction and maintenance of railway projects, and not in operations.

India's Prime Minister Mr Manmohan Singh has sought increased Japanese investment in the country. The two countries are already looking at the possibility of concrete cooperation in areas such as manufacturing and research and development in the electronic industry and energy efficient and energy saving technologies. "I believe there is enormous untapped potential in our business ties, " Mr Singh said following the annual summit level meeting between Japan and India. The presence of Japanese companies in India increased by 16 per cent in 2013.

The Andhra Pradesh State Investment Promotion Board has given the approval to six major investment proposals that will have a total investment of Rs 6, 500 crore (US$ 1.03 billion). The proposals include those by multinational companies such as PepsiCo, Cadbury, Colgate, Johnson & Johnson, Gerdau Steels and ITC. PepsiCo's unit will be the largest beverages plant in India with an investment of Rs 1, 200 crore (US$ 191.06 million). Similarly, Cadbury is establishing its facility in Sri City with an investment of Rs 2, 500 crore (US$ 398.07 million).

In an effort to improve capital flows into the country, the Indian government has allowed 100 per cent FDI under automatic route in storage and warehousing, which includes warehousing of agriculture products with refrigeration. The government has also set up National Centre for Cold Chain Development (NCCD) which will look at standards and protocols for cold chain infrastructure.

Based on the recommendations of Foreign Investment Promotion Board (FIPB) made on December 30, 2013, the Indian government has agreed to five FDI proposals amounting to Rs 1133.41 crore (US$ 180.16 million) approximately. On November 13, 2013, it had approved 12 proposals of FDI amounting to Rs 821.63 crore (US$ 130.73 million) approximately. The FIPB has also approved Swedish clothing major Hennes & Mauritz (H&M) AB's proposal to open 50 stores across India. The investment will be around Rs 720 crore (US$ 114.61 million).

The FDI inflow and GDP in India from the year 1991-92 to 2011-2012(post-liberalization period). The table states that India had showed a large amount of FDI inflow. It showed that FDI inflow has been increased by more than 210 times during the study period because the FDI Inflow has been increased from Rs. 409 crore in 1991-92 to Rs. 173947 crore in 20011-2012. Due to technological up gradation, access to global managerial skills and practices, optimal utilization of human and natural resources, making Indian industry internationally competitive, opening up export markets, providing backward forward linkages and access to international quality goods and services the Indian Government has used many steps to attract more FDI. The highest amount of FDI was received in the year 2011-2012, amounting to Rs. 173947crore. The highest growth rate of FDI inflow is in the year 2006-07 i.e., 186.9622 percent. The FDI as a percentage of GDP was less than one until 2005-06 after then it is increasing year after year.

Future Outlook

India is estimated to require around US$ 1 trillion during the 12th Five-Year Plan period (2012–17), to fund infrastructure in sectors such as roads, airports and ports. The government is in the process of liberalising FDI norms in construction activities and railways, which could bring in investments to meet the target.

The government is also relaxing FDI norms in other sectors for foreign investors to invest. FDI in multi-brand retail has been allowed up to 51 per cent. The minimum requirement for the FDI is US$ 100 million, of which at least 50 per cent must be invested in 'backend infrastructure' within three years following the initiation of the FDI. FDI limit in single-brand retail has been increased to 100 per cent; 49 per cent will be under the automatic route and the rest through the FIPB route.

A Brief Review of The Literature

Agarwal and Khan conducted the study on "Impact of FDI on GDP: A Comparative Study of China and India", the study found that 1% increase in FDI would result in 0.07%increase in GDP of China and 0.02% increase in GDP of India. We also found that China's growth is more affected by FDI, than India's growth.

Kumar and Karthika found out in their study on "Sectoral Performance through Inflows of Foreign Direct Investment (FDI)", that Foreign Direct Investment has a major role to play in the economic development of the host country. Most of the countries have been making use of foreign investment and foreign technology to accelerate the place of their economic growth. FDI ensures a huge amount of domestic capital, production level and employment opportunities in the developing countries, which a major step towards the economic growth of the country.

Balasubramanyam and Sapsford stated in their article "Does India need a lot more FDI" compared the levels of FDI inflows in India and China, and found that FDI in India is one tenth of that of china. The paper also concluded that India may not require increased FDI because of the structure and composition of India's manufacturing, service sectors and her endowments of human capital and the country is in a position to unbundle the FDI package effectively and rely on sources other than FDI for its capital requirements.

Bajpai and Jeffrey stated attempted the paper on "Foreign Direct Investment in India: Issues and Problems", to identify the issues and problems associated with India's current FDI regimes, and also the other associated factors responsible for India's unattractiveness as an investment location. Despite India offering a large domestic market, rule of law, low labour costs, and a well working democracy, her performance in attracting FDI flows have been far from satisfactory. The conclusion of the study is that a restricted FDI regime, high import tariffs, exit barriers for firms, stringent labor laws, poor quality infrastructure, centralized decision making processes, and a verylimited scale of export processing zones make India an unattractive investment location.

Conclusion

India's Foreign Direct Investment (FDI) policy has been gradually liberalised to make the market more investor friendly. The results have been encouraging. These days, the country is consistently ranked among the top three global investment destinations by all international bodies, including the World Bank, according to a United Nations (UN) report.

For Indian economy which has tremendous potential, FDI has had a positive impact. FDI inflow supplements domestic capital, as well as technology and skills of existing companies. It also helps to establish new companies. All of these contribute to economic growth of the Indian Economy.

CURRENT CHALLENGES AND IMPROVEMENT AREAS

India is definitely a lucrative place for FDI, but there are certainly some challenges and areas for improvement still present. Until, these areas are honed to perfection, India will not become the number one place for FDI.

India is focusing on maximizing political and social stability along with a regulatory environment. In spite of the obvious advantages of FDIs, there are quite a few challenges facing larger FDIs in India, such as:

- Resource challenge: India is known to have huge amounts of resources. There is manpower and significant availability of fixed and working capital. At the same time, there are some underexploited or unexploited resources. The resources are well available in the rural as well as the urban areas. The focus is to increase infrastructure 10 years down the line, for which the requirement will be an amount of about US$ 150 billion. This is the first step to overcome challenges facing larger FDI.

- Equity challenge: India is definitely developing in a much faster pace now than before but in spite of that it can be identified that developments have taken place unevenly. This means that while the more urban areas have been tapped, the poorer sections are inadequately exploited. To get the complete picture of growth, it is essential to make sure that the rural section has more or less the same amount of development as the urbanized ones. Thus, fostering social equality and at the same time, a balanced economic growth.
- Political Challenge: The support of the political structure has to be there towards the investing countries abroad. This can be worked out when foreign investors put forward their persuasion for increasing FDI capital in various sectors like banking, and insurance. So, there has to be a common ground between the Parliament and the Foreign countries investing in India. This would increase the reforms in the FDI area of the country.
- Federal Challenge: Very important among the major challenges facing larger FDI, is the need to speed up the implementation of policies, rules, and regulations. The vital part is to keep the implementation of policies in all the states of India at par. Thus, asking for equal speed in policy implementation among the states in India is important.
- India must also focus on areas of poverty reduction, trade liberalization, and banking and insurance liberalization. Challenges facing larger FDI are not just restricted to the ones mentioned above, because trade

relations with foreign investors will always bring in new challenges in investments.

INDIA AND EUROPE: SCOPE FOR BREAKING NEW GROUND

To provide a much-awaited fillip to India's interaction with Europe, Prime Minister Narendra Modi visited two key member states of the European Union (EU) – France and Germany – from 9 to 12 April 2015. His visit took place in the backdrop of slowdown of India-EU strategic partnership and recent cancellation of India-EU summit. Although New Delhi, reportedly, initiated the process of holding the India-EU summit, it was cancelled due to EU's no response to India's suggestion on dates. 'Logistical reasons' as given by the European Commission is unlikely, as reports point out that the Italian marine issues and 'future personal ambitions' led to the cancellation. Such approach of the European Commission was criticized within the political establishment of the EU. Neena Gill, Vice-Chair, Delegation for Relations with India,

European Parliament, said, "Any deterioration in (India-EU) relations is incredibly unfortunate, given that India is leapfrogging towards major importance on the global scene." Scholars point out that the EU's approach to Italian marine case happened to be 'spoilsport' in the India-EU partnership.

There is also an observation that India-EU strategic partnership is 'underperforming' and India and the EU are not able to arrive at a mutually acceptable solution. As expected, Prime Minister Modi's visit to France and Germany has had more of a 'bilateral' agenda, but it was appropriate to discuss the current state of India-EU strategic partnership with the two prominent Member States of the EU. India should convey to its European strategic partners that its judicial process must be honoured, for instance, the Italian marine case is sub-judice. The extra-judicial strategic intervention, therefore, would undermine the virtues of the rule of law and free and fair justice system, which are supposed to be the normative basis of India-EU relations. In such a context, the issue brief argues that Prime Minister Modi's visit to Europe offers scope for breaking new ground in their relationship.

Emphasis on Greater Economic Engagement

Expanding economic engagement and sharing advanced technology were high on Prime Minister Modi's agenda. On his visit to these nations, Prime Minister Narendra Modi himself tweeted, "My France, Germany and Canada visit is centred around supporting India's economic agenda and creating jobs for our youth." After coming to power, the Prime Minister has emphasized on his reform agenda to revive growth and create an enabling environment for better business prospects in the country. Narendra Modi once argued, "I believe a strong economy is the driver of an effective foreign policy... We have to put our own house in order so that the world is attracted to us." The comprehensive 'Make in India' programme has immense potential to revive economic growth, harness demographic dividends and open huge business opportunities and international collaborations as well. On the other hand, the primacy of geo-economic factor has further been enhanced in external relations of the EU and its member states; the domestic economic scenario-internal austerity measures-of the EU member states pushes for more external trade promotion.

In the broader ecosystem of contemporary foreign policy, he rightly emphasizes on the 'Look East, Link West' policy, which pushes for the country's greater integration in global value chain, larger and sustained investment and advanced level of technological cooperation. India has been criticized for cumbersome bureaucratic process and 'policy paralysis'. Today, qualitative change in business environment of the country has been well recognized. The credit rating agency, Moody's has upgraded India from 'stable' to 'positive'. During G-20 summit in Brisbane, Herman Von Rompuy, the then President of the European Council, discussed the India-EU Broad-based Trade and Investment Agreement (BTIA) and how it was stalled due to 'lack of political will'. Referring to major reform initiatives taken by his government to push economic growth and create an out-looking approach, Prime Minister Modi said, "There is a new wind of change. Test it for yourself." In the west as well, India is considered as a 'bright spot in the global economy'.

India already shares a vibrant and dynamic relationship with these countries. India and France have been expanding their cooperation in a number of areas ranging from space technology, civil nuclear cooperation to the defence sector. During the visit, a wide range of issues including space cooperation, tourism, international terrorism, smart cities, defence manufacturing, etc. were discussed. As the key element of 'Make in India' initiative, defence manufacturing is an important area of cooperation. With regards to the MMRCA deal, offsets and life cycle cost and technology transfer were the major issues in the disqualification of other contenders. Negotiations on Rafale deal have been stuck on these issues. India and France have, now, decided to buy 36 fighter planes in flyaway condition. Considering urgent operational requirements of the Indian Air Force, India decided to go for government to government deal for speedy delivery of Rafale jets. New Delhi and Paris also moved a step ahead on nuclear energy cooperation. Both countries attempted to bring clarity on all technical aspects of the Jaitapur plant related to price and provisions for risks. India also made an attempt to attract French businessmen to invest in India. Although the figure is not high as Japan, France also announced an investment of two billion euros in the country.

French President Hollande extended his support for partnering in infrastructure and urban development.

Germany is the largest trading partner in Europe and a major source of advanced technology to India. It has been the 8th largest foreign direct investor in India since 2000.19 Total German investment in India accounts for approximately $3.9 billion since August 1991.20 When India embarked on the path of new economic process in early 1990s, Berlin figured as an 'important component' in the larger India-EU framework. Today, more than two decades of beginning of economic reforms,

Germany would be considered a crucial partner in India's renewed efforts to usher new growth momentum, and consequent socio-economic transformation. The 'Make in India' initiative offers new avenues to expand cooperation in multiple spheres. Germany has strong technological base and vibrant inventive system, which provide huge impetus to its industrial growth. German expenditure on research and development is higher than that of the EU's average. German small and medium-sized enterprises – 'Mittelsand' – are very productive and offer large employment opportunities. Apart from investment, India-Germany cooperation in technology, capacity building, research and development, and promotion of SMEs would be crucial for enhancing prospects of growth in the Indian manufacturing sector and generating more employment in the country.

European countries have made substantial progress in the field of cyber security, innovation, start-ups, digital governance, e-governance, etc., in which India can benefit from their experience. Both Prime Minister Modi and German Chancellor Angela Merkel called for deepening economic cooperation between the two countries. It is pertinent to note that Germany-India trade accounted for 15.9 billion Euros in 2014, far behind that of Germany and China, which was estimated at close to 154 billion Euros. The German Chancellor Merkel favoured re-launching talks on India-EU FTA. It is perceived that the FTA between India and the EU would have the potential to expand the trade between India and the EU. India has also expressed its readiness to start the negotiations on FTA, but prospects for its conclusion, as Anand Menon argues, seem to be 'very slim'.

India's call for pushing the manufacturing sector has not only a favourable domestic environment, but also suits the changing dynamics of global manufacturing centres. For instance, as Zhao Gancheng, Director of South Asia Studies, Shanghai Institute for International Studies, argued, "...the roaring labour costs and stricter environment regulations in China have pushed enthusiastic investors to look away and eye India as a more desirable destination, particularly those from small and medium sized businesses. And the widespread English proficiency in

India also gives a fillip to their interest...." New Delhi's political message to global investors is loud and clear that 'Make in India' is not a 'mere slogan' for the government. The global business community is getting assurance from the highest political level that the regulatory regime is much more transparent, responsive and stable.

Strategic Dimension of 'Link West' Prime Minister Modi's visit was primarily dominated by economic and commercial issues. The strategic issues and current security and humanitarian challenges from West Asia to Afghanistan are also crucial in the relationship with Europe. Although economic engagement will form the 'core' of the India-Europe relations, New Delhi should be also looking towards developing greater synergies at the global level as well as addressing the regional humanitarian and security challenges. India is also keen to expand this relationship beyond economic engagement. The support of France would be crucial in the permanent membership of the UNSC, facilitating greater role for India in the global forums. India has long been a victim of international terrorism. Multicultural societies of India and Europe are anxious about the rise of extremism, fundamentalism and international terrorism. The French President criticized the Mumbai attack mastermind Zaki-ur-Rehman Lakhvi's release by Pakistan. Both India and Europe have fundamental political and economic interests in West Asian and African regions. Growing instability, terrorist activities and violence in the African continent and West Asia are matters of great concern for both the countries, which warrant a common approach to effectively deal with these challenges. New Delhi will be hosting Africa Summit this year and wishes to further widen its engagement in West Asia. C Rajamohan argues, "If geographic regions are one way of organising foreign policy, there is no substitute for boosting bilateral ties to a few pivotal countries around the world."

The Prime Minister's visit to Germany and France raises hope for reenergizing India's interaction with Europe. After assuming office in May 2014, Prime Minister Modi has been proactive in recalibrating India's foreign policy. His foreign visits ranging from the South Asian countries, Japan, Australia and the US, to Indian Ocean Countries or participation in the multilateral and regional summits were considered to be successful in enhancing India's relations with the respective countries. Intellectual discourses on the Europe-India interactions reflect that Prime Minister Modi's tour to Europe was a positive development in shaping the future course of relations. A vibrant 'Link West' policy would effectively complement the 'Act East' policy' in facilitating the country's economic development, technological advancement and political stature on the international arena. The growing middle class in the country wishes more global exposures in areas of education, skill

development, professional activities, tourism, etc. The European economy would be greatly benefitted if they adopt a judicious approach with a viable business model in harnessing such business potentials and shaping the aspiration of the Indian society. Agreements signed with France and Germany from education to skill development to urban development have much relevance to social and professional aspects of younger generation of the country.

Conclusion

The European Central Bank has raised this year's eurozone growth forecast to 1.5 per cent, up from one per cent, and the German government annual report says that economy is also in a 'good state'. But there would be diversity in economic performance in eurozone. Considerable change has already been noticed in the political trends in Europe. The rise of Eurosceptic and far-right parties in elections to the European Parliament 2014 was termed as a "political earthquake". The political base of traditional parties seems to be shifting. Geo-political competition between Russia and the EU over Ukraine adds strategic concerns in the region. How New Delhi will shape its relationship with Europe amidst such political and strategic scenarios will depend on its policy objectives and future synergies in its approach towards regional and global issues. Both countries – France and Germany – are of significance not only in contributing to economic transformation of India, but also in facilitating India's aspiration for greater role at the global stage. India's democratic credentials, demographic dividends and economic vibrancy would be imperative in developing greater compatibility with European political and economic values and policies at both the bilateral and global levels. Expanding the economic linkages with emerging markets offers substantial opportunities for European nations to spur their economic growth. An European Commission paper on trade, growth and jobs explicitly notes that trade has become 'an important means of achieving much needed growth and creating jobs without drawing on public finances' in current economic crisis. '... (Trade) links Europe to the new global growth centres and is a unique source of productivity gains.' India could be a major market with huge middle class populace and governed by the democratic system based on liberal values, which are similar to the West. Prime Minister Modi's visit has given big boost to the 'Link West' policy. The agreements signed and commitments expressed in the negotiations have potential for breaking new ground in India's partnership with Europe, but their effective and speedy transformation into reality would hold the key.

MAKE IN INDIA VS. MAKE IN CHINA

Last Tuesday, Tata Motor's Jaguar Land Rover (JLR) opened its first plant in Changshu, China. The luxury car-maker's $1.78-billion Make-in-China push has come a little over a month after Tata Group chairman Cyrus Mistry confessed to be greatly encouraged under Prime Minister Narendra Modi's leadership to join the "Make In India" programme that, he said, brings together industry and government for crafting a new future.

This was at the glittery launch of "Make in India" in Delhi where a galaxy of global corporate leaders ranging from Mukesh Ambani of Reliance Industries Ltd. to Lockheed Martin India CEO Phil Shaw in response to Mr. Modi's call had pledged to invest and manufacture in India.

The pitch had its origin in the Prime Minister's Independence Day speech when he invited global companies to pick India to locate factories, promising to replace red tape with red-carpet welcomes.

The jobs and incomes for Indians these factories would generate, he said, would in turn create the market for their output.

The goal the Modi government has set is to make India break into the top 50 in the World Bank's ease of business index ranking from the current 134th position.

When companies such as Tata Motors choose where to locate a new factory, they consider a range of factors. But India fares badly on most of the counts. For instance, contract enforcement takes 1,420 days and going through the 12 procedures for starting business typically takes 27 days.

India's chronic infrastructure and logistics deficit with inefficient transport networks makes it tough for manufacturing companies to achieve just-in-time production.

The Modi government has said it wants to radically de-bureaucratise, deregulate, change officers' mindsets, cut paperwork and remove the notorious legal and infrastructure hurdles to starting and doing business in India. This is not the first time India is focussing on its manufacturing sector. In 2006, the UPA government put out a national strategy for manufacturing. It even dubbed 2006-15 as the "decade of manufacturing in India." The five-year period of 2005-06 to 2009-10 was one of a smart 10 per cent plus growth for the manufacturing sector when several advantages — engineering skills, a growing domestic market, a raw material base and a large pool of skilled labour — trumped the vast barriers to doing business in India.

JLR's China launch has set alarm bells ringing for the Modi government: "Make in India" will have to go quickly from being a statement of intent to real action on the ground. Markets across Indian towns and cities that are flooded with Chinese products, more so around festivals such as Deepavali, are grim reminders of how Made-in-China has come to dominate homes and offices. From furniture and gadgets to industrial equipment,

India is importing almost all products from its neighbour, even yarn for saris. It is estimated that over 99 per cent of Bangalore silk saris are being made with Chinese silk yarn.

As a result, the rapidly growing bilateral trade between the two neighbours is tilting heavily in China's favour, at a rate that India has termed unsustainable. Bilateral trade crossed $65 billion in 2013, but while India exported $15 billion worth of goods to China, but imported $51 bn. The quality of trade also goes against India. India exports raw materials such as iron ore but imports manufactured goods.

In pursuit of its reforms agenda of 1979, China has followed a more-exports-at-any-cost policy to boost its economy. The Chinese government's support to manufacturing in the form of affordable cost of funds, cheap inputs and world-class infrastructure gives it an advantage over Indian manufacturers. The Confederation of Indian Industry estimates that Chinese manufacturing as a result enjoys a cost advantage of about 10 per cent over Indian manufacturing.

A fallout of which is dumping of products on big markets like India. To protect domestic manufacturers, India has been imposing an anti-dumping duty on 159 products — ranging from chemicals, petrochemicals, pharmaceutical, steel, fibres and consumer goods — imported from China since 1992.

The spurt in factory imports from China has coincided with a sharp slide in India's manufacturing sector despite the UPA government's efforts to push the sector.

Manufacturing output grew barely 1 per cent in 2012-13. In 2013-14, factory output contracted (-) 0.7 per cent. The share of the jobs-creating sector in the GDP has declined to 14.9 per cent in 2013-14 from the peak level of 16.2 per cent in 2009-10.

India's advantage

But there is hope still. A new index of manufacturing costs, including productivity-adjusted wages, electricity, natural gas and currency movements, created by the Boston Consulting Group (BCG) of the world's 25 biggest exporters shows China's traditional cost advantage is now under pressure denting its attractiveness. Under pressure from the U.S., China has had to appreciate its currency by 30 per cent since 2006, which is eroding its exports' cost competitiveness. Just-in data from the International Monetary Fund show that China is no longer the largest trade surplus economy in the world.

Therein lies an opportunity "Make in India" must tap. India's labour costs are among the lowest in the world. According to the U.S. Bureau of Labor Statistics, average labour compensation (including pay, benefits, social insurance, and taxes) in India's organised manufacturing sector increased only marginally, from $0.68 an hour in 1999 to $1.50 an hour currently.

The average compensation in China's manufacturing sector in contrast rose 20 percent year-on-year in the same period to $3 an hour.

Besides, the cost competitiveness, India boasts a nearly 500-million-strong labour force comprising unskilled workers and English-speaking scientists, researchers, and engineers, making it a potential destination for cost-effective research and development-oriented manufacturing.

Recent sporadic instances of the odd Chinese manufacturer setting up shop in India and a few Indian companies moving production bases back home from China are encouraging. Havells, Godrej, Micromax and auto-components maker Bosch are amongst a handful of companies that have recently moved back to India some part of their manufacturing or outsourcing in China owing to currency, labour and other cost advantages.

As Chinese factories move up the value-chain to hi-tech manufacturing, opportunities would open up for Indian entrepreneurs but they are up against stiff competition. On the BCG ranking, however, several countries, including the U.S. and Mexico, are better poised and ranked above India as of now to take gain from China's loss of competitiveness. The coming together of smart entrepreneurs, employees, infrastructure and know-how could overtime become a durable advantage, as had happened in China's case.

MODI'S MAKE IN INDIA PUSH TO TAKE ON CHINA FACES RED TAPE

Prime Minister Narendra Modi is seeking to turn India into a global manufacturing hub by curbing red tape. Tell that to Tata Steel Ltd., which closed one of its largest iron-ore mines in September over permit delays.

India's largest maker of the alloy isn't alone. Steel Authority of India Ltd. shut one of its top-yielding quarries the same month pending renewal of its lease. JSW Steel Ltd.'s plan to start mining in eastern Jharkhand state has been hampered by a probe begun last month into mine allocations.

Modi is set to trumpet his "Make in India" initiative at the Group of 20 summit in Australia this week as he vies with China to woo manufacturers. The mine closures show lingering bureaucratic obstacles to his push, stemming from court rulings and officials in India's 29 states that lie beyond Modi's direct control. India slid two places to 142nd out of 189 economies in the World Bank's latest ease of doing business rankings.

"There are things beyond the government's control," said Taimur Baig, chief economist at Deutsche Bank AG in Singapore. "If a court makes a pronouncement there is nothing really that the executive can do. For better or for worse, India has many more layers of checks and balances."

Steel Authority of India's shares fell 0.5 percent to 82.60 rupees at the close in Mumbai. JSW Steel rose 1.2 percent to 1,246.70 rupees, while Tata Steel gained 2 percent to 480.30 rupees. Steel Authority is up 14 percent this year, JSW Steel 23 percent and Tata Steel 13 percent, less than the benchmark S&P BSE Sensex's 32 percent increase.

Abundant Supplies

Modi introduced the "Make in India" drive in September to lure investment and revive economic growth after sweeping to office in a landslide victory in May. His government aims to boost manufacturing's share of India's $1.9 trillion gross domestic product to 25 percent from about 15 percent currently.

The government needs abundant iron ore supplies as it vies with nations such as Thailand and Indonesia to become a production hub. The ore is used to make steel, which in turn is used to manufacture everything from cars to railway lines.

Photo: India's Prime Minister Narendra Modi introduced the "Make in India" drive in September to lure investment and revive economic growth after sweeping to office in a landslide victory in May.

Yet judicial mining bans over environmental and regulatory lapses led to a drop in iron ore production in four of the past five years. That's stoked local prices even as global rates fell, and some buyers are turning to imports.

Spot prices of iron ore in Odisha, the biggest producing state, have gained 31 percent in the past year to 3,200 rupees ($52) a ton, said Gunjan Aggarwal, an analyst at commodities consulting firm CRU Group. Prices at China's Qingdao port have slid 44 percent to less than $76 a ton as of yesterday.

Local Purchases

Tata Steel said it's coping with shortages through local purchases and imports of the material.

"There are challenges in procurement due to logistics constraints and hence we are facing difficulty in operations," spokesman Chanakya Chaudhary said in an e-mailed reply to questions.

Steel rebar from China at Indian ports cost 37,000 rupees a metric ton in October, compared with Steel Authority of India's price of 44,000 rupees, the company's data show.

"Steel is the most crucial element," said Surinder Kapur, chairman at New Delhi-based automobile-parts maker Sona Koyo Steering Systems Ltd. "Steel plants running at lower capacity run contrary to the prime minister's vision."

Modi's changes since taking power include faster environmental approvals for major investment projects, more market-based energy pricing, fewer foreign-investment curbs and steps toward ending the state's grip on commercial coal mining.

Hurdles Continue

He expanded his cabinet two days ago as he seeks faster decision-making to speed up growth in Asia's third-largest economy. His administration has vowed to press ahead with amending land, labor and investment laws to make business easier.

At the same time, regulatory hurdles continue to constrain iron ore production. CRU estimates iron ore imports may surge to 15 million tons in the year ending March 31 compared with the prior 12-month period.

Tata Steel is set for record iron ore imports this year. JSW Steel has scaled up its target for overseas purchases to as much as 900,000 tons a month, from an earlier plan of 500,000 tons, Group Chief Financial Officer Seshagiri Rao said Oct. 21.

"We are being squeezed," said Jayant Acharya, marketing director for JSW Steel. "While international iron ore prices are at a five-year low, our own domestic prices are going in an opposite direction."

About 20 percent of India's steel capacity isn't being used, the Steel Ministry's Economic Research Unit estimates.

"That's not a good sign for any investor," said A.S. Firoz, the chief economist at the unit. "We have to fix the raw materials issue and take care of infrastructure for smoother movement of raw materials and finished products."

CAN MODI DELIVER A NEW INDIA?

On the surface, Narendra Modi has had a dream run in his first year as India's prime minister. In May 2014, his Hindu-right Bharatiya Janata Party (BJP) won 281 of the 543 seats in the Lok Sabha, the lower house of Parliament. This marked the first time since Rajiv Gandhi's victory of 1984 that a party won a clear majority of its own and did not need coalition partners to form a government.

After this triumph, Modi managed to install his trusted lieutenant, Amit Shah—who ran the interior ministry in Gujarat when Modi was chief minister of the state—as president of the BJP. Together with Shah, he has since gone on to win important state elections in Haryana, Maharashtra, and Jharkhand. In Jammu and Kashmir, the BJP did spectacularly well in the December 2014 elections and is now in government as part of the ruling coalition headed by the Peoples' Democratic Party.

Reduced to a mere 44 seats in the Lok Sabha, the opposition Congress party has struggled to find its political footing. Front-line leaders from party president Sonia Gandhi and her son, Rahul, to former A-list ministers like P. Chidmabaram, Kapil Sibal, and Jairam Ramesh have retreated into a shell, leaving the task of opposing the Modi government inside and outside Parliament to junior leaders and other parties.

On the economic front, global crude oil prices began to decline soon after Modi assumed office, reaching low levels that have helped his government save foreign exchange and bring the wholesale inflation rate down to more manageable levels, from 5.7 percent in June 2014 to about has welcomed his victory, and the lavish investment commitments made by Indian and foreign companies have buoyed the financial markets and lifted animal spirits all around. Thanks to the Central Statistical Office's decision to recalculate India's growth rate by shifting the base year for the measurement of inflation-adjusted growth from

2004–5 to 2011–12, Modi can claim that he is already growing the economy by an annual rate of over 8 percent.

Globally, Modi is seen by major world powers as a leader who can achieve the great transformations that his predecessor, Manmohan Singh, failed to bring about: creating a more dynamic economy and a policy environment that is more receptive to foreign capital. The United States and Japan have enormous strategic expectations, too. China and Pakistan may have some concerns, but in the main, most countries see Modi's ascent as good for themselves and the international system.

And yet, despite the global goodwill, economic good fortune, and political triumphs Modi has enjoyed, questions are increasingly being asked about his capacity to deliver on the promises that won him the election. Worryingly for the prime minister, it is not just his political opponents or critics who are expressing these doubts, but his supporters as well.

Three Contradictions

The reason for the growing cynicism about Modi is the contradictory expectations that his election campaign generated among diverse constituencies. Before 2014, the BJP's share of the popular vote since the 1990s had averaged approximately 20 percent. In 1999, the last time the party won a national election and formed a government, Atal Bihari Vajpayee managed to boost that vote share to 23.8 percent. It fell to 22.2 percent in 2004 and finally 18.8 per cent in 2009, when L. K. Advani, a leader with the image of a Hindu hard-liner at the time, served as the standard-bearer. Modi's contribution to the BJP in the 2014 election was to single-handedly win 31 percent of the vote, a swing of 12 percentage points over the previous election and 11 points more than the party's historical mean.

How did a man with a reputation for being even less inclusive than either Vajpayee or Advani succeed in attracting so many new voters to his party? He managed this task by deliberately steering clear of communal messaging and presenting himself as someone who stood for *vikas*, or development— and *vikas* alone. In doing so, Modi accomplished two goals. He tapped into the aspirations of young voters who blamed the corruption and ineptitude of the Congress party for an economic slowdown and a lack of opportunities to better themselves. But he also managed to rebrand himself as a politician concerned about all Indians and not just the welfare of one section of the population—certainly of their exclusivist political and cultural agenda, a significant section of the urban electorate that might otherwise be suspicious of the divisiveness of that agenda believed the BJP leader would not allow Hindutva to endanger the pursuit of development.

The RSS, which sensed it was on the cusp of a historic victory, deployed its cadres across the country to mobilize voters for Modi. The cadres saw his emphasis on development as a brilliant tactical exercise and did not demur when key Hindutva demands—the construction of a temple to the Hindu god Rama at the site of the demolished Babri mosque in Ayodhya, the adoption of a Uniform Civil Code (in which Muslim personal law, particularly in relation to marriage, would no longer apply), and the abrogation of constitutional safeguards for Jammu and Kashmir's autonomy—found little or no space in the party manifesto or campaign. They knew there would be ample scope to press ahead on these fronts once Modi came to power.

The rival priorities of development and Hindutva not the "minorities" the BJP accuses the Congress of pandering to, but also not "the Hindus," the constituency did not constitute the only contradiction inherent in Modi's election victory. There was also tension between the BJP usually cultivates.

Sabka saath, sabka vikas— aspirations of the poor that Modi tapped into and the "Together with all, development for all"—became the slogan of his campaign, and it struck a chord with voters who had already been bombarded with the claim that Modi was a great administrator who had turned Gujarat into an economic miracle. To be sure, the BJP campaign was not always on message, and there were regions and constituencies such as Assam, West Bengal, and western Uttar Pradesh where

Modi and Shah made sectional appeals aimed at mobilizing Hindu voters by accusing other parties of backing Muslims involved in violence, cow slaughter, and "infiltration" from Bangladesh. For the most part, however, Modi worked hard to maintain the new image he had cultivated.

The *vikas* slogan was clever for another reason. It allowed Modi to position himself as an inclusive leader without disavowing Hindutva, the Hindu nationalism in which he, his party, and the Rashtriya Swayamsevak Sangh (RSS)—the parent "cultural" organization of the BJP—continued to believe. Thus, even as the Hindutva faithful saw in Modi's candidature a vehicle for the furtherance expectations of corporate India, which funneled hundreds of millions of dollars into his election campaign. India's captains of industry had defected en masse from the Congress party early in Manmohan Singh's second term as prime minister, blaming the economic slowdown on the governments pursuit of a social democratic agenda that seemed to privilege the protection of the environment and the rights of farmers and the rural poor, as well as tribal communities and forest dwellers, over the demands of big business for land and fiscal frugality.

Corporate chieftans backed Modi because they saw in him not just a leader who was sympathetic to their needs but also one with the ability to push through politically difficult decisions. This was considered an indispensable quality, since satisfying the expectations of corporate India would necessarily mean making it easier for farmers and tribals to be displaced from their land to clear the way for mining and manufacturing projects. It would also mean pruning, or "rationalizing," public expenditure on health, education, food security, and employment generation, which would adversely affect the poor. Modi recognized the fraught political consequences of the corporate support he solicited and received, but hoped the circle of expectations could be squared by the millions of jobs his business-friendly measures would presumably generate.

To these two contradictions that were hard-wired into the new government was added a third: The aim of using the "Modi wave" to grow the BJP at the state level, especially in those regions where it has historically had a negligible presence, threatened to tread on the toes of regional parties whose support might still be needed in the Rajya Sabha, Parliament's upper house, where the BJP was well short of a majority. The framers of the Indian constitution deliberately structured the composition of the Rajya Sabha in such a way that a party which swept the Lok Sabha would need to sustain its public support for at least six years in order to gradually build a majority in the upper house. Ruling parties have traditionally overcome this structural impediment through skilful political management. But the task is made harder when a ruling party has a "take no prisoners" approach to potential rivals.

Under Modi and Shah, the BJP is looking to grow in West Bengal and Odisha, where its political ambitions clash with those of the Trinamool Congress and Biju Janata Dal, respectively. Its extremely antagonistic approach to the Congress and other political parties in north India, especially Bihar, has prompted the opposition to seek comfort in numbers. If the non-BJP parties collectively undertake to block the passage of legislation in the upper house—as they seem inclined to do—the only option Modi will have is to repeatedly convene a joint sitting of Parliament to pass pending bills, a contrivance that has been resorted to only once in the 64-year history of the Indian republic. The precedent was in 2002, when the BJP-led government used this device to pass the controversial Prevention of Terrorism Act.

Hindutva Asserts Itself

In its first year, the Modi government has unsuccessfully struggled to find a way around these contradictions. So far, the tension between *vikas* and Hindutva has been resolved largely in the latter's favour, given the prime minister's reluctance to curb the communal politics of the *Sangh Parivar*, the family of organizations associated with the RSS. In the face of dozens of provocative comments by RSS head Mohan Bhagwat, senior leaders of the Vishwa Hindu Parishad (an RSS front organization), his own ministers, and BJP legislators, Modi has kept a studied silence. On August 15, 2014, India's Independence Day, he called for a "10-year moratorium" on divisive politics and utterances, but said nothing when members of his own political flock flouted this advisory soon afterward.

In recent months, the RSS has used various ruses to poison the communal atmosphere. There have been only a few instances of overt violence, but the stridency of the rhetoric has created a palpable sense of insecurity among the religious minorities. Last year, Sangh activists spread rumours of a supposed Muslim plan to seduce and convert Hindu girls, and managed to turn their own made-up name for this plot, "Love Jihad," into a widely used term. They have disrupted church meetings and urged the passage of a national law to ban religious conversions, failing which they will supposedly try to convert all Muslims and Christians to Hinduism in a process they call *ghar wapsi*, or homecoming.

The only time Modi has publicly criticized someone for a communal remark was when Sadhvi Niranjan Jyoti, his minister of state for food processing industries, used an epithet—*haraamzaadon*, or bastards—during an election meeting in Delhi to describe those who do not follow the Hindu god Rama. Even then, Modi made light of this shocking utterance by citing Jyoti's rural background as an extenuating factor. After several months of anti-Christian propaganda by the RSS and its front organizations, the prime minister in February 2015 finally spoke out in defense of religious freedom and the right to propagate one's faith. But days later, Bhagwat of the RSS muddied the waters by accusing the late Mother Teresa, who is respected by most Indians for her work among the poor, of using charity as a cover for converting people to Christianity. Again, there was no statement from Modi in response.

The Hindutva agenda has explicitly come to the fore in BJP-ruled states like Maharashtra, where the government of Devendra Fadnavis, a Modi nominee, has pushed through a law prescribing stringent penalties for the slaughter of cows and bullocks and for the sale or possession of beef. Since beef is a source of relatively cheap protein for poorer Indians—and especially Muslims, whose income levels tend to be lower than the national mean and whose religion does not enjoin them to revere the cow—the new law is clearly seen as a salvo against non-Hindus. The Maharashtra government has also withdrawn an affirmative action program for Muslims in state-aided educational institutions that was launched by the previous Congress-led administration (despite a ruling by the Bombay High Court upholding the scheme's legality) while simultaneously granting reservations to a Hindu caste, the Marathas, which the courts had explicitly excluded from the purview of such programs.

The same partisan attitude toward the rule of law is visible elsewhere, too. The Central Bureau of Investigation (CBI) has all but lost interest in two murder cases it was pursuing against Amit Shah.

The BJP president was indicted by the agency in 2010 following a Supreme Court–ordered investigation into the extrajudicial killings of a Muslim man, Sohrabuddin Sheikh, described by the police as a gangster; his wife, Kauserbi; and his Hindu associate Tulsiram Prajapati. Shah, who was the interior minister in Gujarat at the time of risen to 46 percent in the 2014 general election, fell back to 32 percent, its historical average for the capital, in the 2015 assembly election.

It was almost as if every new voter Modi brought on board in 2014 had deserted him within a year. Although a number of factors were at play in the assembly election, the perception that growth and development were less of a priority for the BJP than Hindutva cost the party dearly. Voters opposed to the BJP decided not to waste their ballots on parties unlikely to win, and the AAP was the beneficiary of this de facto consolidation of the opposition vote.

What's Good For Business

While there has been an electoral cost to pay, the high-decibel madness of Hindutva activists has helped Modi in at least one indirect way: During the winter session of Parliament, the opposition spent more time confronting the government on that issue than debating Modi's economic policies.

Acting largely under the radar, the Modi government the murders, was accused of being party to a conspiracy to kill the three and cover up the crime. In a December 2014 hearing at which the has tried to satisfy a key demand of the corporate sector by relaxing environmental norms for a range of industrial and mining projects. In January, it promulgated ordinances facilitating dismissed the charges against Shah without a trial.

That verdict can be appealed in the High Court, but so far the investigative agency—which reports directly to the Modi government—has failed to file the necessary paperwork. Meanwhile, the senior policemen accused of the murders have been reinstated in the Gujarat police force and given responsible positions. In contrast, the police have lodged a flimsy charge in a bid to arrest Teesta Setalvad, a human rights activist who has spent years collecting evidence on the anti-Muslim massacres that took place in Gujarat in 2002 when Modi was chief minister.

One of the conundrums of India's present-day politics is why Modi has chosen not to confront or act against those pushing sectarian divisions. His silence has cost him the support of many of the new voters who flocked to his side in 2014. In the February 2015 Delhi state elections, the BJP was routed by the Aam Aadmi Party (AAP), a populist party that grew out of a major anticorruption movement. The AAP won 67 of the 70 assembly seats. The BJP's share of the Delhi vote, which had the acquisition of farmland for private projects and reducing the social obligations of mining companies. By allowing the dual use of "social and commercial infrastructure in non-processing areas of special economic zones [SEZs]" by a simple gazette notification—an executive decision that requires no legislative approval—Modi made it easier for the Adani Group, an Indian conglomerate, to monetize the vast tracts of land it had acquired earlier for its port and SEZ projects. (SEZs are aimed at promoting export-oriented industries and usually involve tax concessions.)

The Adani Group is a long-standing backer of Modi. While financial contributions to political parties are difficult to quantify or monitor, the company's billionaire founder and chairman, Gautam Adani, was one of the first Indian businessmen to openly say that Modi should be prime minister.

The flip side to this accommodative approach to corporate interests is a growing intolerance toward activists who challenge the violation of environmental norms by big business. The government has gone after Greenpeace—which has taken on the Essar Group, another conglomerate, for the manner in which it is conducting its mining operations in the Mahan region of Madhya Pradesh—by freezing its funds and stopping one of its activists from traveling abroad. The activist, Priya Pillai, was not allowed to board a flight to London, where she was due to testify before a panel of British members of Parliament about violations by Essar, which is listed on the London Stock Exchange.

Asked to explain its decision, the Modi government has told the Delhi High Court that Pillai was prevented from going abroad because "she was going to project the image of the Indian government negatively," which in turn could lead to sanctions being imposed on the country. The Home Ministry said it would allow her to travel only if she gave a written undertaking not to speak about human rights violations. She refused to provide such an undertaking, and the High Court eventually backed her. "The state may not accept the views of the civil right activists, but that by itself cannot be a good enough reason to do away commensurate with Modi's repeated promises of better access to health care and education, and of "sanitation for all by 2022" (he has vowed that every home will have a toilet by then). Allocations for some key programs like the provision for school meals have been cut.

The BJP says the shortfall will be made up by the states, which will get a greater percentage of national tax revenue thanks to a new revenue-sharing formula. As the economist Jean Drèze noted in *The Hindu*, however, this is easier said than done: "Anyone with a minimal understanding of Centre-State relations is likely to hear alarm bells. Also, it is not clear how State governments are supposed to make instantaneous adjustments in their 2015–16 Budgets to fall in line with this cold turkey approach."

Health-related transfers to the states have been cut by around 15 percent, and funding for education by 16 percent. Funds for "women and child development" have been slashed by 51 percent. The allocation for rural roads has not been increased, while funds for sanitation—supposedly the with dissent," it said, ordering the government to lift its travel ban.

Prevented from traveling signature social infrastructure priority of the government, which announced a "Clean India" campaign—to London, Pillai spoke to the British parliamentarians via have been cut by half. Despite these cuts, which run Skype. This leaves open the question of whether the government might some day seek to proscribe not just travel by activists but the very act of criticizing India, since information is fungible and criticism produced for an Indian audience could just as easily be "misused" by foreign powers. If that seems a bit of a stretch, the manner in which the Modi government has sought to ban a documentary about rape in India is not a good omen for free speech. The documentary, produced for the BBC and based on interviews with the family members of a young woman who was gang-raped and killed in Delhi in December 2012, was banned from being broadcast in India after the government objected to the fact that the rapists had also been interviewed and made statements which it felt portrayed the country in a bad light.

While the government has delivered concrete benefits to corporate India on a number of issues, including in the budget presented on February 28, 2015, by Finance Minister Arun Jaitley, public expenditure under key budgetary headings like sanitation, health, and education is certainly not ter to Modi's development rhetoric, the finance minister has been forced to postpone his stated target of a 3 percent budget deficit by two years, to 2018, because of a push for physical infrastructure, especially roads and railways.

Diplomatic Successes

If there is one area where Modi has exceeded the expectations of his supporters and confounded many of his critics, it is foreign policy. He began his tenure as prime minister by inviting all of India's South Asian neighbours to his inauguration, including Prime Minister Nawaz Sharif of Pakistan. In his first 10 months, he has visited Bhutan, Nepal, and Sri Lanka; no Indian prime minister had paid an official visit to the latter two countries in over two decades. Modi has reversed his party's opposition to a crucial border agreement with Bangladesh that was negotiated by Manmohan Singh but never implemented. All indications are that the agreement will be finalized this year.

Modi paid high-profile visits to Japan, Australia, and the United States, where he was feted by the Indian diaspora and by investors anxious to hear firsthand about how many doors his government was now willing to open for them. His visit to the United States was especially significant, since it demonstrated his willingness to put aside the rancor caused by Washington's decade-long refusal to grant him a visa due to allegations that he was complicit in the 2002 Gujarat massacres. The fact that President Barack Obama returned Modi's visit within months suggests the two countries have found a way to steer the bilateral relationship away from the rut it had entered over the past few years.

A rough-and-ready solution to the problem of nuclear liability—a key obstacle in the way of American reactor sales to India—has been hammered out, though doubts remain about the legal viability of the fix. The two sides appear ready to take their defense cooperation to a higher level. More importantly, Modi and Obama issued a Joint Strategic Vision for the Asia-Pacific and Indian Ocean Region that would appear to formalize India's willingness to endorse the US pivot to Asia.

But the jury is still out on how ready Modi may be to risk antagonizing the Chinese by drawing closer to the United States, Japan, and Australia. While in Tokyo, he publicly described China as an "expansionist" power that was "encroaching on the seas of others." A few weeks later, however, he rolled out the red carpet for Chinese President Xi Jinping despite a provocative incursion Chinese troops made into the Ladakh region of Jammu and Kashmir during that visit. Modi is due to visit Beijing later in 2015, where he will no doubt make a pitch for greater Chinese investment in India.

Lack Of Clarity

For all his sure-footedness in dealing with the outside world, Modi does not seem to have made up his mind about how to engage with Pakistan. In May 2014, he and Nawaz Sharif agreed to have their foreign secretaries restart the stalled dialogue process between the two countries. However, one week before they were to meet, India abruptly pulled the plug. The grounds cited were flimsy—Pakistan's high commissioner in Delhi had gone ahead and met a Kashmiri separatist leader despite a warning from India not to do so. Such meetings had been taking place for years without India making an issue of them. In February 2015, Modi abruptly reversed his stand again. Under the pretext of seeking to further South Asian cooperation, he sent the Indian foreign secretary to Islamabad for talks with his counterpart.

It is hard to say where the bilateral relationship will go, given the lack of clarity on Modi's part. His corporate constituency would favour a process of engagement with Pakistan, but his Hindutva constituency would not. The tension between these two sections can be managed so long as there is not another major terrorist attack in India that is traced back to jihadist elements based in Pakistan. Having spent the past decade berating the Congress party for being soft on terrorism emanating from across the border, Modi will come under enormous pressure from within the Sangh Parivar for a muscular response to any such provocation.

The truth is that Modi's willingness to play the ultranationalist card with Pakistan (or even China) will be inversely proportional to his successes on the economic front.

Five years of sustained growth will help him resolve the contradictions between development and Hindutva, popular aspirations and corporate expectations, and the BJP's desire to expand in new regions and the need to avoid alienating local allies. Conversely, a failure to deliver growth, or jobs, will turn the Modi project into an unstable compound, one in which religious chauvinism and jingoism become dangerous and unpredictable political elements.

Bibliography

Aiyar, S.: *Accidental India*, New Delhi: Aleph Book Company, 2012.

Albert N.: *Evaluating Economic Damages, A Handbook for Attorneys*, Westport, CT, Quorum Books, 1992.

Arrowsmith, S.: *Government Procurement in the WTO*, London: Kluwer Law International, 2003.

Balasubramanyam, N.: *"Conversations with Indian Economists,"* London: Macmillan, 2001.

Bhagwati, Jagdish: *India in Transition: Freeing the Economy*, Oxford, Clarendon Press, 1993.

Chaudhuri, Pramit: *The Indian Economy: Poverty and Development*, New York, St. Martin's Press, 1979.

Dhingra, C.: *The Indian Economy: Resources, Planning, Development, and Problems*, Delhi, Sultan Chand, 1983.

Fernandes, Vivian: *Modi: Leadership, governance and Performance*. Orient Publishing. Delhi, 2014

Gaur, Sanjay: *Narendra Modi : Change We can Believe In*, Yking Books, Delhi, 2014.

John A, Marcell, *Handbook of Small Business Valuation Formulas and Rules of Thumb*, Valuation Press, 1993.

Kamath, M.V.; Randeri, Kalindi: *The Man of the Moment: Narendra Modi*. Vikas. Delhi, 2013

Ray, S.K.: *Indian Economy*, New Delhi, Prentice-Hall, 1987.

Schumpeter, J. A., *The Theory of Economic Development*, Harvard University Press,Cambridge, Massachusetts, 1934.

Ullman, D. G.: *Making Robust Decisions*, Trafford, 2006.

Index

❑❑❑